I0831701

SOUTHERN FRONTIER HUMOR

SOUTHERN FRONTIER HUMOR

New Approaches

EDITED BY ED PIACENTINO

University Press of Mississippi
Jackson

www.upress.state.ms.us

The University Press of Mississippi is a member of the Association of American University Presses.

Manufactured in the United States of America

First printing 2013
∞

Library of Congress Cataloging-in-Publication Data

Southern frontier humor : new approaches / edited by Ed Piacentino.
pages cm
Includes index.
ISBN 978-1-61703-768-9 (cloth : alk. paper) —
ISBN 978-1-61703-769-6 (ebook) 1. American wit and humor—Southwest, Old—History and criticism. 2. American literature—Southwest, Old—History and criticism. 3. American literature—Southern States—History and criticism. 4. Southwest, Old—Humor. 5. Southern States—Humor. 6. Southwest, Old—In literature. 7. Southern States—In literature. I. Piacentino, Edward J., 1945–, editor of compilation.
PS437.S68 2013
817.009'976—dc23 2012044873

British Library Cataloging-in-Publication Data available

CONTENTS

PREFACE

SINCE ITS INCEPTION IN THE EARLY 1830S, THE HUMOR OF THE Old South or Old Southwest has attracted the curiosity of readers, and since the 1930s, the investigative and critical efforts of scholars as well. In the nearly one hundred eighty years since the first southern frontier sketches began appearing in William Trotter Porter's New York *Spirit of the Times*, the most significant venue for the genre, and in other newspapers, nearly five hundred publications—reviews, books, journal articles, chapters in books, anthologies, scholarly editions and reprints, and even websites—have appeared as testaments to ongoing interest and critical inquiry. This book, the work of many inquiring minds, represents an attempt to generate further scholarly efforts. First of all, there would be no book if it were not for the contributors—Jennifer Hughes, Gretchen Martin, Bruce Blansett, Katie McKee, Tracy Wuster, Win Morgan, John Lowe, Jim Bishop, and Mark Graybill—each of whom has added considerably to our understanding of the southern frontier humor genre and its contextual consequence. I extend my utmost gratitude to these scholars for their work, which has opened up some new territory for scholarly research. I am also deeply indebted to Walter Biggins of the University Press of Mississippi, to the press's outside reader, who offered valuable recommendations and insights for revision, to others at the press who, in various ways, were involved in bringing this project to fruition, and to copyeditor Lisa Paddock for her discerning and meticulous work. I am also grateful to my friend and fellow humor scholar, Tom Inge, of Randolph-Macon College, who encouraged me to pursue this project and who read an early draft of the introduction, providing useful suggestions. I am most appreciative of the exemplary staff of the Smith Library at High Point University for their many kindnesses in aiding my research, and especially grateful to Bob Fitzgerald, reference librarian, for handling my interlibrary loan requests. As always, my principal supporter is my wife and partner, Diane, to whom I dedicate this book. Her patient understanding, cheerful spirit, and unconditional love make life richer and all the more worthwhile.

SOUTHERN FRONTIER HUMOR

INTRODUCTION

ED PIACENTINO

SOUTHERN FRONTIER HUMOR, WHICH EMERGED IN THE 1830S primarily in the lower South and the then Southwest, enjoyed popularity from its inception through the period of the Civil War, though its influence on later American writers and forms of popular culture would continue after that time and has been ongoing ever since. According to intellectual historian Michael O'Brien, the genre "was mostly sensitive to what was East and West, what followed rivers and penetrated forests. It was very interested, therefore, in the scenes of travel, in steamboats, taverns, hotels, strangers talking. Everything moved, and the world was made intelligible by story. Or, to be more precise, a man's world was made intelligible" (2: 758–59).

Serious scholarly interest in this humor genre began in the 1930s with the pioneer work of Walter Blair, Franklin J. Meine, and Constance Rourke, who laid the foundations for further study. The impetus of their work was carried on by Norris Yates and Kenneth S. Lynn, in the 1950s and in the 1960s by Milton Rickels, John Q. Anderson, and Hennig Cohen and William B. Dillingham (editors of what would become the standard anthology in the field, *The Humor of the Old* Southwest). In 1970s and 1980s, substantial scholarly contributions by M. Thomas Inge, Blair and Hamlin Hill, William E. Lenz, and Nancy Snell Griffith would further solidify and validate the importance of antebellum southern humor as a worthy field for study. And in the 1990s, Fritz Oehlschlaeger's anthology on southwest humor in the *St. Louis Reveille*, and David Rachels's expanded edition of Longstreet's *Georgia Scenes*, titled *Georgia Scenes Completed*, became major scholarly contributions.[1]

Yet the big decade for the resurgence of scholarly interest in southern frontier humor coincided with the onset of the new millennium, which saw publication of seven book-length contributions. In 2001, Crockett scholar Michael Lofaro published a collection of tall tales featuring women from the Crockett Almanacs, *Davy Crockett's Riproarious Shemales and Sentimental Sisters* (Tennessee). Lofaro's book includes 122 tales (many previously uncollected) showcasing the masculine attributes and prowess of backwoods women (or, as he dubs them, "shemales") with numerous complementary woodcut illustrations. Organizing his selections into eight categories—"Wild and Grotesque Description," Battle with Animals," Battles with Humans," "Courting Stories and Amorous Adventures," "Sentimental and Religious Stories," True Adventure Stories," "Stereotypes, Stock Figures, and Jokes," and "Recipes and Household Hints"—Lofaro offers for the first time under one cover this significant and rich lode of almanac pieces about mythic women. His substantive and well-researched introduction contextualizes these materials within the emerging women's movement toward greater freedom and opportunity. Also in 2001, M. Thomas Inge and Ed Piacentino published *The Humor of the Old South* (Kentucky), a collection including both several previously published pieces (some revised) representing the most significant scholarship on southern frontier humor published between 1975 and 2000, as well as ten new essays, examining gender, race, Longstreet (two), Thompson, Crockett, Noland, and Thompson, Baldwin, O. B. Mayer, and J. Ross Browne. This book also offers the most extensive bibliography on the subject.

In 2004, James H. Justus published *Fetching the Old Southwest: Humorous Writing from Longstreet to Twain* (Missouri), a book that has been widely touted as the most compelling study of the genre. Justus examines most of the antebellum southern humorists currently recognized as most significant: Longstreet, Thompson, Hooper, Harris, Lewis, Thorpe, Baldwin, Crockett, Noland, Taliaferro, Sol Smith, and Twain (the latter often regarded as the principal legatee and culmination of the southern frontier humor tradition). Divided into three sections—"Mythmakers and Revisionists," "The World the Humorists Found," and "The World the Humorists Made"—Justus's book brilliantly illuminates the varied nature of the southern frontier humor genre, arguing that "[d]espite its imaginative latitude, conceptual intensity, and stylistic exaggeration of the writing, the humorists' created world is a reliable index to the social and cultural actualities of the lower South in the thirty-odd years before the Civil War" (3). Justus also focuses on the importance of women in the world the humorists created, more so than most previous scholars, and challenges once again long-held perspectives such as Kenneth Lynn's thesis of the *cordon sanitaire.*

This concept, first introduced and discussed by Lynn in his 1959 book, *Mark Twain and Southwestern Humor*, posits that the frame device often used by the southern frontier humorists—who he claims were Whig supporters and whom he calls "morally irreproachable Gentlem[e]n"—created a *cordon sanitaire*, a barrier enabling the gentlemen writers to separate themselves "outside and above the comic action" (64) and simultaneously to satirize the yeomen characters they featured in their sketches and tales. Controversial and widely disclaimed, Lynn's thesis has been a locus of contention for over fifty years now among scholars of southern literary studies, especially those knowledgeable about the primary texts of the southern frontier genre. On the other hand, several historians, such as Michael O'Brien and John Mayfield, are strong advocates of Lynn's claim. Unlike the literary scholars and folklorists, Mayfield, who has most recently addressed Lynn's postulation, contends that "the Southern humorists *were* hard on the plain folk and took particular delight in portraying them as yokels and hicks," and that "[h]istorians find . . . [the] dichotomies [of the Lynn thesis] useful" (xxii).[2]

Another new book in the new millennium, Ed Piacentino's *The Enduring Legacy of Old Southwest Humor* (LSU Press, 2006), is a collection of fourteen original and previously unpublished essays on writers and popular culture artists who seemed to have been inspired by the genre of southern frontier humor. This book, the first devoted exclusively to this subject, features essays on legatees William Faulkner, Erskine Caldwell, Flannery O'Connor, Eudora Welty, Woody Guthrie, Harry Crews, William Price Fox, Fred Chappell, Barry Hannah, Cormac McCarthy, and African American writers Zora Neale Hurston, Ralph Ellison, Alice Walker, Ishmael Reed, and Yusef Komunyakaa. The popular culture legacy includes coverage of the comic strip, *Li'l Abner*, comedians Andy Griffith, Dave Gardner, Justin Wilson, Jerry Clower, and Jeff Foxworthy, the sitcom, *The Beverly Hillbillies*, and the Internet (the so-called "electronic frontier"). This ongoing legacy provides a substantive and reliable indicator of the continuing fascination with the tropes, character types, and conventions of the genre.

The year 2007 saw the publication of Gretchen Martin's *The Frontier Roots of American Realism*, a title in Peter Lang Publishing's Studies on

Themes and Motifs in Literature series. Martin's book validates, better than any other to date, what scholars have generalized about for many years: namely, that southern frontier humor provided the foundation for American literary realism, inaugurating some of the techniques that would evolve into postbellum realistic writing. Viewing the sketches and tales of antebellum southern humor as protorealism that "confront[s] life directly . . . fly[ing] under the radar of the moral and secular guards of literary propriety" (3), and that features "the daily activities and social events of the 'plain folk,'" Martin argues that such creations "provide access into the language and values of rural communities and feature the plain folk of the antebellum South as a culture worthy of artistic treatment" (4).

In 2009, John Mayfield's *Counterfeit Gentlemen: Manhood and Humor in the Old South* (University Press of Florida) and Ed Piacentino's *C. M. Haile's "Pardon Jones" Letters: Old Southwest Humor from Antebellum Louisiana* (LSU Press) were published. Part of the New Perspectives on the History of the South series, Mayfield's monograph examines the social function of humor and how it intersects with southern manhood and identity. He focuses on John Pendleton Kennedy (who had not previously been considered a humorist), Augustus Baldwin Longstreet, Johnson Jones Hooper, Joseph Glover Baldwin, Thomas Bangs Thorpe, Henry Clay Lewis, and G. W. Harris—each of whom "negotiated manhood in his own special way" (xxi). In doing so, these authors presented material "centered on 'manly' pursuits . . . [that] were competitive" (xxi) to an audience of other men typically belonging the same social class as themselves. Piacentino's *C. M. Haile's "Pardon Jones" Letters* is a recovery project, consisting of an introduction contextualizing Haile within the antebellum southern humor genre and sixty-seven of Haile's extant and previously uncollected mock dialect comic letters, which the editor has copiously annotated. Most were published initially in the New Orleans *Picayune* between 1840 and 1848, appearing under the pseudonym of Pardon Jones or of one of his fictive relatives or friends. Many of these mock letters to the editor employ subjects common in the humor of the Old South, focus on local and national issues, and feature three separate venues: Louisiana, Massachusetts, and Mexico—the latter serving to establish Haile as the only southern frontier humorist who can be regarded as transnational.

At the end of this active decade, Tom Inge and Ed Piacentino collaborated on a new anthology, *Southern Frontier Humor* (Missouri 2010). This collection of primary pieces not only features writers and texts long associated with the southern frontier humor genre, but also works of some lesser figures not previously represented in Cohen and Dillingham's *Humor of the Old Southwest*. New to this anthology are works by Ham Jones, Joseph Gault, Orlando B. Mayer, James Edward Henry, Marcus Lafayette Byrn, C. M. Haile, William Gilmore Simms, Adam Geiselhard Summer, and tall tales from the Crockett Almanacs featuring frontier women. The editors' introduction incorporates recent scholarly views on the subject and offers several new contexts for examination.

Southern frontier humor, not surprisingly, has made it onto the "electronic frontier" of the Internet, where several websites are devoted to southern frontier humor. Angel Price's *Southwestern Humor and Mark Twain* (http://etext.virginia.edu/railton/projects/price/southwes.htm) includes links to some well-known primary texts in the genre, including Twain's "The Dandy Frightening the Squatter," "The Celebrated Jumping Frog of Calaveras County," and "Jim Blaine and His Grandfather's Old Ram," and a short selective bibliography of books on the topic. Donna Campbell's *Southwestern Humor, 1830–1860* (http://public.wsu.edu/~campbelld/amlit/swhumor.htm), whose website is located at Washington State University, lists characteristics of the genre, with links to some of the key figures and their representative texts. Another useful web resource, *Southwestern Humor: Criticism and Defense of an American Character* (http://xroads.virginia.edu/~HYPER/DETOC/sw/front.html), has links to a generous sampling of antebellum southern humor texts, character types, and brief biographical sketches of some of the principal humorists.

The present collection of essays, *Southern Frontier Humor: New Approaches*, builds on the momentum of the productive scholarly activity generated during the last decade. Consisting of ten new and original essays, this book investigates several areas of promising and fertile inquiry in the field. Such a study is important for several reasons. New primary materials, some previously unknown and/or having fallen into oblivion in southern periodicals archives, have been recovered and are now readily accessible for scholarly consideration. Among these primary materials are some of the humorous pieces of James Edward Henry, Joseph Gault, Christopher Mason Haile, and of Longstreet's "completed" *Georgia Scenes*. As scholars continue to explore both traditional and digital archives, more long forgotten sketches, tales, and anecdotes will likely be recovered, collected, and made available, prompting new avenues for critical inquiry.

While the authors featured here sometimes reference some of the major practitioners of antebellum southern humor, only one of them makes any of the canonical figures the principal or sole emphasis of an essay. Instead, the essays collected here cover topics ranging from recovery, to the intersection between laughter and cultural conquest, to legacy pieces showing affinities between the South's frontier humor and southern local color writers, to Mark Twain, to the appropriation of the rascally imposter by contemporary southern fiction writers, an amalgam of the affable Jack of the Jack Tales and his ambivalent trickster cousin of Old Southwest humor. Essays also address intersections between Jamaican Anancy tricksters and their southern frontier counterparts, or adapt and apply contemporary critical methodologies to Old South hunting yarns and to George Washington Harris's Sut Lovingood tales. All tap into previously unexplored territory. Each essay, in its own way, justifies its choice of appropriate literary, socio-historical, socio-cultural, or critical contexts and answers the underlying question that frames and defines this book: What are some of the directions future research in southern frontier humor might follow? Moreover, the essays—individually as well as collectively—expand and therefore contribute to humor studies discourse, providing a strong rationale for continued scholarly scrutiny and dialogue.

The first essay, "Henry Junius Nott and the Roots of Southern Frontier Humor," my own contribution, reexamines the little-known work, *Novelettes of a Traveller; or, Odds and Ends from the Knapsack of Thomas Singularity* (1834), authored by Nott. Focusing on the longest of the novelettes, "Biographical Sketch of Thomas Singularity," I argue that it contains a rich lode of materials that Longstreet and his fellow frontier humorists would appropriate and similarly employ in some of their own sketches and tales to create a body of work embodying the southern frontier humor genre. Nott's pioneering work features character types (dandies, rural roughs, gamblers, con artists and their would-be victims); subjects such as hunts, gambling, horse racing, courtship, pranks and deceptive practices, and drunkenness; the frame device; and popular thematic and plot appropriations—most notably a variation of Washington Irving's "The Legend of Sleepy Hollow," the most widely imitated script of southern frontier humor. This writing is arguably not as lively or entertaining as the work of many of Nott's southern frontier humor successors. Still, before Longstreet's *Georgia Scenes,* Nott's "Biographical Sketch of Thomas Singularity" is probably the best representation of what would become the humor of the Old Southwest.

Jennifer Hughes, in "Hysterical Power: Frontier Humor and Genres of Cultural Conquest," views frontier humor as engaged "in the battle for national and even world ideology, going to the fronts against the visions of other widely read literatures." Beginning in the 1830s, she argues, laughter was a "radical utterance," helping to broaden democracy and expand social empowerment. Antebellum southern frontier humor, in particular, played a significant role in promoting what Hughes calls the "Laugh and Grow Fat," or "laughter is the best medicine" philosophy, an anodyne to improve rather than harm the emergent American society, no easy task. Humor, Hughes points out, had to fight for legitimacy, just as sentimental literature once did. Longstreet, Thorpe, the anonymous writers for the *Crockett Almanacs,* and Henry Clay Lewis were among the southern frontier humorists whose works helped "to uphold the ideology that hilarity was to be the salvation of the nation as opposed to sentimentality and intellectualism." In advocating what Hughes calls the "hysterical power" of laughter, the humorists saw the possibility for the effects of their comic characters to entice hilarity out of others.

In his recent biography on Mark Twain, Jerome Loving has argued that southern frontier humor, which shaped Twain's development as an artist, "divided into two complementary streams—one a shallow and rough-and-tumble brook, the other a deeper and more sedate stream, but both leading to the great sea change in American literature, Realism." The first, Loving goes on to point out, were the literary comedians "who manipulated language with misspellings and malapropisms to satirize political events of the day. . . . The other stream of development led to the rise of the local colorists" (266–67). Heretofore, with the exception of Kathryn McKee, scholars have paid little attention to the intersection between antebellum southern humor and southern local color fiction. Three essays in this collection, however, do address that subject. They, in fact, extend the legacy of southern frontier humor to include three of Twain's contemporaries: Joel Chandler Harris, Charles W. Chesnutt, and Sherwood Bonner. In the first essay, "'Bawn in a Brier-patch' & Frontier Bred: Joel

Chandler Harris's Debt to the Humor of the Old South," Gretchen Martin perceives in some of Harris's lesser-known stories the "intertextualization of southern folk culture, black and white," the latter that of southern frontier humor. Martin shows that Harris, who knew the work of some of the several Georgia humorists who predated him, discernibly draws on the antebellum southern humor genre in a variety of ways. In "Teague Poteet: A Sketch of the Hog Mountain Range," the central character's views on manhood similarly mirror those of the frontier humorists, and in "A Conscript's Christmas," Harris uses the familiar frontier trope of defiance of authority. Also, in "Blue Dave," the principal character, a black slave named Dave, employs verbal wit and cross-racial collaboration to defy the upper class, and in "Balaam and his Master" the slave Balaam survives through his use of the type of trickster wisdom evident in the slave folktales. Finally, in "Where's Duncan?" Harris, employing the frame device, successfully creates a hybrid, fusing traits of southern frontier with those of the African American trickster.

In "From Swamp Doctor to Conjure Woman: Exploring 'Science' and Race in Nineteenth-Century America", the second of three essays examining a southern local colorist, Bruce Blansett develops important intersections between Henry Clay Lewis's *Odd Leaves from the Life of a Louisiana Swamp Doctor* and Charles W. Chesnutt's *The Conjure Woman.* Blansett sees the two works as not only sharing similar themes and stylistic and narrative strategies, but also presenting subversive attitudes toward scientific and medical contexts of the time—the latter often colored by blatant racist ideologies. Lewis's *Odd Leaves*, Blansett argues, was a "subversive antecedent" to *The Conjure Woman*, and in it Lewis, a humorist-physician, "disrupts traditional scientific and medical discourses by juxtaposing the compassionate swamp doctor with the posturing professional man, the city physician," exposing in both errors and mistakes in judgment. As Blansett carefully demonstrates, "Chesnutt, though revolutionary in his subversive techniques and highly respected as one of the first prominent African American authors, reworks various techniques, forms, and subversive strategies already employed by a Southwest humor antecedent, Henry Clay Lewis." Sharing common concerns and humorous strategies, both Lewis and Chesnutt debunk the medical status quo, questioning the treatments—many of which cruelly and unnecessarily victimized African American patients—to which slaves were subjected, and laying bare the racist "medical discourse" on which such practices were predicated.

The third essay devoted to a local colorist, Kathryn McKee's "Sherwood Bonner and the Postbellum Legacy of Southern Humor," treats a writer less known than Harris or Chesnutt. In examining four of Sherwood Bonner's stories—"Hieronymus Pop and the Baby," "Dr. Jex's Predicament," "Aunt Anniky's Teeth," and "The Gentlemen of Sarsar"—McKee shows their close affinities to the genre of southern frontier humor. Bonner's humor, McKee argues, "exposes the fault lines of southern culture, in her case as they destabilized expectations for both race and gender in an uncertain postbellum world. In this grouping of stories, Bonner explores, not just changing roles for black and white men and women, but also humor as a means of resisting the simultaneous instantiation of restrictively contoured white womanhood at the center of nascent Lost Cause ideology." In doing this, Bonner significantly modified and expanded the "conventions" of antebellum southern humor, reconfiguring them in such a way as to challenge some of the "prevailing expectations for both women's writing and regional writing at the time."

Any collection of new essays on southern frontier humor predictably will include a piece on Mark Twain, and *Southern Frontier Humor: New Approaches* does not disappoint in this regard. Tracy Wuster's "'I wa'n't bawn in de mash to be fool' by trash!': Mark Twain's 'A True Story' and the Culmination of Southern Frontier Humor" sharply takes issue with the prevailing claim that Twain represents the apogee of the antebellum southern humor genre. Such a notion, Wuster posits, "obscures key aspects of Mark Twain's career, of the relationship between antebellum and postbellum Southern writing, and of the representation of American culture in humor." Wuster asserts that "A True Story" (1874), one of Twain's first pieces to use African American dialect, represents a "central transition point in Twain's oeuvre and in the transition from antebellum to Gilded Age representations of race in local color fiction." Perceiving "A True Story" as a transitional piece between antebellum southern frontier humor and postbellum local color fiction, Wuster argues that Twain's story challenges the limitations inherent in writings featuring former slave narrators, such as those of Thomas Nelson Page and Joel Chandler Harris. While drawing on certain conventions associated with the southern frontier humor sketch—the frame and prominent vernacular voice—Twain "used [them] to address questions of race and gender in ways that more closely linked him with northern traditions that linked artistic work with moral aims." In Wuster's view, shifting the "narrative" from the authorial narrator to the black vernacular speaker and the "powerful dramatization of the sorrow of slavery" in "A True Story" resulted in establishment of "a considerable distance between the cultural work of Twain's humor and that of the Old Southwest." In giving voice to the black female vernacular speaker, Twain "literally and figuratively breaks the mold with her narrative, reversing the cultural work of southwestern humor by refusing the containment of political and cultural threats central to frame tales."

The next two essays extend the legacy of southern frontier humor beyond the southern local color tradition. Winifred Morgan's "Morphing Once Again: From Jack to Simon Suggs to Aunt Lucille" and John Lowe's "Anancy's Web/Sut's Stratagems: Humor, Race, and Trickery in Jamaica and the Old Southwest" concentrate on the trickster, a familiar, ambivalent, and recurring character in antebellum southern humor. Acknowledging the ongoing cultural vitality of and interest in the ubiquitous trickster—from the likeable Jack of the Appalachian Jack Tales, to the rogues of southern frontier humor, to the con artists featured in contemporary southern fiction—Morgan explores some of the intersections between these variations. As in its earlier southern manifestations, the contemporary trickster is a fortune seeker or timeserver, hoping to enhance his/her own aggrandizement or satiate his/her personal desires. In showing the reemergence of the trickster as con artist in contemporary southern literature, Morgan sees the continuation of the legacy of a Euro-American counterpart, a literary cross of the traits of both Jack and antebellum southern rogues like Simon Suggs and Sut Lovingood. In her examination of tricksters in John Kennedy Toole's *A Confederacy of Dunces* (1980), Mark Childress's *Crazy in Alabama* (1997) and *Georgia Bottoms* (2011), and Clyde Edgerton's *Walking Across Egypt* (1987), *Killer Diller* (1991), and *The Bible Salesman* (2008), Morgan perceives a similar pattern in their function, which provides yet another link to the old southwestern con artist/prankster: "[S]ingle-minded pursuit of their own self-interest alters and often improves the world they live in."

John Lowe's essay focuses on transnational intersections between the Anancy trickster of Jamaica and his counterpart in southern frontier humor. The Anancy folktales feature the trickster as a spider and are the product of the diasporan dispersal of the Ashanti people of West Africa, who were forcefully transported to the New World as slaves. Anancy, according to Lowe, "represents humor, chaos, and ambiguity," traits often associated with the trickster in the many and diverse folk traditions in which he appears. Lowe's essay opens up new territory, for it is the first scholarly investigation to explore connections and differences between the southern frontier humor trickster and the Jamaican Anancy. In terms of similarities, Lowe notes, among other things, that both humor genres feature orality, are subversive, employ vernacular discourse, headline liars, accentuate the laziness of the trickster, favor cleverness and the underdog, were told at social gatherings, and sometimes use reversal (with the trickster being tricked). There are also some distinctions. For example, whereas Anancy tales were initially told by slaves, antebellum southern humor tales and sketches typically feature poor white storytellers. Moreover, the appearance of the trickster figure in the American South and Southwest and in Jamaica created the possibility for change, a point on which both Morgan and Lowe agree. As Lowe observes, "Southern frontier humor scoundrels and Anancy, as spirits of the disorder, nevertheless give man hope, for their boisterous, irreverent, often chaotic interventions demonstrate the possibility of creating rupture in rigid cultures, which can lead to new forms and modes of being."

The final two essays, Mark S. Graybill's "Postmodern Humor *ante Litteram*: Self-Reflexivity, Incongruity, and Dialect in George Washington Harris's *Yarns Spun*," and James E. Bishop's "The Real Big Kill: Authenticity, Ecology, and Narrative in Southern Frontier Humor," take the subject of southern frontier humor into the exciting realm of contemporary critical theory, postmodernism and ecocriticism. Drawing on the contexts of semiotics, comedy, and self-reflexivity from Jerry Palmer's *Taking Humour Seriously* (1994), Graybill re-examines Harris's *Sut Lovingood: Yarns* within a postmodern context, seeing Harris as employing "a kind of pre-postmodern self-reflexivity" and arguing that "Harris's linguistic gymnastics . . . fit rather comfortably beside those of postmodern writers" such as John Barth, Kurt Vonnegut, and Thomas Pynchon. Graybill also observes that incongruity calls for what Palmer describes as "a bifurcated logical process, which leads the listener to judge that the state of affairs portrayed is simultaneously highly implausible and just a little bit plausible," a "logic of the absurd." The question that Graybill poses and successfully answers is: "To what degree . . . does Harris's use of self-conscious or self-reflexive language account for the humor in his stories?"

Bishop's "The Real Big Kill: Authenticity, Ecology, and Narrative in Southern Frontier Humor" explores selected southern frontier humor sketches and tales with an emphasis on ecological awareness. The hunting and slaughter of large numbers of animals, a frequent script in antebellum southern humor, is, from the current ecocritical perspective that Bishop applies, politically and socially unacceptable. Acknowledging the influence of Rudolph Raspe's *Baron Münchhausen's Narrative of His Marvelous Travels and Campaigns* (1785) as a catalyst in shaping the southern "real big kill" and its variations, the "mythic beast" and the "extravagant slaughter" narratives, Bishop argues that while southern frontier humor cannot be blamed "for perpetuating the ideology of environmental devastation that dominated nineteenth-century American policy and practice . . . it did play a role in enabling and ennobling it." Focusing his analysis on Thorpe's "The Big Bear of Arkansas," C. M. Haile's "Letter from Curnel Pardon Jones, To Curnel Tom Owen of the Agricultural Society, with a Tail," William Gilmore Simms's "How Sharp Snaffles Got His Wife and Capital," Hardin E. Taliaferro's "The Pigeon Roost," and the bear-hunting segments of the fictionalized autobiography, *A Narrative of the Life of David Crockett*, Bishop provocatively claims that the "big kill" narrative (and its variants), when "placed in its historical context, enables us to see that humorous renderings of embellished hunting stories may have obscured Americans' ability to see the real environmental destruction that was happening around them, much in the way that frontier humor may have blunted their attentiveness to racism, gender inequality, and rural poverty."

As the purpose of this collection of new essays on southern frontier humor is to generate further exploration of the topic, I would like to mention some potential directions future scholarship might examine. Promising areas for investigation include:

- critical biographies on Thompson, Hooper, Baldwin, Harris, and Noland;
- more retrieval work from antebellum newspapers archives, which contain literally hundreds of sketches and tales authored pseudonymously;
- more application of contemporary critical methodologies to the humorous texts;
- the ongoing legacy of this genre to contemporary literature and popular culture;
- intertextuality both within the genre and beyond it;
- intersections between the genre and similar contemporary humorous materials featured on the Internet;

- attention to groups of humorists who wrote for the same newspapers and who knew one another personally, as did the Dutch Fork correspondents to the Columbia *South Carolinian* or Louisiana humorists Thomas Bangs Thorpe, Christopher Mason Haile, and George Wilkins Kendall;
- a comparative study of the mock epistle to the editor in humorists such as Fenton Noland, William Tappan Thompson, Haile, Thorpe, Phillip B. January, and John S. Robb;
- the relation to and relevance of southern frontier humor on New Southern Studies;
- the exploration of transnational links of the genre to folk humor genres in Native American, Black Atlantic, circum-Caribbean, and other cultures;
- examination of the genre in the context of the history of the book studies (the production, circulation, and reception of texts in their material forms);
- more emphasis on studies examining some of the minor humorists;
- the relationship of southern frontier humor to Down East humor, Civil War literary comedy, or local color humor;
- further conversation about gender and ethnicity issues in the genre;
- connections between the early nineteenth-century British sporting magazines and their articles and similar materials published in the New York *Spirit of the Times*; and
- intersections between southern frontier humor and other antebellum American popular culture forms, particularly forms addressed to male readers.

Moreover the time is ripe to address a topic of broader and more profound concern: the need to situate southern frontier humor in the sociocultural and historical contexts of the South. While not exhaustive, these topics represent a promising and challenging agenda that southern cultural studies and southern frontier humor scholars might pursue.

NOTES

1. See Meine's *Tall Tales of the Southwest: An Anthology of Southern and Southwestern Humor, 1830–1860* (1930), Rourke's *American Humor: A Study of the National Character* (1931), Blair's *Native American Humor* (1937), Yates's *William T. Porter and the Spirit of the Times: A Study of the Big Bear School of Humor* (1957), Lynn's *Mark Twain and*

Southwestern Humor (1959), Rickel's *Thomas Bangs Thorpe: Humorist of the Old Southwest* (1962); Anderson's *Louisiana Swamp Doctor: The Writings of Henry Clay Lewis alias "Madison Tensas, M. D."* (1962), Inge's *The Frontier Humorists: Critical Views* (1975), Blair and Hill's *America's Humor from Poor Richard to Doonesbury* (1978), Lenz's *Fast Talk and Flush Times: The Confidence Man as a Literary Convention* (1985), Griffith's *Humor of the Old Southwest: An Annotated Bibliography of Primary and Secondary Sources* (1989), Oehlschalaeger's *Old Southwest Humor from the St. Louis Reveille, 1844–1850* (1990), and Rachels's *Augustus Baldwin Longstreet's Georgia Scenes Completed* (1998).

2. A few years earlier, O'Brien, in *Conjectures of Order: Intellectual Life and the American South*, while generally commenting on the southwestern humorous sketch, also affirmed Lynn's *cordon sanitaire*: "[T]he structure is . . . Federalist; the civilized narrator looks out on an unsafe and uncontrollable world disfigured by passionate license and 'moral discord,' occasioned by the pell-mell pace of social mobility and change. The chaos never quite reaches him, but he knows about it, has stood on the scene, and so thinks it important to tell the monitory tale" (2: 755).

WORKS CITED

Anderson, John Q. *Louisiana Swamp Doctor: The Writings of Henry Clay Lewis alias "Madison Tensas, M. D."* Baton Rouge: Louisiana State University Press, 1962. Print.

Blair, Walter. *Native American Humor*. New York: American Book Co., 1937. Print.

———, and Hamlin Hill. *America's Humor from Poor Richard to Doonesbury*. New York: Oxford University Press, 1978. Print.

Campbell, Donna M. "Southwestern Humor 1830–1860," Washington State University. Web. 27 Oct. 2011. http://public.wsu.edu/~campbelld/amlit/swhumor.htm.

Cohen, Hennig, and William B. Dillingham, eds. *Humor of the Old Southwest*. Boston: Houghton Mifflin, 1964. Print.

———. *Humor of the Old Southwest*. Athens: University of Georgia Press, 1975. Print.

———. *Humor of the Old Southwest*. Athens: University of Georgia Press, 1994. Print.

Griffith, Susan Snell. *Humor of the Old Southwest: An Annotated Bibliography of Primary and Secondary Sources*. Westport, CT: Greenwood Press, 1989. Print.

Inge, M. Thomas. *The Frontier Humorists: Critical Views*. Hamden, CT: Archon Books, 1975. Print.

Inge, M. Thomas, and Edward J. Piacentino, eds. *The Humor of the Old South*. Lexington: University Press of Kentucky, 2001. Print.

———. *Southern Frontier Humor: An Anthology*. Columbia: University of Missouri Press, 2010. Print.

Justus, James H. *Fetching the Old Southwest: Humorous Writing from Longstreet to Twain*. Columbia: University of Missouri Press, 2004. Print.

Lenz, William E. *Fast Talk and Flush Times: The Confidence Man as a Literary Convention*. Columbia: University of Missouri Press, 1985. Print.

Lofaro, Michael A., ed. *Davy Crockett's Riproarious Shemales and Sentimental Sisters: Women's Tall Tales from the Crockett Almanacs, 1835–1856*. Mechanicsburg, PA: Stackpole Books, 2001. Print.

Loving, Jerome. *Mark Twain and The Adventures of Samuel L. Clemens*. Berkeley: University of California Press, 2010. Print.

Lynn, Kenneth S. *Mark Twain and Southwestern Humor*. Boston: Little, Brown, 1959. Print.

Martin, Gretchen. *The Frontier Roots of American Realism*. New York: Peter Lang, 2007. Print.

Mayfield, John. *Counterfeit Gentlemen: Manhood and Humor in the Old South*. Gainesville: University Press of Florida, 2009. Print.

Meine, Franklin J., ed. *Tall Tales of the Southwest: An Anthology of Southern and Southwestern Humor, 1830–1860*. New York: Knopf, 1930. Print.

O'Brien, Michael. *Conjectures of Order: Intellectual Life and the American South, 1810–1860*. 2 vols. Chapel Hill: University of North Carolina Press, 2004. Print.

Oehlschalaeger, Fritz, ed. *Old Southwest Humor from the St. Louis Reveille, 1844–1850*. Columbia: University of Missouri Press, 1990. Print.

Piacentino, Ed, ed. *C. M. Haile's "Pardon Jones" Letters: Old Southwest Humor from Antebellum Louisiana*. Baton Rouge: Louisiana State University Press, 2009. Print.

———. *The Enduring Legacy of Old Southwest Humor*. Baton Rouge: Louisiana State University Press, 2006. Print.

Price, Angel. *Southwestern Humor and Mark Twain*. University of Virginia. 27 Oct. 2011. Web. http://etext.virginia.edu/railton/projects/price/southwes.htm.

Rachels, David, ed. *Augustus Baldwin Longstreet's Georgia Scenes Completed*. Athens: University of Georgia Press, 1998. Print.

Rickels, Milton. *Thomas Bangs Thorpe: Humorist of the Old Southwest*. Baton Rouge: Louisiana State University Press, 1962. Print.

Rourke, Constance. *American Humor: A Study of the National Character*. New York: Harcourt, Brace, 1931. Print.

Southwestern Humor: Criticism and Defense of American Character. University of Virginia. 27 Oct. 2011. Web. http://xroads.virginia.edu/~HYPER/DETOC/sw/front.html.

Yates, Norris W. *William T. Porter and the "Spirit of the Times": A Study of the Big Bear School of Humor*. Baton Rouge: Louisiana State University Press, 1957. Print.

HENRY JUNIUS NOTT AND THE ROOTS OF SOUTHERN FRONTIER HUMOR

ED PIACENTINO

When one thinks of the analogues and antecedents of antebellum southern humor, the usual candidates are: Ebenezer Cook's comical satire, *The Sot-weed Factor; or a Voyage to Maryland* (1708), William Byrd II's Dividing Line histories, Dr. Alexander Hamilton's mid-eighteenth-century satire, "The History of the Tuesday Club," Rudolph Raspe's *Baron Munchausen's Narrative of His Marvelous Travels and Campaigns* (1785), the comic eclogues of William Henry Timrod (the father of the Henry Timrod, often lauded as the poet laureate of the Confederacy), Mason Locke Weems's "Awful History of Young Dred Drake" (1812), and segments of James Kirke Paulding's *Letters from the South* (1817) and his play, *The Lion of the West* (1830). Other precursors include Washington Irving's widely popular "The Legend of Sleepy Hollow" (1820) and "Rip Van Winkle"(1819), Joseph Doddridge's play, *Dialogue of the Backwoodsman and the Dandy, 1st Recited at the Buffaloe* [Creek Va.] *Seminary, July 1, 1821* (1823), the rustic Yankee or Down East humor of Seba Smith and others popular in the early 1830s, and the sporting sketches found in early nineteenth-century British periodicals such as *The London Sporting Magazine* and *Bell's Life in London*, and in British books such as Pierce Egan's two collections, *Anecdotes, Original and Selected of the Turf, the Chase, the Ring, and the Stage* (1827) and *Pierce Egan's Book of Sports and Mirror of Life: Embracing the Turf, the Chase, the Ring, and the Stage* (1836).[1]

There is yet another candidate: Henry Junius Nott of South Carolina, a writer, unlike most of those previously mentioned, who is veritably unknown or forgotten today. When scholars come across the name Henry Junius Nott, few, if any, have ever heard of him. Even fewer have heard of his book, *Novelettes of a Traveller; or, Odds and Ends from the Knapsack of*

Thomas Singularity, published in two volumes by Harper and Brothers in 1834. Still fewer have actually read *Novelettes*, even the long first section, "Biographical Sketch of Thomas Singularity," the most humorously fertile part of Nott's work. Yet, the "Biographical Sketch of Thomas Singularity" preceded Augustus Baldwin Longstreet's *Georgia Scenes* (1835), generally considered the foundational text of southern frontier humor and a book that allegedly featured first some of the themes, subjects, and character types of the genre. What I hope to do, then, is to demonstrate that Nott's "Biographical Sketch" anticipates some of the materials that southern humorists would similarly employ, and in so doing to argue that Nott's work represents an embryonic stage in the development of what would become a new American genre: the humor of the Old South.

But, first, I want to raise a question: Who was Henry Junius Nott? The son of prominent judge Abraham Nott, Nott was born in the Union District of South Carolina on November 4, 1797.[2] Raised in Columbia, South Carolina, Henry Nott attended Columbia Academy and entered South Carolina College in 1810, graduating in 1814. He then read law, and shortly after being admitted to the bar in 1818, Nott and his law partner, Colonel David J. McCord, collected and published *Reports of Cases Determined by the Constitutional Court of South Carolina* (1818, 1819, and 1820). Realizing his interest in literature exceeded his interest in practicing law, Nott abandoned his law practice and in 1821 traveled to Europe, where, for the next three years, he studied in France and Holland, read widely in literary texts, and gained facility in French, German, and other modern foreign languages. After returning to Columbia in 1824, Nott was appointed professor of criticism, logic, and the philosophy of languages at his alma mater, South Carolina College, a position he held until his untimely death in 1837. Given his career path in academe, it is not surprising that Nott became an accomplished scholar, publishing biographical essays on Erasmus, Dr. Samuel Parr, Daniel Wyttenback, and Louis Courier, and articles on D'Aguesseau and Defoe—all in the *Southern Review* and all indicators of the diverse range of his intellectual interests. What we know of Nott's personality seems appropriate for a humorist. Maximilian LaBorde, who apparently knew Nott, writes:

> In his personal and social relations he was most agreeable. He had great amiability of temper, and cheerfulness of spirit. Though

> sportive and playful, fond of telling stories and representing others in such way as to create a laugh, yet it was done with such good nature as never to give offense. . . . He enjoyed life, made the most of it, and was never cast down by present calamity or misfortune. (214–15)[3]

In Nott's most important work, *Novelettes of a Traveler,* he introduced materials that would be more skillfully and artfully adapted and employed in the sketches, tales, and essays of Longstreet, Hooper, Baldwin, Harris, and other southern frontier humorists who succeeded him, though there are no records indicating these authors had direct familiarity with Nott's book. Unknown, too, is the extent of its regional or national popularity, since the archives of Harper and Brothers have no sale records for *Novelettes.* A contemporary review of *Novelettes* in the *American Monthly Magazine* in November 1834 praised Nott as a "very agreeable writer" and described the style of *Novelettes* as "highly graphic, and at times highly humorous" (143–44). Six years after Nott's death, William T. Porter, the editor of the *Spirit of the Times,* then the most famous venue for southern frontier humor, became the first to acknowledge in print a resemblance been Johnson Jones Hooper's "Taking the Census in Alabama" (which he reprinted in the September 9, 1843 issue of the *Spirit*) and Nott's *Novelettes* and Longstreet's *Georgia Scenes.* In an editorial note preceding Hooper's sketch, Porter observed, it "reminds us forcibly of the late Judge Longstreet's 'Georgia Scenes' and of the 'Adventures of Thomas Singularity' by the late Prof. Nott, of S[outh] C[arolina]" (326). Subsequently, in a 1907 biographical sketch on Nott in the *Library of Southern Literature,* St. James Cummings Jr. called Nott "a hearty lover of fun" and saw in the "Biographical Sketch of Thomas Singularity," the first of Nott's novelettes, "[the] author's charitable humor, that clothes with grace the vanity, the follies and vices of a roving ne'er-do-weel" [*sic*]. Though acknowledging that some of Nott's novelettes offended readers, Cummings wisely did not condemn Nott on that count, indicating that to do so "is almost to impeach the sterling worth of the bulk of Southern humor long since taken to our hearts" (3798–99).[4]

Recognized as "a popular book in its day," according to George Armstrong Wauchope (who in all likelihood was thinking of the Thomas Singularity segment), *Novelettes* "overflows with the kind of boisterous humor that was exceedingly popular in the old South" (59). Like Wauchope, Walter Blair, in a brief footnote in his introduction to *Native American Humor* (1937), acknowledged affinities between Nott's book and the picaresque tradition, but his overall impressions of *Novelettes* were negative. "Nott's book," he writes, "is pretty generalized, pretty pallid, and rather dull" (87).[5] Modern scholars have also generally reaffirmed that *Novelettes* is a harbinger of the brand of southern frontier humor that flourished between the mid 1830s and the Civil War. The entry on Nott in *The Oxford Companion to American Literature*, for example, describes *Novelettes* as a "realistic depiction of frontier life [though] a less brilliant but earlier example of the humor of the Southwest, as represented by Longstreet, Hooper, Baldwin, and others" (Hart and Leininger 479).

Better examples of the picaresque and its roguish anti-hero appear in southern frontier humor, such as Hooper's Simon Suggs in *Some Adventures of Captain Simon Suggs* (1845), Baldwin's Simon Suggs Jr. in "Simon Suggs, Jr., Esq: A Legal Biography" in *Flush Times of Alabama and Mississippi* (1853), George Washington Harris's Sut Lovingood in *Sut Lovingood: Yarns*, and Kittrell Warren's Billy Fishback in *Life and Public Services of an Army Straggler* (1865). And Blair's inconsequential and unenthusiastic impression of Nott's *Novelettes* is not unwarranted. Still, *Novelettes*, particularly the "Biographical Sketch of Thomas Singularity," seems worthy of recovery and renewed investigation as a rich domain of materials, which in the mid-1830s better southern humorists would begin to mine and combine with an emphasis on vernacular voice to create a new American genre.

In the "Biographical Sketch of Thomas Singularity," Nott realistically and humorously delineated some of the subjects, character types, and motifs that would become familiar fare in southern frontier humor. Like so many of these humorists, Nott employs a narrative persona or author surrogate in the person of Jeremiah Hopkins, a young journeyman printer and friend of Tommy Singularity who retrospectively describes Singularity's flaws and misadventures—the latter serving as the unifying element that precipitates and helps to sustain the plot's action. Since Jerry (as he prefers to be called) is usually sensitively practical, sometimes noticeably moralistic, and generally reliable in what he tells the reader, as a character he differs in almost every respect from Tommy, and he serves as a foil to Singularity. At the outset of the narrative, Jerry informs the reader of his intent to recount incidents in Singularity's life—many coming from Tommy's friends, from Tommy himself, and from Jerry's "long intimate acquaintance" with him. Jerry hopes "they might amuse many, and be instructive to the ruminating few that chew the cud of reflection" (Nott 1: 6, 5). In describing Tommy's uncomely physical appearance and fastidious manner—particularly in regard to caring for his hair—Jerry notes:

> He was about five feet four inches high, not badly put together, but of a leanness altogether wonderful, and a light tendency to being knock-kneed; his face was pale, and somewhat marked with the small-pox; he had light blue eyes, with a very slight squint; a well-shaped nose, and a mouth not amiss, except a disposition to drop the under-lip, which, with the obliquity of his vision, gave to his countenance rather a sinister expression. What he mainly prided himself on was his hair. It was abundant and curly, of flaxen colour, verging towards red. He always let it grow to a considerable length, combing it with great care, and madefacting [*sic*] it with pomatums and perfumed oils. Adown either cheek hung a corkscrew-curl, that he cherished and nourished with especial affection. (Nott 1:34)

Tommy's actions complement his hideous appearance and manner. As Jerry points out, "He was slovenly, comparatively lazy, and superlatively mischievous" (Nott 1: 14), traits, which along with his disregard of authority, similarly apply to many roguish characters in southern frontier humor. Moreover, Tommy lies, cheats, and deceives for personal gain, frequently gambles at cards and dice, and drinks excessively. In short, Tommy is a scoundrel whose behavior often backfires. Though not of the same social class as Hooper's Simon Suggs, Harris's Sut Lovingood, Warren's Billy Fishback, or Twain's King and Duke, Tommy Singularity, as a picaro and ne'er-do-well, is a close literary cousin to these other characters. Of these, Tommy—though not as shrewd and crafty—probably comes closest to resembling Sut Lovingood, who, in part of his self-description in "Sut Lovingood's Sermon" says:

> "*Fustly,* that I hain't got nara a soul, nuffin but a whisky-proof gizzard. . . . *Secondly,* that I'se too durn'd a fool to come under millertary lor. *Thurdly,* that I hes the longes' par ove laigs ever hung

> to eny cackus, 'sceptin only ove a grandaddy spider. . . . *Foufly*, I kin chamber more cork-screw, kill-devil whisky, an stay on aind, than enything 'sceptin only a broad-bottum'd chun. *Fivety*, and las'ly, kin get into more durn'd misfortnit skeery scrapes, than enybody, and then run outen them faster, by golly, nor enybody." (Harris 138).

Feigning literary dilettantism, a trait distinguishing him from these other rogues—excepting Twain's backwoods con artists in *Huckleberry Finn*—Tommy is vain, ostentatious, self-serving, careless, and without a strong restraining conscience. Freewheeling and shifty—like Simon Suggs, whose governing ethic is "it's good to be shifty in a new country"—Tommy describes himself as "'like a bark without moorings. On a summer sea I float safely; but I am at the mercy of every current of prejudice or gale of passion'" (Nott 1: 24). Even so, his actions, typically innocuous and rarely beneficial to himself, evoke more laughter than disdain. They inflict no serious discomfort on others, for Tommy Singularity is usually the only casualty of his own devices. In fact, the recurring pattern found in his various misadventures in "Biographical Sketch" shows him to be a fool, more often than not a victim of humiliation.

Some of Tommy Singularity's humorous escapades result in his own physical distress and even emotional turmoil. As William Lenz perceptively points out, "Humor based on others' physical discomfort is a conventional southwestern technique for enduring frontier hardships by making light of them" (106–7). Moreover, for most readers such incidents seem tolerably and innocuously amusing. Because of comic distancing, the reader has no trouble laughing at Tommy Singularity, invariably a deserving victim of the hardship and ridicule he experiences. In the "Biographical Sketch," several of Tommy's mishaps involve his unexpected confrontation with potentially menacing animals—snakes, a dog, and yellow jackets.

One such encounter features Tommy, Jerry the narrator, and some friends on a hunting expedition near Columbia, South Carolina, on a Sunday morning, a clear transgression of the communal custom that this day should be reserved for spiritual worship. Things go awry quickly when both Tommy—acting somewhat dandified, obnoxious, and theatrical in his words and actions on this occasion—and Jerry become stuck in the marsh. Tommy is actually bitten several times by a rattlesnake, in part due to his own vanity and lack of caution. What ensues is a veritable comedy of errors, with the humor at Tommy's expense:

> "I am a dead man," said Tommy; "for he has bitten me twice on the legs, and the poison will work before I can get a doctor. "But," said he excited by rage and rum, "I'll not die unrevenged." He thereupon, after looking round, tried to break a small dead sapling which seemed of a suitable size for a pole. With much labour he wrenched it off; and rushed onwards with all the impetuosity of desperate passion. In his trepidation he not only struck beyond where he intended, but hit the ground with such violence that the stick snapped in twain, and, yielding him no support, he pitched forwards at full length, and received . . . another bite on the arm. . . . Doubly sure of death, Tommy now approached more carefully. With the fragment of stick which he retained in his hand, he aimed deliberately a most violent blow at the head of his enemy. The stick did not break this time, but his hand was brought near the ground, and the agile animal, shifting his position . . . avoided the danger and struck Singularity on the wrist. Glowing with anger, and stirred up to desperation, he drew out his knife and cut a cudgel that appeared sufficiently long and strong to ensure his purpose. . . . [W]hen the ground on which his front foot was planted gave way, he sank into the bog, and fell so near the snake that he was bitten full on the cheek." (Nott 1: 37–38)

The apparent seriousness of this situation is defused, however, when one of the other hunters discovers the snake is without fangs and the bites harmless. Moreover, both Tommy's struggles with the snake and Jerry's "muddied clothes" become familiar objects of derision before the townspeople.

Singularity's misadventure with snakes is a harbinger of better tales involving this kind of reptile in three of the Davy Lane tall-taleish sketches—"The Chase," "The Horn-snake," and "The Rattlesnake Bite"—in Hardin E. Taliaferro's *Fisher's River's (North Carolina) Scenes and Characters, by "Skitt," "Who Was Raised Thar"*(1859), in William C. Hall's mock-snake story, "How Sally Hooter Got Snake-Bit" (1850), and most notably in George Washington Harris's "The Snake-Bit Irishman" (1867), involving Sut's prank on an uninvited Irishman who has an obsessive fear of snakes.

Interestingly, snake stories, as Norris Yates points out, would become "one of the most numerous groups of tales," principally of the tall-taleish variety, featured in Porter's the *Spirit of the Times* (177).

Another of Tommy's comical encounters with an animal occurs while he is working as a printer in Norfolk, Virginia. Notorious for his nocturnal excursions—purportedly to a tavern to purchase whiskey—Tommy, upon discovering the gate to the groggery locked, climbs over the fence and is chased by a large bulldog "well known for his uncommon strength and fierceness" (Nott 1: 78). In his attempt to escape the pursuing dog, Tommy jumps into an empty cask that formerly held molasses. He is discovered the next morning by an African American slave gardener who, assuming Tommy to be a thief, threatens to call his master, only to change his mind after Tommy bribes him with five dollars. After a miserable night of confinement, Tommy, "daubed with molasses from head to foot" (Nott 1: 80), arrives at the newspaper office but does not disclose the previous night's humiliating ordeal. He withdraws to his room to sleep, where Tommy's fellow journeymen printers blacken "his face with tallow and soot." Upon awakening and realizing what has happened to him, Tommy becomes an object of ridicule: "He had put on another suit, [Jerry recalls] but old and dirty; his knotted and combined locks were uncombed and well filled with feathers, and his eyes of a fiery redness, gleamed in his sooty visage like balefires athwart a midnight sky" (1:81). Victims of humiliating pranks like Tommy Singularity who are vain and deserving of disgrace recur with some frequency in Old Southwest humor. Among the better-known sketches in this vein are Thompson's "The Major in an Embarrassing Situation" and Harris's "Parson John Bullen's Lizards" and "Sicily Burns's Wedding." Each of the eponymous characters in these sketches becomes an object of ridicule. Also, Tommy's encounter with a bulldog anticipates a similar motif involving characters confronting more dangerous animals, such as bears and panthers, as settlers migrated farther west.

Of all Tommy Singularity's misadventures with animals, the most comical and most often recognizable variation of the script—and one that has become a recurring motif in the genre of southern frontier humor and in Mark Twain, the chief beneficiary of this genre—is his run-in with stinging insects. Walter Blair has noted that Nott's use of a story involving stinging insects in *Novelettes* is possibly its earliest occurrence in American literature (*Mark Twain and Huck Finn* 242). The story the narrator Jerry recounts involves Tommy's acquaintance with a Dutch farmer, Geiermann Schmalbauch, a man of "sufficient property" and the father of two lovely daughters. As a major in the militia, Schmalbauch wishes for Singularity to teach him military tactics. Eager to exploit this new opportunity for romance and its attendant material benefits, Tommy impresses Schmalbauch favorably and is invited to give him further instruction. Prior to his visit to the Schmalbauch farm, however, Tommy, who has agreed to escort the farmer's daughters to a Sunday camp meeting, stops in route to change his soiled clothes. While still on his horse, a steed "young and spirited [but] docile," Tommy prepares to don a "garment of snowy hue . . . [which he] raised aloft on his arms . . . and just envelop[ing] his head," when he and his horse are unexpectedly encircled and attacked by a large swarm of yellow jackets (Nott 1: 97). Chaos ensues, and what follows is a scene of comic inconvenience, pain, and humiliation. In describing Tommy's predicament, Jerry spares no details—especially visual ones—in accentuating the moment and capitalizing on its rich comedic possibilities:

> Alarmed at the fierce assault . . . [Tommy's] courser bounded off like lightning, kicking and plunging in vain to disembarrass himself. Tommy could manage any horse without difficulty; but taken by surprise, with his head effectually muffled [his white garment was about his head when the yellow jackets attack], all he could do was to seize the mane with both hands. Away went the steed, peppered by myriads of the irritated insects—away he went, with a speed that could have distanced Gilpin, young Lochinvar, or Burger's Spectre Bridegroom. (Nott 1: 98)

Afflicted "with fright, surprise, and bodily agony," Tommy, still clinging desperately to his horse, encounters many people in route to the camp-meeting: "ladies and gentlemen, young and old, black and white, tag, rag, and bobtail, in chaises, carriages, and wagons, on horseback, muleback, and footback," [who clear the way] "for the flying horseman, and st[and] gazing with wonder at the unseemly sight." (Nott 1: 98). When the bewildered horse arrives at Schmalbauch's farm, Tommy, embarrassed and with his shirt still about his head, "his extraordinary and indecent appearance at midday, before a gentleman's house," is exposed before Mr.

Schmalbauch and his daughters, whom he had hoped to impress (Nott 1: 98). The comic reversal not only generates much laughter, but results in "pain and shame" as well as disgrace and disappointment for Singularity. Thoroughly humiliated and distressed, Singularity sends the Schmalbauch girls a message asking to be excused from accompanying them to the camp meeting and returns to town instead, never again to renew his pursuit of the farmer's favor or his daughters.

This episode, one of the most humorous in *Novelettes of a Traveller*, calls to mind a similar incident in John Robb's "Hoss Allen's Apology" (*Streaks of Squatter Life, and Far-West Scenes* 1847), in which a judge and his horse, misdirected in the swamp as part of a ruse, are attacked not by bees or hornets, but by a large swarm of stinging mosquitoes. Adventures in southern frontier humor involving stripping—intentional or otherwise—and more overtly risqué than Tommy Singularity's exposure, include the disrobing of the horseracing Mrs. Hibbs in Lewis's "A Tight Race Considerin," the somewhat subdued sexual foreplay in William C. Hall's "How Sally Hooter Got Snake-Bit," and the hunter-raconteur Jim Doggett being caught with his pants down during an interrupted bowel movement in Thorpe's "The Big Bear of Arkansas."

Variations of Nott's stinging insects script, presented as pranks and as accidents, have appeared so many times in southern frontier humor as to become one of the genre's most enduringly amusing motifs. Walter Blair has noted examples of the story in Thompson's version, usually either titled "Into a Hornets' Nest" (1843) or "The Unclad Horseman" (1849), "Deacon Smith's Bull, or Mike Fink in a Tight Place" (1851) by "Scroggins," and Harris's "Sicily Burns's Wedding" (1858) (*Mark Twain and Huck Finn* 242–43). Other antebellum southern humorists who have adopted and modified the story include C. M. Haile in "Letter from Pardon Jones" (20 July 1841), Thomas Bangs Thorpe in "Beyond the Cross Timbers" (Letter 12 in "Letters from the Far West," 1843), Ham Jones in "The Sandy Creek Literary Society" (1846), Lafayette Byrn in "The Way to Keep Folks from Marrying" in his *The Life and Adventures of an Arkansaw Doctor* (1851). and G. W. Harris in three additional Sut Lovingood tales: "Sut Lovengood's [*sic*] Daddy, Acting Horse" (1854), "Old Burns's Bull Ride" (1858), and "Sut at a Negro Night Meetin'" (1867).[6]

Mark Twain—who during his apprenticeship read and learned writing strategies from the southwest humorists, and who is considered their principal literary heir—also adapted the stinging insects motif for a tale featuring a boy riding a bull, intending to use it in *The Prince and the Pauper*. However, on the advice of William Dean Howells, Twain instead published the stinging insect tale in the Hartford *Bazaar Budget* on June 4, 1880, under the title "A Boy's Adventure" (Blair, *Mark Twain and Huck Finn* 243). Subsequently, Twain used a different version of this story "in a style more natural and restrained" in *Personal Recollections of Joan of Arc* (1896) (McKethan, "Mark Twain's Story" 250).[7]

In his portrayal of Tommy Singularity as a vagabond and sometime con man (albeit always an ineffectual one), Nott paved the way for a major character type some subsequent southern frontier humorists would feature. As a freewheeling and self-serving opportunist, Tommy represents an early version of the southern rapscallion, a rudimentary Simon Suggs. Though more cultured and sophisticated than Hooper's Suggs, Tommy shares similar interests and propensities. Like Simon, Tommy is inclined to gambling—particularly in card games—and to drinking, though neither brings him notoriety or material gain. Adventuresome and of questionable character, Tommy is also careless, his carelessness typically leading to his setbacks. Describing Singularity's character early in "Biographical Sketch," Jerry assuredly notes, "Tommy's career was marked by constant accidents and mishaps, arising no doubt, in most cases, from his great impatience, and want of ordinary precaution" (Nott 1: 26). And Tommy's two principal vices—drinking to excess and card playing—often lead to his undoing and humiliation, his failures typically prompting him to flee the scene. On one occasion, Tommy, accompanied by Jerry, frequents the backroom of a local groggery, where he engages "a portly gentleman, with large black whiskers, [and] extremely well dressed" (Nott 1: 41) at cards, and perceiving him an easy mark, intends to cheat the fellow. Misperceiving this man as "one of those good-natured, unsuspicious people that know little about the world" (Nott 1: 41), Tommy himself becomes the dupe, the victim of a comic reversal of expectations in which the would-be trickster is himself tricked. Giving the appearance of self-assuredness, Tommy proves vulnerable, drinking too much too quickly. As it turns out, the apparently clueless stranger is actually a "famous Virginia sportsman" . . . [who] was in the habit of visiting [the groggery] . . . placing marked cards in the way, by which more than one had been swindled" (Nott 1: 42). In this instance of comic turnaround, Tommy, Jerry reports, is "caught in his own trap by the land-shark" and loses virtually everything of value he has: his "cash, watch, breast-pin, rings, and gold sleeve-buttons" (Nott 1: 43, 42). A victim of situational irony and vanity, Singularity is deceived by someone he assumed was easy prey, but who actually is a better player, one more capable than he of effecting trust and actuating duplicity. Variations of the trickster-tricked motif, which Nott employs here, occur with some frequently in southern frontier humor and in Mark Twain—most notably in Longstreet's "The Horse-Swap," Baldwin's "Simon Suggs, Jr., Esq.: A Legal Biography," Harris's "Rare Ripe Garden Seed," and Twain's "Jim Smiley and His Jumping Frog" and *Adventures of Huckleberry Finn.*

Nott's Singularity also shares literary kinship with another brand of southern frontier humor character with an anti-heroic stripe: Kittrell J. Warren's Billy Fishback, a Confederate soldier and deserter who is the conscienceless rogue featured in *Life and Public Services of an Army Straggler* (1865). Unpatriotic and unscrupulous, Fishback is consumed by his own self-aggrandizement and regularly employs nefarious tactics for personal gain or advantage. Singularity, especially in his army service, closely resembles Fishback. Both are army deserters and bungling con artists whose scams and deceptions generally go awry. During his brief tenure in the army, Singularity proves to be shameless, unpatriotic, and hypocritical, displaying the same character traits Warren would subsequently feature in Fishback. In 1817, Singularity volunteers as part of a patriotic military group formed by Gregor McGregor, a Scotsman, who purportedly seeks to liberate the Spanish colonies in Florida seeking independence from Spain. Consisting of men of mixed nationalities and races—who, as Jerry ironically points out, "dignified themselves with the name of patriots"—this so-called "patriot army" "looked . . . like a mob assembled to pull down a jail. Many of them had never seen service, and many of them were drunk" (Nott 1: 56) as they prepared for their first military engagement at Amelia Island,. During this encounter, which turns out to be a travesty of military propriety and dignity, Tommy displays cowardice, lagging behind the rest of the group and informing McGregor, his commander, that he is sick with the colic and needs to lie down. But once McGregor threatens him, Tommy, colic or no, moves forward with the rest of the troop—though he soon falls to the rear again. Ultimately, the Spanish enemy capitulates without a shot being fired and seems ready to surrender the fort. Tommy, timeserver that he is, realizes that the anticipated danger is tenuous, even non-existent, and then advances to rally the patriot troops with pretended enthusiasm and braggadocio: "'No capitulation, fellow soldiers. . . . Let us storm the fort! [A]re patriots to listen to any terms of despots'" (Nott 1: 59). When McGregor informs his rag-tag soldiers that the Spanish cannon in the fort are likely pointed at them and would "produce destruction at the first fire," Tommy reverts to duplicity and faint-heartedness. Indubitably a charlatan, Tommy fails to back up his eloquence and headstrong words with exemplary action. Instead, Tommy's only action at Amelia Island is reprehensible: He unnecessarily plunders the homes of private citizens and steals their valuables, doing so covertly in defiance of McGregor's orders forbidding this kind of activity.

During the remainder of his volunteer army service, Tommy continues to show cowardice. Upon learning that the Spanish governor is marching from St. Augustine "with five hundred regular troops" (Nott 1: 64), Tommy and various other patriots desert, with the intent of fleeing to Georgia. Always looking out for his own self-interest, Singularity perceives himself as an undeserving victim. He facilely rationalizes his desertion by noting that "the heroic ardour with which he had proposed [earlier] to storm the fort [at Amelia Island] . . . [resulted neither] with promotion [n]or even commendation [and] had frequently been turned most cruelly into ridicule by McGregor and his officers" (Nott 1: 64). Even so, Tommy abandons his desertion plan once again, overcome by sickness, "a kind of dizziness [Jerry notes] which [Tommy] attributed to the bad quality of the Spanish brandy he had used that day . . . , [though] he often took the same quantity of good cognac without discomfort" (Nott 1: 65). While sickness prevents his desertion, it also provides him a face-saving opportunity to be physically present for the subsequent bloodless battle against the invading Spanish troops. Claiming affliction with another bout of the colic, Tommy is accorded permission to go to bed and not participate in the fray. But when he hears guns and assumes his fellow soldiers "were gathering fresh laurels, and that he alone was excluded from the rich harvest" (Nott 1: 66), Tommy, consumed by vanity, rejoins them. But as Jerry mockingly insinuates, Tommy yields again to his cowardly propensities, desiring to avoid any impending danger a battle with the Spaniards may bring. And as the context makes clear, Singularity never sincerely intended to risk his life in a confrontation with the Spanish:

> [Tommy] [d]uring the rest of the battle . . . stood manfully at his post; but, like a veteran, tempering his natural impulses by that discretion which one of the deepest searchers into the human heart has pronounced the better part of valour, when a sortie was proposed, he resolutely opposed the wanton loss of a single life, when it could easily be preserved by a prudent ensconcement. (Nott 66)

Even though Tommy eventually joins the regular army, he does so for unpatriotic and practical reasons, "having lost all of his money in "a run of ill-luck at cards" (Nott 1: 68). Needing money to return to the United States, he enlists for purely expedient and selfish reasons: by joining up, he receives fifty dollars. Predictably, he becomes disenchanted with military life—particularly when he hears his troop will be sent to Georgia to fight against the Seminoles—and then deserts the army, escaping by boat with three other soldiers. Consistently the scapegrace, Tommy Singularity shows by the end of his army sojourn that he possesses neither heroic fortitude nor moral fiber.

Wherever Tommy Singularity goes and whatever adversity he encounters, he shows a recurring predilection to pursue and achieve personal advantage—often with the intent of satisfying some avaricious design. One such activity involves horseracing, which for Tommy turns into a betting scam. Actually, horseracing was to become one of most familiar subjects featured in sketches and tales of southern frontier humor.[8] Porter's *Spirit of the Times*, the most famous venue for southern frontier humor, published numerous turf reports and even fictive accounts of horse races written by southern correspondents (usually in the form of sporting epistles), which began appearing in the *Spirit* in the mid-1830s. By including such materials, Porter sought to model the *Spirit* after the popular British sporting magazine, *Bell's Life in London* (Fienberg 271). He thus opened the door to showcasing materials, both true and fictive, written in response to the popular fascination with horseracing in the antebellum South, especially among men. Of the numerous humorous contributors to the *Spirit*, Charles F. M. Noland was not only the first southern correspondent, whose first sporting epistle appeared in 1836, but also a horse and racing enthusiast. Noland's many turf reports and fictive contributions to the *Spirit* (over three hundred), written under his pseudonyms, "N. of Arkansas" and "Pete Whetstone," often contain amusing references to and conversations about racehorses and horse races (Williams 23–24). Other well-known works of southern frontier humor, some also published in the *Spirit*, concern horse racing and/or the aftermath of races. For instance, "A Quarter Race in Kentucky," published in the *Spirit* in 1836 under the pseudonym "A North Alabamian," became the title story for one of Porter's two anthologies of humorous writing, both featuring comic sketches and tales previously published in the *Spirit*. Other humorists of the Old South who likewise included references to horseracing are Sol Smith who, in "The Consolate Widow," describes a drunken man in a quarter-mile race who runs into a whiskey house, killing both himself and his horse. Afterward, his widow laments the loss of the whiskey, rather than the loss of her husband. Also, Johnson Jones Hooper penned a sketch about Simon Suggs racing his father's plough horses. And Henry Clay Lewis wrote the highly dramatic and visually engaging "A Tight Race Considerin," featuring a race between an old farmwoman whose father used to own a racehorse and a circuit preacher. Most notably, Mark Twain, in "Jim Smiley and His Jumping Frog," features among Smiley's animals a mare that starts slowly but always wins races.

None of this background on horseracing is meant to suggest that Tommy Singularity's ill-fated episode with a racehorse in "A Biographical Sketch" directly inspired any of the sketches and tales of antebellum southern humorists who subsequently treated this subject. Still, Tommy's scam closely resembles the one involving Simon Suggs Jr. described above. Moreover, Nott's comical treatment of Tommy's horseracing debacle may be one of the first appearances of this scenario in southern writing. Having some knowledge of horses, Tommy purchases a racehorse with an unbecoming appearance and discovers it to be good racer—though no one, given the steed's "rough-looking" condition, would ever expect as much. Tommy even intends to keep the horse's coat in its unkempt state so as to deceive would-be bettors, hoping to entice them to wager against him in a race. He even uses Jerry as an accomplice to carry out this scheme, telling his friend "to bet against the horse; plenty will take you up, and I can make our rider hold in" (Nott 1: 101). Convinced his ploy is foolproof (as no one knows about the horse's potential capabilities except Jerry), on race day Tommy makes sure his horse appears "rough as a jackass" (Nott 1: 102), instructing the rider, Jerry reports, "to hold in [Sturgeonigger] from the start, and to let our rival merely gain the race by a neck or length at most, so as to give the appearance of a hard contest" (Nott 1: 102). Yet as it turns out, Sturgeonigger's rider has trouble holding him back, and Sturgeonigger wins the race by a length. Both Tommy, who had bet on his rival's horse as part of the stratagem, and Jerry, who bet against Tommy's horse, end up "penniless," losing all the money their friends had invested in this knavery.

A variation of this script would subsequently be employed by Simon Suggs Jr. in Baldwin's "Simon Suggs, Jr., Esq.: A Legal Biography," in which the title character attempts to hold back his horse because he has bet money on a competitor's horse. In Nott's episode, Tommy also loses the horse, having borrowed two hundred dollars from a man before the race, thereby mortgaging Sturgeonigger. When the lender, who believes that "Tommy had won handsomely" (Nott 1: 103), comes to collect the debt, Tommy has no money and is obliged to relinquish his horse. Another venture gone wrong, Tommy and Jerry find themselves in trouble with their friends, financial supporters of their scam, and fearing altercations and lawsuits, both quickly flee to Washington. Unlike so many con artists in southern frontier humor—most notably Simon Suggs and Sut Lovingood—Tommy Singularity proves worthless.

There is yet another link between Nott's "A Biographical Sketch of Thomas Singularity" and antebellum southern humor. Nott adopts a triangular love plot, which seems to come directly from Washington Irving's widely known "The Legend of Sleepy Hollow." This may be the first instance where Irving's story inspired a southern humorous text. Singularity's affairs of the heart form part of his humorous misadventures in "A Biographical Sketch," and one notable instance seems to share character types and plot elements that Irving first popularized in "Sleepy Hollow." Soon after he moves to Raleigh, North Carolina, one of the many places where Tommy, an itinerant journeyman printer, practices his trade, Singularity becomes attracted to Rebecca Kingman, the "only daughter of an honest farmer" and an apparently ingenuous young woman who has "not seen any thing of town-life" (Nott 1: 70, 73). In these respects she resembles Irving's Katrina Van Tassel. Like his literary prototype, Ichabod Crane, Tommy seems confident he can charm Rebecca and sure that his romantic conquest will be successful. Sharing Tommy's optimism, Jerry observes, "[I]n absence of other suitors, she might be dazzled with my friend's dandyish appearance, and amused with his jokes and tricks" (Nott

1: 71). Nott employs several other elements of the "Sleepy Hollow" script, including the lucrative benefits of marrying a wealthy farmer's daughter. Rebecca's father owns an inn, as well as a farm, slaves, and other property, and Rebecca "would get a good round sum of money when married, with an equal certainty of finally inheriting all her father's goods and chattels" (Nott 1: 71). In fact, it is Jerry who urges Tommy "not to let such a prize slip through his fingers" (Nott 1: 71). Though Rebecca appears naïve and inexperienced, Jerry questions her sincerity, noting that "with a prodigious show . . . of modesty and simplicity, I saw that she had a strong perception of the ridiculous, and frequently I was left in doubt whether her conversation with Tommy was downright artlessness or adroit quizzing" (Nott 1: 72). In short, Rebecca is likely a coquette and conniver, not the naïf she appears to be. To complete the "Sleepy Hollow" triangle, Nott does include a formidable rival for Tommy, a literary descendant of Irving's Brom Bones, in the character of Roger Saunders, "an awkward bumpkin" and a "stout, well-made fellow, with a pleasant face, and [who], in the midst of most helter-skelter rattling, made strong remarks and good hits in the way of a joke" (Nott 1: 71, 73). Through some collaborative dissembling on the part of Rebecca, Roger, and her father, Nott weaves a conflict-of-cultures subplot wherein the literate and literary townsman, outsider, and opportunist Tommy Singularity believes he is superior to the country bumpkin, Saunders. And like Irving, Nott executes a comical reversal in which Tommy actually becomes the dupe, losing Rebecca to Saunders in a marriage that seems to have been arranged even before Tommy began his romantic conquest. With the advantage of hindsight, Tommy indicates that rather than Roger Saunders being the one he and Jerry were "going to roast for our sport," the bumpkin Roger Saunders "was in very good-humour, kept up the fire manfully; and it seemed to me from the significant glances that were exchanged among him, the father, and daughter, that they were quizzing my friend most egregiously" (Nott 1: 73). Tommy becomes even more vulnerable on this occasion, as "seen in the incoherency of his conversation and faltering of his tongue" (Nott 1: 74) owing to excessive indulging in Mr. Kingman's spirits. And at the end of this episode, Mr. Kingman, fully cognizant of Tommy's inadequacies as a potential husband for Rebecca, explains to Jerry and the humiliated Tommy that Singularity is essentially a drunk and timeserver: "'As for my friend Tom, here,' . . . giving Singularity a thwack between the shoulders, 'if I don't get his money [the bill for the lodging, food, and hospitality] it will run down his throat somewhere else'" (Nott 76).

Washington Irving first used this script featuring the self-confident town dandy who becomes the victim of country artifice and conspiracy in "The Legend of Sleepy Hollow," and Nott may have been the first southerner to appropriate and transform it in "A Biographical Sketch of Thomas Singularity." The plot would subsequently appear in numerous other humorous rescriptings, becoming one of the scenarios most favored by Nott's antebellum southern frontier humor successors. Adaptations of the courtship triangle and refitted versions of the clash-of-cultures pattern—apparently conscious imitations of the "Sleepy Hollow" narrative—may be found in such southern frontier humorous sketches and tales as James Edward Henry's "The Kiss" (1843), William Tappan Thompson's "The Runaway Match; or, How the Schoolmaster Married a Fortune" (1848), Orlando Benedict Mayer's "The Corn Cob Pipe: A Tale of the Comet of '43" (1848), and Joseph Beckham Cobb's "The Legend of Black Creek" (1851) and "The Bride of Lick-the-Skillet" (1851). Several other pieces—Thompson's "Adventures of a Sabbath Breaker" (1839), Augustus Baldwin Longstreet's "The Turn Out" (1833), Francis James Robinson's "The Frightened Serenaders; or, the B'hoys in a Fix" (1853), and William Gilmore Simms's "How Sharp Snaffles Got His Capital and Wife" (1870)—likewise include echoes of "Sleepy Hollow," though to a lesser extent.[9] Mark Twain learned his craft from the southwestern humorists, and in his second published sketch, "The Dandy Frightening the Squatter" (1852), also seems to have drawn on the clash of genteel civilization and backwoods society that informs "Sleepy Hollow." And many years later William Faulkner, who was inspired by these humorists and seems to have known "Sleepy Hollow," used a variation of Irving's tale in the Labove, Eula Varner, and Hoake McCarron episode in *The Hamlet* (1940).[10]

As every student of southern frontier humor knows, Longstreet and his southern humorous contemporaries, "la[id] the foundations of a new style in American writing" (Cohen and Dillingham xxxi), giving their yeoman characters freedom to speak in their own vibrant vernacular idiom. "Rich in similes and metaphors and in exaggerations," Cohen and Dillingham observe, "this backwoods language is characterized by concreteness, freshness, and color. It was effective, too, because it rang true where the pale or pompous dialogues of the genteel novels were contrived and unrealistic" (xxxi). While Nott's contribution to the incipient robust style associated with southern frontier humor is minimal, and while in "Biographical Sketch" his narrator, Jeremiah Hopkins, principally employs a formal and literate voice, Nott occasionally creates a comic impression by turning to figurative language in an attempt to deliver an exaggerated or accentuated effect—most notably through incongruous comparisons, one of the familiar discourses Longstreet and his successors would also employ. For example, early in the narrative, Tommy Singularity feigns a headache because he does not want to attend a Sunday church service. When Mr. Shepherd, Tommy's employer, who has excused him from church attendance, asks to borrow his prayer book, Singularity "instead . . . jerked out of his pocket an old dog-eared pack of cards" (Nott 1: 18–19). Jerry, dropping his former demeanor, reports that Mr. Shepherd, who cannot tolerate card playing and who regards gambling as morally objectionable, angrily "flew at Singularity, and applied slaps with both hands as rapidly as a weaver ever plied the fly–shuttle, and with a noise not unlike it" (Nott 1: 19). In a similar instance involving the interweaving of physical comedy, violence, and consequent humiliation, Nott employs incongruous comparison again, using Jerry as his mouthpiece. Mr. Murray, nicknamed "Little Hercules," a man of "great strength, which was kept in full power by hunting and athletic pursuits," and of "ruddy complexion" and standing "about five feet six inches high, with a breadth of shoulder, expansion of the chest, and powerful but well-modeled regularity of limb" (Nott 1: 48), publicly whips Tommy in retaliation for the latter's romantic pursuit of his niece. In a visually figurative and lightly amusing description of Tommy's predicament and subsequent helplessness, Jerry, again dropping his formal pose, creates the desired exaggerated impression by invoking a flurry of successive animal images: "All struggling was bootless in the grip of one who held his prey as firmly as the line does a deer, or, the cat a mouse." Caught off guard by the "sudden attack" of his stronger adversary, Tommy, as Jerry further notes, "raised a faint yell of mingled fear and pain, like the bleatings of a suffering kid." When the pain of the flogging begins to torment Tommy, "he proffered bellowings as loud as 'the wolf's long howl from Onalaska's shore'" (Nott 1: 50–51). While such hyperbole pales in comparison to the elaborate figurative descriptions of Harris, Thorpe, and some of their contemporary southern frontier humorists, it nevertheless represents the rudimentary beginnings of colorful and unrestrained backwoods speech.

In 1985, William E. Lenz, in *Fast Talk and Flush Times: The Confidence Man as a Literary Convention,* observed that Nott's "Biographical Sketch of Thomas Singularity" "displays its descent from periodical and picaresque fiction, borrowing from American soil only its ostensible location. At best Thomas Singularity's misadventures with snakes, bees, and women appear diluted versions of Teague O'Regan's" in Hugh Henry Brackenridge's 1804 novel, *Modern Chivalry* (40). And while Lenz subsequently observes that Tommy Singularity represents a stage in the emergence of the confidence man as a literary type, he ultimately sees the con artist as an "inherited" stock character or device. Regarding the development of the confidence man as a literary convention, one evolving from a "vertical model of historical continuity," Lenz claims, "the desire to create a native literature led writers in 1820s and 1830s to insert in American settings inherited conventions like the prankster with little more than a change of clothes; the continuity from Brom Bones to Thomas Singularity to Ned Brace [the latter the con-prankster in Longstreet's "The Character of a Native Georgian"] is direct or vertical" (64–65). While Lenz's attempt to establish a line of descent in the evolution of the confidence man character seems astute and incisive, it does not take into account the full significance Nott's work as a seminal stage in the emergence of the genre of antebellum southern frontier humor. Though by no measure a work of significant literary artistry, Nott's "Biographical Sketch of Thomas Singularity" may be the long overlooked link between American Down East humor of the early 1830s—particularly Seba Smith's comic epistles of Major Jack Downing—and Longstreet's *Georgia Scenes,* the latter most often credited with inaugurating the humor of the Old South upon its publication in 1835.

Even though in "Biographical Sketch of Thomas Singularity" Henry Junius Nott offers an elemental rendering of the southern confidence man in a humorous context, clearly suggesting the outlines of characters like Hooper's Simon Suggs, Baldwin's Simon Suggs Jr., Kittrell Warren's Billy Fishback and other southern backwoods rogues, this novelette offers still more components significant to the emergence of southern frontier humor. It features many of the subjects antebellum southern humorists would subsequently treat—including the hunt, courtship, fighting, horse races, card games and gambling, pranks and deceptions, cowardice, drinking and drunkenness, and the humorous confrontation between men and animals—and in so doing may be related to them intertexually.[11] Moreover, Nott, at least in book form, seems to have employed most of these topics first, perceiving in them materials potentially useful for humor. Nott also was probably the first southern writer to appropriate for comical purposes the themes, character types, and several of the plot parallels from "The Legend of Sleepy Hollow," Washington Irving's classic clash-of-cultures sketch. In doing so, Nott seems to have recognized the comic possibilities inherent in several character types appropriate to southern frontier humor: the dandy, the prankster, the con artist, and the rural rowdy. While "Biographical Sketch of Thomas Singularity" does not exhibit the raucous energy, stylistic flair, and earthiness of backwoods vernacular discourse that would become a signal trait in many of the sketches and tales of Longstreet, Hooper, Thorpe, Lewis, Harris, and lesser practitioners of the southern frontier humor genre, Nott's text does occasionally show flashes of humorous exaggeration effected through incongruous comparisons. In using figurative discourse in this way, Nott anticipated—though less brilliantly than his southern humorist successors—the comic possibilities of hyperbolic language. After considering all these connections, if we still have doubts about Henry Junius Nott's modest but essential contributions to shaping the outlines of what would become the humor of the Old South, we run the risk of overlooking an important stage in the historical evolution of what would become the dominant strain in American humor.

NOTES

1. Several sources examine the analogues and precursors of antebellum southern humor. Lemay's *Men of Letters in Colonial Maryland* 1357–61 and Davis's *Intellectual Life in the Colonial South* Volume 3, 1357–59, discuss Cook's *The Sot-Weed Factor*; Cohen and Dillingham in their introduction to *Humor of the Old Southwest* discuss James Kirke Paulding, Parson Weems, Timothy Flint, Raspe's Baron Munchausen, Joseph Doddridge, and Irving's "Sleepy Hollow." More extensive exploration of the Munchausen connection is found in Blair's "A German Connection: Raspe's Baron Munchausen," and of the "Sleepy Hollow" influence in Piacentino's "'Sleepy Hollow' Come South: Washington Irving's Influence on Old Southwestern Humor." Lemay's "The Origins of the Humor of the Old South" focuses on Henry Timrod's poetry. Though little has been written on the influence of the British sporting epistle, one can find brief treatment in Blair's "Traditions

in Southern Humor," 20–21 and in Wimsatt and Phillips's "Antebellum Humor" chapter in the *History of Southern Literature*, 136. Concerning the contents and subtitles of Egan's books, as Walter Blair has noted, they resemble the sporting epistles and subtitle of William Trotter Porter's New York weekly, the *Spirit of the Times: A Chronicle of the Turf, Agriculture, Field Sports, Literature, and the Stage*, which began publication in 1831 and which became the major venue for southern frontier humor ("Traditions in Southern Humor" 20, 19).

2. The principal sources for biographical information on Nott are Cummings's essay, 3797–802 in *Library of Southern Literature* and the section on Nott in Wauchope's *The Writers of South Carolina*, 209–17. For other brief biographical accounts of Nott, see LaBorde's *History of the South Carolina College*, 209–14 and the Duyckincks's *Cyclopedia of American Literature*, 30–31.
3. O'Neall 513 corroborates LaBorde's assessment of Nott's personality, writing, "He was of a lively, cheerful disposition, fond of anecdote, and a companionable man."
4. O'Neall 513 confirms that the Thomas Singularity section "although . . . a sprightly tale, well written, yet there was much in it which was displeasing to the religious community."
5. Wauchope 59 may have been the first to point out the literary lineage of *Novelettes*, dubbing Thomas Singularity as a "lineal descendant of the rogues of the early picaresque romances."
6. Haile's "Pardon Jones Letter" was published on 20 July 1841 in the New Orleans *Picayune*; Thorpe's "Beyond the Cross Timbers" was published in the Vidalia, Louisiana, *Concordia Intelligencer* under the pseudonym P. O. F. on 10 Feb. 1844; Jones's "The Sandy Ridge Literary Society" appeared on 15 Aug. 1846 in the *Spirit of the Times*; Harris's "Sut Lovengood [*sic*], Acting Horse" was initially published in the *Spirit of the Times* on 4 Nov. 1854; "Old Burns's Bull Ride" was published in the *Nashville Union and American* on 22 Apr. 1858; and "Sut at a Negro Night Meeting"' was published in *Sut Lovingood: Yarns* in 1867.
7. D. M. McKethan, in "Mark Twain's Story of the Bull and the Bees" and in his subsequent article, "Bull Rides Described by 'Scroggins,' G. W. Harris, and Mark Twain," provides the most detailed account of the bull and bees story and points out that either Harris's "Sicily Burns's Wedding" or Scroggins's "Deacon Smith Bull, or Mike Fink in a Tight Place" may have influenced Twain's adaptations of this script, though McKethan indicates Twain's versions seem more similar to Harris's story than to Scroggins's ("Bull Rides" 243).
8. Cohen and Dillingham xxiv include horseracing with the category of games and contests among the twenty-two subjects commonly used by the southwestern humorists.
9. My article, "Sleepy Hollow Comes South: Washington Irving's Influence on Old Southwestern Humor," examines the Irving influence in all of these tales, except Henry's "The Kiss." For a brief analysis of the "Sleepy Hollow" connection in that story, see Piacentino's "The Comic Voice of James Edward Henry: Reclaiming Another Writer for the Tradition of Southwestern Humor" 57–58.
10. The most recent and substantive examination of *The Hamlet* and "Sleepy Hollow" is Sarah Clere's "Faulkner's Appropriation of 'The Legend of Sleepy Hollow' in *The Hamlet*."
11. The subjects that Nott treats might be favorably compared to the general list of topical categories mentioned in Cohen and Dillingham xxiv.

WORKS CITED

Blair, Walter. "A German Connection: Raspe's Baron Munchausen." *Critical Essays on American Humor*. Ed. William B. Clark and W. Craig Turner. Boston: Hall 1984. 123—39.

———. *Mark Twain and Huck Finn*. Berkeley: University of California Press, 1960. Print.

———. *Native American Humor*. Chicago: Chandler, 1960. Print.

———. "Traditions in Southern Humor." *Essays on American Humor: Blair Through the Ages*. Ed. Hamlin Hill. Madison: University of Wisconsin Press, 1994. 15—24. Print.

Clere, Sarah. "Faulkner's Appropriation of 'The Legend of Sleepy Hollow' in *The Hamlet*." *Mississippi Quarterly* 62.3 (2009): 443—56. Print.

Cohen, Hennig, and William B. Dillingham. Introduction. *Humor of the Old Southwest*. Athens: University of Georgia Press, 1994. xv—xl. Print.

Cummings, St. James, Jr. "Henry Junius Nott." *Library of Southern Literature*. Ed. Edwin Anderson Alderman and Joel Chandler Harris. Vo. 9. Atlanta: Martin Hoyt, 1907. 3797—825. Print.

Davis, Richard Beale. *Intellectual Life in the Colonial South*. Vol. 3. Knoxville: University of Tennessee Press, 1978. Print.

Duyckinck, Evert A., and George L. Duyckinck. "Henry Junius Nott." *Cyclopedia of American Literature*. Vol. 2. 1854. Print.

Fienberg, Lorne. "*Spirit of the Times*." *American Humor Magazines and Comic Periodicals*. Ed. David E. E. Sloane. Westport, CT: Greenwood Press, 1987. 271—78. Print.

Harris, George Washington. "Sut Lovingood's Sermon." *Sut Lovingood's Yarns*. Ed. M. Thomas Inge. New Haven, CT: College & University Press, 1966. 138—43.

Inge, M. Thomas, and Edward J. Piacentino, eds. *The Humor of the Old South*. Lexington: University Press of Kentucky, 2001.

LaBorde, Maximilian. *History of the South Carolina College From Its Incorporation December 19, 1801 to Nov. 25, 1857*. Columbia, SC: P. B. Glass, 1859. Print.

Lemay, J. A. Leo. *Men of Letters in Colonial Maryland*. Knoxville: University of Tennessee Press, 1972. Print.

———. "The Origins of the Humor of the Old South." Inge and Piacentino. 13–21. Print.

Lenz, William E. *Fast Talk and Flush Times: The Confidence Man as a Literary Convention*. Columbia: University of Missouri Press, 1985. Print.

McKethan, D. M. "Bull Rides Described by 'Scroggins,' G. W. Harris, and Mark Twain." *Southern Folklore Quarterly* 17 (1953): 241–43. Print.

———. "Mark Twain's Story of the Bull and the Bees." *Tennessee Historical Quarterly* 11 (1952): 246–53. Print.

"Nott Henry Junius." *The Oxford Companion to American Literature*. 6th ed. Ed. James D. Hart and Phillip W. Leininger. New York: Oxford University Press, 1995. Print.

Nott, Henry Junius. "A Biographical Sketch of Thomas Singularity." *Novelettes of a Traveller; or, Odds and Ends from the Knapsack of Thomas Singularity*. 2 vols. New York: Harper and Brothers, 1834. 2–110. Print.

O'Neall, John Belton. *Biographical Sketches of the Bench and Bar of South Carolina*. Vol. 2. Charleston, SC: S. G. Courtenay, 1859. Print.

Piacentino, Ed. "The Comic Voice of James Edward Henry: Reclaiming Another Writer for the Tradition of Southwestern Humor." *Studies in American Humor* 3.10 ns (2003): 51–64. Print.

———. "'Sleepy Hollow' Comes South: Washington Irving's Influence on Old Southwestern Humor." Inge and Piacentino 22–35.

Porter, William T. Editorial Note to "Taking the Census in Alabama." New York *Spirit of the Times* 9 Sept. 1843: 326. Print.

Rev. of *Novelettes of a Traveller*, by Henry Junius Nott. *American Monthly Magazine* 1 Nov. 1834: 143–44. Print.

Wauchope, George Armstrong. *The Writers of South Carolina. With a Critical Introduction, Biographical Sketches, and Selections in Prose and Verse.* Columbia, SC: Slate Co., 1910. Print.

Williams, Leonard. Introduction. *Cavorting on the Devil's Fork: the Pete Whetstone Letters of C. F. M. Noland.* Ed. Williams. Memphis, TN: Memphis State University Press, 1979. 1–54.

Wimsatt, Mary Ann, and Robert L. Phillips. "Antebellum Humor." *The History of Southern Literature.* Ed. Louis D. Rubin Jr. Baton Rouge: Louisiana State University Press, 1985. 136–56. Print.

Yates, Norris W. *William T. Porter and the Spirit of the Times.* (1957). New York: Arno Press, 1977.

HYSTERICAL POWER

Frontier Humor and Genres of Cultural Conquest

JENNIFER A. HUGHES

> We consider a feller a flunk and a sneak if he don't take an eye-opener in the morning and an antifigmatic about nine o'clock. . . . If he can't hunt, perhaps he can fight; and if he can't fight perhaps he can scream; and if he can't scream, *perhaps he can grin pretty severe*; and if he can't do that, perhaps he can tell a story.
>
> –*The Crockett Almanac for 1841*

IN THIS PASSAGE FROM THE NASHVILLE SERIES OF CROCKETT ALmanacs, Davy Crockett's definition of the person who is not scorned by Kentuckians as a "flunk and a sneak" is less narrow than a reader familiar with the machismo of southwestern humor might expect. An inability to perform conventional manly activities such as hunting and fighting is forgiven so long as a man has the ability to "scream," "grin," or simply tell a good story. Crockett suggests that to be welcomed into frontier society one might either laugh, or tell the kind of story that could make others laugh. He democratically levels the social values of the uproarious audience and the humorist in this description of how to be accepted into his community. While the Crockett almanacs of the antebellum era were concerned generally with white male experience and often presumed a white male readership, they also joined in a broader ideological vision of the nation as good-humored and laughing. Laughter, which southwestern publications instigated and celebrated in abundance, was figured as the voice of not only the common *man*, but of the common American. In this essay, I argue that the inscription of hilarity upon American bodies—male and female, white and non-white, adult and child—was a revolutionary, ideologically-motivated act on the part of southwestern humorists, who were engaged in vying for cultural conquest regarding how the new United States would envision itself as a nation.

When Jane Tompkins argued in *Sensational Designs* that evangelical, sentimental literature should be seen as a radically orchestrated effort by women and men to conquer and control early American society, she revolutionized the canon of nineteenth-century American literature. Previously dismissed works such as Susan Warner's *The Wide, Wide World* and even Harriet Beecher Stowe's *Uncle Tom's Cabin* were revitalized in the eyes of scholars, who no longer saw them as submissive texts lacking the empowerment and ideological coherence of works already accepted into the canon, such as Herman Melville's *Moby-Dick* or Walt Whitman's *Leaves of Grass*. However, as exciting as Tompkins's work was and still is, it reinforces a critical dichotomy between sentimental "women's literature" and elite "masculine" literature. Tompkins validates literature of the emotions in opposition to literature of the mind, but in doing so she imagines a culture war between these two genres—and these two genres alone. Although this dichotomy has in recent decades shaped much scholarship of nineteenth-century American literature, we alter it substantially by including southwestern humor in the critical picture. When we speak of southwestern humor as a "conquering" literature, we are usually speaking of a literature associated with the conquest of people and of land in America's frontiers. However, southwestern humor was also involved in the battle for national and even world ideology, set against the visions of other widely read literatures. The battle cry was "Laugh and grow fat!" and the proper exercise of the risible muscles was potentially enough to render anyone a valid, successful member of the ideal American society. As Colonel Crockett implies, having hilarity at one's beck and call—in order to make others laugh or to laugh oneself—would be the key to acceptance and to social power. As a genre that celebrates comic embodiment over seriousness and self-control, frontier humor eschews Tompkins's sentimental "vocabulary of clasping hands and falling tears" in order to forward a vocabulary of knee slapping and screaming laughter (132). Additionally, it is not merely a satisfying joke for the masses that frontier humor so frequently ridicules people of privilege; rather, the joke itself implies that people of privilege are weakened by their inattention to hilarity. In the era of its publication, frontier humor was a concentrated force that asserted the moral and practical supremacy of hilarious affect over lachrymose sincerity, struggling against the value shared by both evangelicals and elitists that humor was essentially a waste of time and energy. Frontier humor sought to indoctrinate its readership into a way of being—a way of feeling, a form of embodiment—through its promotion of laughter.

James Justus posits in his introduction to *Fetching the Old Southwest* that of all the facets of the writing of the Old Southwest that we might examine, "in both bulk and interest its humor is the most important" (3). From outrageous hunts to clever pranks, humor is at the center of the genre, but I am arguing that the genre's urge to discuss and promote laughter is more important. That is, for this essay, the question of what *causes* laughter is irrelevant. I do not discuss jokes or any theory—abstract or contextual—of why we laugh at them. Rather, I am delineating the ways in which antebellum authors were engaged rhetorically in an effort to shape their society's beliefs about the importance and significance of laughter itself to the process of imagining an ideal nation. I suggest that many humorist authors considered themselves to be fighting against generalized enemies—sentimental literatures, activist literatures, intellectual literatures—that disparaged or dismissed hilarity. Within the genre of early frontier humor, laughter was viewed as a panacea for human ills, as an utterance that—no matter its cause—rendered the human body both physically and mentally suited to the demands of citizenship within democracy. Within this ideology, laughter was the key to sanity. This view was directly opposed, for instance, to that of many reformers and Christian evangelicals, who construed laughter as dangerous. To their way of thinking, laughter threatened to possess or even colonize the body with a weak will. In its throes, then, one might forget pious duties and responsibilities. Overpowering, hysterical laughter was seen to take over the body and mind, and it was pointed to as evidence of insanity.

To antebellum Americans laughter was, for better or worse, a radical utterance. As it rippled across a body, it could empower the otherwise disenfranchised individual or disenfranchise the empowered. Humorists, above all else, championed laughter as empowering. In an era in which sex, race, and age determined both one's status and citizenship, the idea that an ephemeral utterance might transcend such predetermination was revolutionary. Although this ideological revolution was not restricted to, and did not necessarily even begin with, frontier humor, humorists in the genre promulgated a vision of an expanded democracy through hilarity, carrying it westward and sending it back to the East.

The Emergence of a Battle Cry

As a sub-genre of early American humor, frontier humor emerged in the context of the printing boom of the early 1830s, during which the American public was increasingly offered relatively inexpensive comic materials, including joke books, magazines, gift books, and newspapers, as well as tickets to laughing gas exhibitions, minstrel shows, and comic lectures. Advertisements for these products and services—and the products and services themselves—repeatedly promoted the somatic virtues of laughter. "Laugh and Grow Fat!" became the battle cry of comic publication and performance in the competitive marketplace. Products promised to deliver laughter in order to help consumers—generally, but not always imagined to be white men—as the best way of maintaining the proper body and mind-set for the republican ideal. A laughing body was an empowered body, growing vital, hearty, and reasonable with each salubrious gasp. Notably, this assumption about laughter's powers applied to disenfranchised groups, too, assisting each human body in its growth toward more perfect humanity. Humor and its promotion therefore became a forum for subtle consideration of antebellum anxieties over citizenship and human rights through overt examination of who had the right to laugh.

For example, one of the earliest publications dedicated entirely to humor was the *American Comic Almanac* (the *ACA*), which, beginning in 1831, was published by Charles Ellms of Boston. On the cover of the 1833 edition of the *ACA*, a cartoon of an exceedingly fat man sitting on a platter asks readers to "Sit down and feed and welcome to our table." The cover links the process of "consuming" humorous literature to the process of consuming food; both offer sustenance and put meat on the bones by promoting a sanguine body. Imagery of comic literature spread across plates being lifted up to grinning mouths with oversized forks, or being devoured by grotesquely obese figures, appears over and over again in ads and in the texts themselves. *Turner's Comick Almanack for 1844* contains an exemplary cartoon (see fig. 1). The text accompanying the cartoon explains how the laughing host (at the center) of a dinner party offers a meal of *Turner's* as a cure for his "dyspeptic" guest (the thin, spectacled man who is prodding the almanac with a fork). The host promises that this meal will "shake from their bodies all traces of disease, debility, and blue devils." The cartoon playfully suggests that the guest's digestive and temperamental ailments stem from a dearth of hilarity in his literary diet. Notice, though, in the margins of the cartoon that a woman, a black man, and a young girl are included in the joke and are visibly participating in the healthful laughter. *Turner's* self-advertisement, like many antebellum comic publications, frequently addresses its audience with broad, if careful, inclusivity. While including the maid, the black servant, and the child in the laughter might easily be viewed as merely paternalistic, consider this promotional passage found in the same almanac:

> Be it known throughout the twenty-six sovereign states, and the three territories of Uncle Sam, and to all the men, women, and little boys and little gals thereof, and *to others who desire to laugh, love and grow fat*, that this year will be distributed for the benefit of So-sigh-e-ty, the digestive organs, and the risible muscles, the titter-i-cal, crack-your-side-i-cal, stretch your face-i-cal Comic Almanac of the said Turner and Fisher, known as professors of comic philosophy and laughing salvation. Therefore, come ye forth and laugh, one and all, and the lord save your sides. ("Proclamation X-traordinary," emphasis added)

The advertisement pointedly asks not only men, but also women, children, and "others" to "come ye forth and laugh." Crossing "So-sigh-e-ty's" boundaries of gender and age, this ad's reference to "others who desire" implies both racial inclusion and, indeed, international inclusion—people not living within Uncle Sam's empire—in the prospect of "laughing salvation." This attempt to reach out to all comers creates the possibility of not just an expanded national market, but an expansion of the right to laugh to individuals other than those who would have been generally considered proper consumers or legal citizens. Here, *Turner's* promulgates a vision of people of all genders, ages, races, and nations choosing for themselves a "comic philosophy" as a form of empowered self-improvement.

Veins of this comic philosophy appear repeatedly in early American popular culture, often in opposition to other philosophies. An itinerant performer known as Dr. Valentine advertised his comic impersonations by prescribing laughter as medication, saying, "In order to decide on things and matter properly, the internal organs should be maintained

Figure 1: From *Turner's Comick Almanack for 1844*. Courtesy of the American Antiquarian Society.

in a healthy state of action," adding that laughing at his performance "may be relied upon as a complete antidote to THE HORRORS, THE BLUE DEVILS, and a thousand other evils that the flesh is heir to" ("Dr. Valentine" Broadside). His argument pertains to both the personal and political; it imagines laughter to be good for his audiences' bodies, and also for preserving their ability to make good decisions—a critical skill for the democratic masses to maintain. Laughing gas exhibitions, during which members of the audience inhaled nitrous oxide until they laughed and danced in a state of giddy intoxication, drew crowds of people who heeded the call: "Care to our coffin adds a nail no doubt, / While every grin so merrily draws one out" ("Scientific Amusement" Broadside). Not only do such advertisements promote the benefits of hilarity, they subtly denigrate seriousness and sentimentality. They imply that sober publications or performances potentially endanger the well-being and decision-making prowess of consumers.

Comic publications were not the only voice discussing laughter in antebellum popular print culture. The assertion of laughter's benefits to society was often opposed from within what Ronald Walters calls "an incredible proliferation of reforms in the pre–Civil War years"—a proliferation of activists who advanced abolition, women's rights, temperance, prison and asylum reform, and many other causes (xi). In reformist and other serious-minded American publications, laughter was characterized as trivial at best and morally distracting or degenerate at worst. As we will see below, comic materials were often considered morally suspect, and laughter was represented in terms of superfluity and moral laxity. These differences of opinion about laughter show up in advertisements like the following:

> We caution our readers, who want new Almanacs, not to pay their sixpences for useless trash under the name of *Comic Almanacs,* or any similar collection of nonsense, while the Anti-Slavery Almanac may be obtained for the same price, at the Anti-Slavery Office, 143 Nassau street. ("The Anti-Slavery Almanac" in *The Colored American*)

This brief 1839 ad for the *American Anti-Slavery Almanac* (the *AASA*) directly acknowledges competition between itself and comic almanacs, frankly addressing the financial stakes. Money was not the only reason reformers were anxious about the comedy industry, though. Frustration with exuberant language promoting and celebrating laughter—a language glib, light, and frequently dismissive of the sobering aspects of life—also leads the promoters of the *AASA* to encourage consumers to spend for a cause. This sincere and succinct advertisement is cast as a benevolent warning, a "caution" against wasting one's money on "useless trash" and "nonsense." It hints at an anxiety about material that elicits laughter, an anxiety the following blurb from the *New Bedford Mercury* expounds upon in condemning humorous personalities, or jesters:

> They have, of all people, the least real knowledge of the human heart—though they often make it their boast, that they know human nature thoroughly; the least tenderness for those little infirmities which cling to the best of human beings; the least sympathy in bodily or mental affections; the least reverence for the image of God in the mind of man. When once the spirit of ridicule has taken possession, thenceforth farewell high and noble feeling . . . We often feel affection for the individual who has extorted from us tears; but he who drags forth, hour after hour, *unwilling laughter*, is never regarded with complacency. ("Pleasant Companions," emphasis added)

That one might be joshed, unwillingly, into moral degeneracy is a striking suggestion. The anonymous author here is anxious about the jester using laughter to colonize the minds of otherwise godly people, usurping all good things: tenderness, sympathy, reverence. In this formulation, he who laughs is sick because hilarity conquers all the virtues—at least those we find celebrated in sentimental literature. Indeed, laughter-as-illness is viewed in this passage as not far from demonic possession, a semi-Satanic obstruction between a human being and God. Similar language in an 1861 article from the *Christian Recorder* is evidence of the persistence of the idea that laughter is wickedly overpowering. Hilarity is vividly described, again, in terms of "fiendish" demonic possession: "It [laughter] arouses the most fiendish passions; the eye flashes, the bosom heaves tumultuously over the feverish fire that rages within it, the heart beats wildly, and all control is gone" ("On Ridicule"). The unsigned author presents the bodily act of laughing—forgetting what sort of risibility created it—as excessive, grotesque, and insane. Here, laughter is a terrifying loss of control.

The pro-laughter and anti-laughter blurbs discussed above represent a small sampling of a conversation about hilarity found in the almanacs, advertisements, broadsides, and newspapers of the antebellum popular print marketplace. These publications record an avid disagreement about the values of laughter and of seriousness of purpose, which are envisioned by some as diametrically opposed. However, I aver that such texts as the Crockett almanacs, Augustus Longstreet's "The Horse-Swap," Thomas Bangs Thorpe's "The Big Bear of Arkansas," Mary Clavers's *A New Home–Who'll Follow?* and other works of frontier humor are pro-laughter, while also remaining quite serious about creating a national literature that addresses political, social, and artistic concerns. If we understand elite, masculine literature as "serious about" conquering culture in order to define great American literature, and sentimental literature as "serious about" conquering culture for a perfect Christian society through abundant tears and earnest supplication to God, then frontier humor was "serious about" conquering culture in order to create a more perfect, laughing citizenry. Such a citizenry would be interested in individual empowerment and the expansion of democracy through practical efforts to be healthy in mind and body. Hence the giddily disingenuous and sometimes sacrilegious writings of frontier humorists would have been viewed much like literary enemies on a strategically important battlefield. While Stowe or Hawthorne saw a casualty or a prisoner of war each time hysterical laughter overtook a reader's body, frontier humorists saw a new subject or convert.

Manifest Hilarity

In 1847 a reviewer of the Christy Minstrels, a blackface minstrelsy troop, declared to the readers of the *Spirit of the Times*:

> We do not go to see these gentlemen, no matter what band they belong to, for the expansion of our sentimentalism, but to laugh and grow fat. At Palmo's, we listen and are pleased, but leave with little desire to return. At the Mechanic's Hall, we listen and laugh, and have a desire to go again, and again. And in this feeling, we believe the great majority of the people is with us. ("Christy's Minstrels")

Here we see a direct affront to sentimental culture coming from the journal that propelled so many southwestern humorists to fame. Sentimental productions are deemed acceptably pleasant but ultimately dismissible, while the preference for comic over sentimental production is presented as a natural preference confirmed by the wise majority. Eric Lott's research into minstrelsy demonstrates that "assertions of the genuine fun inspired turn up with some frequency in the commentary on blackface, and they offer compelling evidence of the kind of pleasure minstrelsy afforded—so supremely infectious that it begged to be repeated" (*Love and Theft*, 141). However, what Lott sees as a compulsive Freudian drive to repeat "infectious" pleasure, the reviewer—by citing the axiom "laugh and grow fat"—construes as a drive towards healthy activity. One returns to laughing just as one returns to eating—or to anything that enriches one's life. Laughing bodies, growing steadily heartier and happier through risibility, are placed in the foreground by humorists and consumers of humor. Notably, due to the fact that it is an unsigned blurb in his own paper, the appreciative reviewer who believes that the "great majority of people" agreed with him on the virtue of laughing is most likely the influential William T. Porter himself, founder of *Spirit of the Times* and avid promoter of southwestern humor.

Frontier humorists responded to the invocation to "Laugh and Grow Fat," writing against the fear of what laughter could do to an individual body, and seeking to inculcate the idea that laughter would strengthen American society rather than weaken it. Texts crawl with hilarity on all levels: The protagonists and narrators giggle and guffaw, the narratives' audiences laugh with or at them, and the external reader is invited to join in the cachinnating fun. As the epigram from the Crockett almanac that appears at the top of this essay shows, a "comic philosophy" of inclusion traveled west with southwestern humor, and the genre touts the panacean, empowering promise of laughter in its own language. The New York publisher of racy papers and comic materials, R. H. Elton, for example, picked up on the craze for Davy Crockett tales and began publishing *Crockett's Yaller Flower Almanac*, telling jokes in dialect. Elton also borrowed Crockett's punchy voice to cross-advertise his other comic almanac:

> Oh cricky! What lots of Fun, ki eye! If that 'ere Elton's Comic All-my-nack for '36 aint a screamer, I'm blessed; the way it takes with me is a caution. There now, if you've got the hypo, cut your stick, marvel I say, up to 134 Division street, and the way you'll be cured is no man's business. (*Elton's Comic All-my-nack for 1841*)

Elton puts the language of "laughter as the best medicine" in the colonel's mouth, and the tall tales of the Crockett almanacs uphold the idea that this laughing ideology was moving southwest. They link the idealization of healthy, democratic masculinity to gut-shaking, profuse laughter. Indeed, laughter is as much the language of the "common man" as is unorthodox orthography in these texts, while a tendency toward illness or even a belief in illness ("the hypo") is aligned with effete elites. Here, laughter bespeaks vigor and vitality. Tales of Davy Crockett boast that he could "run faster, dive deeper, stay longer under, and come out drier than any other chap this side of the big swamp; and can *grin the bark off a tree*—look a panther to death—take a steam boat on his back" (*Crockett's Yaller Flower*). Remarkably, we see that Davy includes hilarity in his list of exuberant athletic feats. In another almanac, the size and duration of the Colonel's laugh relates just how heroically hearty he is:

> While I was in Texas, I met my old friend General Jimmy Raymond, the wild beast collector for all creation; he wanted about fifty men to go into Mixico, to catch an all tearin she tiger, and her young cubs for his great Zoological Institute. Well, soon as he spoke o' fifty men, I broke out instinctively into a horse laugh fit that lasted nearly an hour. It fairly shook the clothes off my back. (*Crockett's Almanac for 1846*)

Such dynamic manliness does not merely laugh off danger; it "instinctively" ridicules to excess what would otherwise be considered conventional masculine pursuits. Crude, healthy, and audacious, the Crocketts, Finks, and other "gamecocks of the wilderness" repeatedly express a belief that laughter renders a man masculine, muscular, and American. As Constance Rourke put it in her 1931 classic, *American Humor*, "Comic resilience swept through [the backwoodsmen] in waves, transcending the past, transcending terror, with the sense of comedy, itself a wild emotion" (44). The wildness of this transcendence furthered the power of the laughter beyond what had been imagined in the earlier comic publications of the East.

Other memorable characters of frontier humor, if not quite so outrageously prone to laughter as Crockett, are remarkable for their amiable ability to coax hilarity out of others. Jim Doggett, the "Big Bear" of Thorpe's "The Big Bear of Arkansas," has the ability to captivate an audience within minutes of his appearance. When he makes his entrance, "in a moment every face [is] wreathed in a smile" (269). He clearly has the ability to tell a story, to make other laugh with him, and his personage, described by the narrator as looking like "a man enjoying perfect health and contentment . . . good-natured to simplicity," suggests that he himself has laughed and grown fat (269). The shifty Simon Suggs, while living "as merrily and as comfortably as possible at the expense of others," is also noted to have a "quick and ready wit" that "makes him whenever he chooses to be so—and that is always—very companionable" (Hooper 12–13). In his "Preface," Sut Lovingood tells his readers he knows that a preface is a place to apologize for any errors or offensive moments in the text and to pray for his own salvation, but instead he paints a picture of a suffering soul—poor, hungry, despairing—and declares, "ef sich a one kin fine a laugh, jis' one, sich a laugh as is remembered wif his keerless boyhood, atwixt these yere kivers—then, I'll thank God that I *hes* made a book, an' feel that I hev got my pay in full" (Harris xi). George Washington Harris allows Sut to suggest in his own language that "atwixt these yere kivers" is a form of sustenance and redemption for both readers and storytellers, should the text engender laughter.

Henry Clay Lewis and Hysterical Power

The voices of Davy Crockett, Jim Doggett, Simon Suggs, and Sut Lovingood are certainly voices of conquest—conquest of land, of beasts, of peoples, of the frontier. One might say that they would submit to no one and to nothing—except perhaps to the hilarity of a good joke. Just as their stories imagined the expansion of the borders of the nation, they also imagined the expansion of the borders of a laughing society, bearing witness to the empowering benefits of submitting to laughter and urging readers to follow their lead. The culture of the frontier distrusted and discouraged melancholic personalities that resisted hilarity and welcomed laughter as salutary, benevolent, useful, and right-minded. Giving in to laughter simultaneously affirmed one's full humanity by exhibiting the healthfulness of one's body and mind and allowed one to be heard. Such submission could therefore empower anyone, regardless of class, age, race, or gender. Hence we find unexpected moments of transgression in frontier humor, moments where the era's marginalized figures appear at the center, humanized. Edward J. Piacentino, in an article that explores moments in Old Southwestern humor during which minority characters transgress society's boundaries, asks:

> Were authors consciously aware that they were defying convention? If they were cognizant of what they were doing, then why were they being rebellious? Of what significance were their transgressions, deliberate or unintentional, of prevalent attitudes endorsed by southern society? (66)

Piacentino offers some excellent answers—readers expect and allow humor to be rebellious and shocking; authors themselves had social lives which enabled transgression—but I argue that such defiance was necessary to uphold the ideology that hilarity, rather than sentimentality or intellectualism, was to be the salvation of the nation(67–68).

One especially fascinating moment of transgression, as scholars such as Piacentino and Alan Rose have pointed out, is the hysterical laughter of the title character of Henry Clay Lewis's "The Curious Widow." The gist of the story is that Madison Tensas, the narrator who is at this point of the book a medical student, boards in the home of a widow and her several daughters. In an effort to monitor potential correspondence between her daughters and her tenants, the widow rifles through Tensas's possessions whenever he leaves the house. Tensas and fellow boarders (other male medical students) resolve to scare the widow out of her intrusive habit by hiding a horrifying artifact in Tensas's room for her to find. The comic turn of the story comes when Tensas's diagnosis of the widow's response to their prank proves dramatically incorrect. The construction of this practical joke narrative utilizes ironies that highlight errors produced by the narrator's elitism, misogyny, and racism. Ultimately, though, the narrative leads to a denouement that reveals both the expressive power of laughter and the importance of its potential illegibility to those who attempt to "read" laughter through a faulty lens that blocks its ability to empower because of who is doing the laughing.

In "The Curious Widow," Lewis merges the convention in southwestern storytelling of the elaborate prank with Tensas's educated medical perspective, a perspective that Lewis subtly mocks throughout the story. Tensas and his fellow medical students essentially prescribe shock treatment for what they have diagnosed as the widow's "illness," curiosity. The students themselves are engaged in research into anatomical dissection—ironically, an invasive and ethically-charged exercise of curiosity about what lies beneath the human exterior, justified by the language of scientific progress and discovery. As is common in frontier humor, the narrator is unaware that his privileged education renders him more ignorant and prone to silliness than other characters he views with disdain. For example, Tensas's own fearful curiosity serves as inspiration for how he imagines he will cure the widow:

> The subject that we were engaged upon was one of the most hideous specimens of humanity that ever horrified the sight. The wretch had saved his life from the hangman by dying the evening before the day

> of execution, and we, by some process or other, became the possessors of his body . . . he was so hideous that nothing but my devotion to anatomy, and the fineness of the subject, could reconcile me to the dissection; and even after working a week upon him, I never caught a glimpse of his countenance but what I had the nightmare in consequence. He was one of that peculiar class called Albinoes, or white negroes. (76–77)

Tensas presumes, from his position of authority, that his horror of the Albino's deformed face is natural and universal. The young medical student often looks at living people as mere bodies; however, *this* body is potent with dreadful meaning for him due to its ambiguous racial classification. He does not realize that it is his own desperate clinging to the supremacy of his knowledge that causes his fear. The albino disturbs his notion of clear racial classification, causing him nightmares. Notice that Tensas elides the medical school's method of attaining the body—"some process or other"—revealing the degree to which Tensas dismisses black humanity. However, the student is clearly disturbed by the whiteness that "hides" the albino's race as much as by what he supposes to be the correspondence between the physical and moral deformity of the albino. While claiming that he would prefer not to dissect the body, he cannot conceal his interest in the body, a curiosity that borders on the sublime. Tensas admits no relation between his anxiety about probing this corpse and the widow's relatively innocuous, unabashed probing into the affairs of the living. Still, he does believe that his "cure" will work, due to a belief that the widow will share his fear of the dead man's face and that it will affect her as it does him. That is, he believes a confrontation with this particular face makes one hesitate to pursue curiosity.

With this peculiar "prescription" in mind, the students surgically remove the face from the corpse and proceed to wrap it elaborately, so that it may prove an enticingly secret item to the widow. Tensas finds himself in possession of the face for one night, holding it until he will leave it for his landlady to find the next day. Its proximity possesses his distraught imagination. He passes a sleepless night "nervous and irritated," nearly repenting his plans (78). His dread of the face makes him reconsider with some degree of sympathy what he believes the face will do to the widow, but he thinks, "then—she is a widow! My heart at this last reflection, became immediately barred to the softening influences of forgiveness, and I determined in all hostility to *face* her" (78). Tensas's logic resonates with antebellum misogynist conventions as much as with his racist fear of the not-black, black face. The stereotype of widowhood—the social woman construed in southwestern humor and elsewhere in antebellum literature as over-sexed, over-powered, and hence ridiculous—provides Tensas with his justification for endeavoring to dose her so unkindly.

The rest of the story chronicles Tensas's mental state as he anxiously, curiously, waits for the widow's discovery of the face. He sits through his medical classes in a state of distraction, neglects duties, and hastens home to witness the outcome of the prank. However, Tensas and the other medical students do not witness the denouement that they expected. Always a man of science, Tensas watches the widow discover the face and details the responses he witnesses—as well as his interpretation of them as symptoms of his prank:

> Ay, but she was a firm-nerved woman. . . . She did not faint—did not vent a scream—but gazed upon its awfulness in silence, as if her eyes were riveted to it for ever. We felt completely mortified to think that our well-laid scheme had failed—that we had failed to terrify her; when, to perfect our chagrin, she broke out into a low laugh. (80)

After an unwrapping which blatantly parallels the process of anatomical dissection, the landlady's initial silence upon finding a disembodied face beneath the layers of material perplexes and disappoints the students. They had imagined an inevitable correspondence between fear and this face, but she does not express fear. Tensas consoles himself with the thought that his elite logic of cause and effect is undermined only by the unforeseeable fact that the widow is a "firm-nerved" anomaly. As she begins to laugh, though, the students take her low chuckling as evidence of the failure of their "cure," the laugh of an unflappable character dismissing fear. However, her laughter quickly progresses into something that again piques Tensas's medical imagination: hysterical laughter.

> [W]e noticed her laughter was becoming hysterical. We spoke to her—shook her by the shoulder—but still she laughed on, increasing in vehemence and intensity. It began to excite attention in the

> lower apartments, and even in the street; and soon loud knocks and wondering exclamations began to alarm us for the consequences of our participation. We strove to take the fearful object from her, but she clung to it with the tenacity of madness, or a young doctor to his first scientific opinion. (80)

Unresponsive, unshakable, unsocial—the widow's escalating laughter is to Tensas a socially inappropriate but medically explicable response that expresses the widow's reception of a shock so violent that it transcends screaming or fainting. Interpreting laughter in a manner that weds the views of intellectuals and sentimentalists, he sees the laughter as a form of possession explained by the anatomy of a woman's body. Her susceptible nervous system is deranged, and the laughter "speaks" more aptly of the enormity of the shock. Tensas diagnoses the laughter as a symptom, referring to a break in the woman's mind—madness or dementia caused by confrontation with the horror of the face.

Curiosity compels the widow to snoop, the doctor to dissect, and finally, the masses to listen. Passersby, "impelled by the ramrod of curiosity," recognize this laughter as something notably peculiar and elect to become spectators to the laughter. A crowd enters the house seeking to discover the object of her cacophonous hilarity. Finally, in the presence of this sizeable audience, she puts an end to the scene:

> [T]he widow ceased her laughter, and, putting on an expression of the most supreme contempt, coolly remarked: — "Excuse me, gentlemen, if I have caused you any inconvenience by my unusual conduct. I was just *smiling aloud* to think what fools these students made of themselves when they tried to scare me with a dead nigger's face, when I had slept with a drunken husband for twenty years!" (80–81)

The widow knows that her laughter is "unusual conduct" in the eyes of her boarders. By using laughter in an "unusual" manner she manages to communicate her point. She permits the students to believe that the face, the face that is so emphatically full of horror for them, is the reason for her reactions. She then dramatically utilizes this misunderstanding, proving that their assumptions about signification are wrong. The face is not inherently frightening; a woman's profuse laughter is not inherently evidence of insanity. The joke is on a medical doctor who believes that laughter—particularly when it emanates from a widow's body—is a sign of disorder rather than vigor. While Lewis's story certainly—and unconventionally—questions both racist fears and belittling misogyny, the story primarily rescues laughter from interpretations that weaken its "hysterical" power.

The denouement of Lewis's story is not accidental. In the frontier humor tradition of cultural conquest, the story advances a narrative in which laughter contains sufficient authority and force to subdue any opponent, including a traditionally privileged figure like the narrator. The text is comic, but the message about the necessity of comedy is serious: He or she who laughs is the victor. With laughter, the widow triumphs over her erudite enemies, banishes them from her property, and protects her goods (her daughters) from their threat of romantic conquest. Furthermore, her laughter draws in a democratic crowd to witness, confirm, and perhaps emulate her victory.

Southern frontier humor promotes the idea that submission to laughter is empowering, no matter who laughs. The stories, by celebrating laughter within their narratives and causing laughter for their readers, bolster the idea that the nation and its citizenry should embrace a risible perspective during the nineteenth-century period of conquest, growth, and expansion. The fact that anybody—black, white, old, young, male, or female—could be possessed by laughter opened up the possibility that anybody might possess the virtues which entitled him or her to social power within frontier humor's ideology, even when other social conventions demanded these individuals be subjugated. To hysterically "smile aloud," like Lewis's curious widow, was an utterance of nothing less than conquest.

NOTE

This essay revises and expands upon research found in my unpublished 2009 dissertation, "Telling Laughter: Hilarity and Democracy in the Nineteenth-Century United States," which is held at Emory University.

WORKS CITED

The American Comic Almanac for 1833: With Whims, Scraps and Oddities. Boston: Charles Ellms & Willard Felt, 1832. Print.

"The Anti-Slavery Almanac." Advertisement. *The Colored American.* 12 Jan. 1839. Print.

"Christy's Minstrels." Unsigned review. [William T. Porter?] *The Spirit of the Times.* 16 October 1847. *Uncle Tom's Cabin and American Culture.* Web. 29 May 2011.

The Crockett Almanac for 1841. Nashville: Ben Harding, 1840. Print.

Crockett's Almanac for 1846. Baltimore: J. B. Keller, 1845. Print

Crockett's Yaller Flower Almanac for '36. New York: R. H. Elton, 1835. Print.

"Dr. Valentine." Broadside. United States: s. n., 1846. *American Broadsides and Ephemera.* Series 1. Web. 8 June 2009.

Elton's Comic All-my-nack for 1841. New York: R. H. Elton, 1840. Print.

Harris, George Washington. "Preface." *Sut Lovingood: Yarns Spun by a "Nat'ral Born Durn'd Fool."* New York: Dick & Fitzgerald, 1867. ix–xi. Print.

Hooper, Johnson Jones. *Some Adventures of Captain Simon Suggs, Taking the Census, Etc.* Philadelphia: Carey & Hart, 1845. Print.

Justus, James H. *Fetching the Old Southwest: Humorous Writing from Longstreet to Twain.* Columbia: University of Missouri Press, 2004. Print.

Lewis, Henry Clay. "The Curious Widow." *Odd Leaves from the Life of a Louisiana Swamp Doctor.* 1851. Ed. with introduction by Edwin Arnold. Baton Rouge: Louisiana State University Press, 1966. 75–81. Print.

"On Ridicule." *The Christian Recorder.* 10 Aug. 1861. *America's Historical Newspapers.* Web. 10 July 2009.

Piacentino, Edward J. "Contesting the Boundaries of Race and Gender in Old Southwestern Humor." *The Humor of the Old South.* Ed. M. Thomas Inge and Edward J. Piacentino. Lexington: University Press of Kentucky, 2001. 52–71. Print.

"Pleasant Companions." *The New-Bedford Mercury.* 27 Feb. 1829, vol. 22, issue 34: 1. *America's Historical Newspapers.* Web. 10 July 2009.

Rose, Alan. "Blackness in the Fantastic World of Old Southwestern Humor." *Demonic Vision: Racial Fantasy and Southern Fiction.* Hamden, CT: Archon, 1976. 19–38. Print.

"Scientific Amusement!" Broadside. United States: July 1862. *American Broadsides and Ephemera.* Series 1. Web. 8 June 2009.

Thorpe, Thomas Bangs. "The Big Bear of Arkansas." *The Hive of the Bee-Hunter.* 1854. *Humor of the Old Southwest.* Ed. Hennig Cohen and William B. Dillingham. Athens: University Press of Georgia, 1975. 268–79. Print.

Tompkins, Jane. *Sensational Designs: The Cultural Work of American Fiction, 1790–1860.* New York: Oxford University Press, 1985. Print.

Turner's Comick Almanack for 1844. New York: Turner & Fisher, 1843. Print.

Walters, Ronald. *American Reformers, 1815–1860.* Consulting ed. Eric Foner. New York: Hill and Wang, 1978. Print.

"BAWN IN A BRIER-PATCH" AND FRONTIER BRED

Joel Chandler Harris's Debt to the Humor of the Old South

GRETCHEN MARTIN

JOEL CHANDLER HARRIS'S MOST WELL KNOWN CHARACTER, Uncle Remus, has been and continues to be a critically polarizing figure in American literature, and the Uncle Remus collections have dominated scholarly attention to Harris's work. While Alice Walker condemns Harris as a cultural thief and refers to the Uncle Remus character as "a creature," other scholars like Ralph Ellison and James Weldon Johnson commend Harris for recognizing the aesthetic artistry of black folk tales. Yet Harris was also familiar with and indeed drew from another important antebellum literary tradition, southern frontier humor, praising in particular Augustus Baldwin Longstreet's *Georgia Scenes* and William Tappan Thompson's *Major Jones's Travels* in his book *Stories of Georgia* (250). Throughout his work, including but not limited to his Uncle Remus collections, Harris employs a wide range of the literary and aesthetic techniques commonly practiced by frontier humorists, such as double-ended narrative frames, dialect, and wit rather than formal education used to demonstrate a character's exceptional intelligence. Harris's short stories are also largely indebted to frontier humor, as is evident in his depiction of various classes, particularly his sympathetic treatment of non-elite whites and his regard for the cultural values of the plain folk. And, like many frontier humorists, Harris is also often critical of ruling class planters, particularly of those who abuse their power. In this essay, I explore Harris's intertextual negotiations of a range of antebellum southern literary traditions, black and white, and contend that Harris's work demonstrates quintessential aspects of southern literature. Harris's work is a literary hybrid committed to the artistry of the story, told from many angles, in many forms, with sensitivity to voice, perspective, humor, but above all, the dignity of his featured characters.

The hybrid nature of a text is, as Roland Barthes notes, "plural" and "depends, that is, not on the ambiguity of its contents but on what might be called the stereographic plurality of its weave of signifiers (etymologically, the text is a tissue, a woven fabric)" (1328). Julia Kristeva explains that intertextuality is not simply a matter of textual or authorial influences, but involves a "transposition of one (or several) sign system(s) into another" (59–60), a particularly important "transposition," given that various signifying systems evident in Harris's work are cultural and oral signifying networks and thus lack definitive sources. Indeed, as a newspaper editor, fiction writer, avid reader—and perhaps most importantly—an attentive listener, Harris was uniquely knowledgeable about the culture and discourses he often covertly criticized. Several of his short stories are set prior to the war, but function to allegorize many of the problems of the post-Reconstruction period—particularly the shift from the conservative racism prevalent in the antebellum era to a highly charged and often deadly radical racism. Other stories are set during the war and offer the perspective of the backcountry plain folk, "many of whom supported the Confederacy with great reluctance, if at all" (Hahn 45).

As several scholars have demonstrated, Harris was highly influenced by the black oral tradition as well as by the antebellum plantation tradition, and his Uncle Remus tales have been regarded as a frame combining these incompatible literary genres. Robert Hemenway contends that Harris utilized "a medium that he could mimic but never fully comprehend (30–31), whereas Ashleigh Harris claims that Harris

> completely isolated the Brer Rabbit tales from their present African-American context as well as from the historical trajectory from which they originated. Through providing a depoliticized, decommunalised, deracialised and emasculated narrator, Harris's tales fundamentally changed the social and political significance of the Brer Rabbit tales . . . . Harris caricatures African-American plantation and slave identity and culture, and this in turn ridicules and distorts the significance of the characters and narratives of the stories. (66)

These scholars suggest what Kenneth Lynn describes as the predominant narrative structure of the frontier humor tradition, a *cordon sanitaire* separating the narrator from the antics of the characters featured in the embedded tales (64).

While many scholars have challenged what the *cordon sanitaire* separation implies or asserts, as a narrative device the frame would become representative of the genre, as well as an important structural model for postbellum plantation authors, including Thomas Nelson Page, Joel Chandler Harris, and Charles Chesnutt. Chesnutt, however, distinguishes himself by the subversive quality of his tales, while Harris and Page are typically grouped together as authors whose fiction "served to perpetuate the carefully fabricated myth of genteel plantation owners and contented slaves with nothing but fond memories of bondage, which was created by Southern writers after the Civil War" (Watkins 72). Lucinda MacKethan, however, cautions, "Harris's Uncle Remus stories are in some measure complicated by the old story-teller's dual role; in one guise, he speaks to a postwar generation of whites about the good old days, but in a quite different voice he tells, and obviously identifies with, the folktales of that subversive animal anarchist, Brer Rabbit" (651). Robert Cochran also identifies subversive elements in the Remus collections and contends, "Uncle Remus's control of the story-telling context and his persistent, if oblique, critique of plantation values" (23) reveals Harris "quietly but insistently pursuing an anti-racist agenda" (23). Moreover, by examining Harris's intertextualization of southern folk culture, black and white, his non-Remus fiction emerges as more subversive than has traditionally been thought.

In spite of many obvious differences between black and white folk culture, these groups shared many values, such as community unity, family loyalty, a distrust of outsiders (for the black community, this distrust included all whites), resistance toward authority, a keen sense of personal worth, and embracing wit rather than formal education as a highly regarded social value. Furthermore, Harris's familiarity with black folk culture not only enabled him to understand signifying strategies at work in the embedded tales, but additionally enabled him to understand signifying as a creative device. He employs signifying together with a wide range of literary traditions to debunk nostalgic fantasies of the Old South, particularly stereotypes of African Americans and non-elite whites, in order to promote greater sensitivity between the races and defuse white America's growing hostility toward its black citizenry.

Because Harris had to be careful to avoid offending his audience or failing to find publication outlets, he adopted the signifying tactics of the trickster. Robert Cochran notes that "George Terrell and Harbert, telling Brer Rabbit's wonderful tales to the listening boy, taught him not only the covert critique of their subject matter, but also the even more subversive lessons of their Signifying method," adding, "Harris went to the world as the trickster Brer Rabbit" (29). Signifying, as Henry Louis Gates Jr. notes, "turns on the play and chain of signifiers, and not on some supposedly transcendent signified" (52). In the black vernacular tradition, "the signifier is emptied out—or opened up—to include a multiplicity of rhetorical figures. Thus, standard English signifying is transmuted into black vernacular Signifyin(g), a multivalent and multivocal trope that is skillfully wielded by the folkloric trickster" (Lee 462). Harris's use of signifying as a methodology gives him far more freedom to play on the sign systems of antebellum literary traditions and cultural discourses—black and white, written and oral—to undermine, ultimately, the myth of the Old South. This myth was coming to be regarded as history rather than fiction and perpetuating largely demeaning stereotypes of African Americans and non-elite whites that developed from antebellum proslavery discourses, most notably the plantation tradition.

The genre of frontier humor stands in sharp contrast to traditional plantation fiction—particularly with regard to depiction of the plain folk. Ed Piacentino and Thomas Inge note:

> [S]ome of the defining features of the humor of the Old South are the prominence of plain folk—lower-class rustics, backwoodsmen, and other marginal types, some of whom may be disreputable—as the principal players in the action. In addition, the situations depicted tend to be outlandish and sometimes bizarre, and the folk characters are given extensive voice, speaking in a colorful vernacular discourse. Moreover, the humorists favor the dialect of the vernacular speakers over the formal English of genteel characters, the latter usually relegated to the tale's or sketch's frame and consigned to the periphery. (2)

Harris prominently features the plain folk in several short stories. Specifically, he concentrates on backcountry mountain culture and the animosity many mountain communities felt regarding outside interference—particularly what may perceived as a threat to their intense sense of independence. Steven Hahn notes that throughout the backcountry, "'Liberty' was more than a catchword. At heart, it meant a specific sort of independence—ownership of productive resources, control over farming operations, an emphasis on household self-sufficiency, and lack of subservience to outsiders or outside forces" (45). During the antebellum era, the backcountry regions of southwest Virginia, as well as the Carolinas, Georgia, Tennessee, Alabama, Mississippi, and Louisiana were, as James Webb explains in *Born Fighting*, predominantly settled by Scots-Irish, "a quick-tempered but sensual and playful people [that] often dressed provocatively, acted with a volatile belligerence, drank to excess, engaged in constant and open competition in every form, and adamantly defied the attempts of outsiders to control them" (133). While there were no mountain men who reached the level of defiance demonstrated by George Washington Harris's Sut Lovingood of Frog Mountain, Tennessee, Joel Chandler Harris sets several stories in the Georgia mountains and depicts many characters who have much in common with Sut. Joel Chandler Harris also offers a unique perspective on backcountry culture by developing narratives that often begin where the genre of frontier humor ends: with the Civil War.

In several short stories published in various collections, Harris features mountain culture and demonstrates the animosity many mountain communities felt about secession, particularly the view that the Civil War was a rich man's war to defend property rights of slave owners. In "Teague Poteet's: A Sketch of the Hog Mountain Range," for example, the featured character is in the year 1859 described as a "young man of thirty or thereabouts" and is depicted "tilling, in a half serious, half-jocular way, a small farm on Hog Mountain" (14). Harris creates a character portrait representative of backcountry characters and identifies a clear distinction between the culture of "the mountains of North Georgia" and the town culture of the Valley by establishing physical, linguistic, cultural, and ideological distinctions, notably the "contempt which the Mountain entertained for the Valley," (15) or as Teague Poteet puts it, "them dad-blasted Restercrats" (16).

In addition to his contempt for Valley politics, Poteet is also critical of "the young men who wore ready-made clothes, starched shirts, and beaver hats; nor was his ideal of feminine beauty reached by the village belles, with their roach-combs, their red and yellow ribbons, and their enormous flounces. In the mountains, he was to the manner born" (14). Teague Poteet prefers the backcountry plain style and "wore a wool hat, a homespun shirt, jeans pantaloons, and cotton suspenders," and chooses for his wife Puss Pringle (14). Their excursion into the Valley to get married is met with disdain by the town girls, who "greeted the bridal procession with a little explosion of giggles, and when Puss Pringle pushed back her gingham sun-bonnet and innocently gazed upon them, they turned up their noses, sniffed the air scornfully, and made such demonstrations as no feminine mind, however ignorant in other directions, could fail to interpret" (15). Puss Pringle is at a disadvantage because she has "not learned the art of tossing her head and sniffing the air," but "Teague saw the whole affair and he was cut to the quick. In addition to the latent pride of his class, he inherited the sensitiveness of his ancestors." Following the wedding, he "thereafter avoided Gulletsville" (15). Harris's highly unflattering depictions of town snobbery suggest that the plain folk of the mountains are far more genuine and worthy of respect.

Harris also introduces characteristics of manhood—commonly featured in the tradition of frontier humor—that function as indicators of class status. Throughout the backcountry, reputation is determined by values like honesty, courage, and fair play. Michael Oriard notes that reputation is not a matter of lineage, formal and social education, or wealth, characteristics that contribute to reputation among upper-class southern gentlemen. Instead, a good backcountry reputation is earned by fair play, often depicted as physical brawls to demonstrate backcountry honor, to "determine the 'best man,' or for proof of manhood" (18). Teague Poteet represents these values and has earned "the reputation of being a man of marked shrewdness and common-sense" by "knocking the sheriff of the county over the head with a chair, and putting a bullet through a saloon-keeper who bullied everybody" (14). Harris characterizes Poteet as exemplifying the backcountry values of manhood that are lauded throughout the genre of frontier humor.

The mountain community's attitude toward the approach of war is depicted when, in spite of Teague Poteet's aversion to town culture, a year or more after his wedding, he "was compelled to ride down to Gullettsville under whip and spur for a doctor" (15). Harris notes that on "the very day that Teague Poteet's wife presented him with the puzzle of a daughter, Fate presented his countrymen with the problem of war" (16). Neighbors visit and ask: "'What's them Restercrats in the Valley cuttin' up the'r scallops fer?'" Poteet replies, "'Whoopin' up secession. Sou' Ca'liny done plum gone out, an' Georgy a-gwin'" (16). He adds emphatically, "'Them air Restercrats kin go wher' they dang please; I'm a-gwine to stay right slam–bang in the Nunited States'" (16). Another mountaineer makes a similar inquiry, asking, "'What's up down yan?'" Poteet replies, "'Them dad-blasted Restercrats a-secedin' out'n the Nunited States'" (16). The class distinction between Poteet and the town's aristocrats is suggested by the response, "'They say they ar airter savin' of the'r niggers,'" and Poteet replies, "'Well, I hain't got none, and I hain't awantin' none; an' it hain't been ten minnits sense I ups an' says to Dave Hightower, s'I, 'The Nunited States is big enough for me'" (16). Furthermore, town snobbery dissipates as the need for recruits grows, and as the war

> surged nearer and nearer, and the demand for recruits became clamorous, the people of the Valley bethought them of the gaunt but sturdy men who live in the Mountain. A conscript officer, representing the necessities of a new government, made a journey thither, —a little excursion full of authority and consequence. As he failed to return, another officer, similarly equipped and commissioned, rode forth and disappeared, and then another and another. (17)

These new officials eventually realize "that the fastnesses of Hog Mountain concealed a strong and dangerous organization of Union men" (17). The mountain men are, however, equally defiant of the assertion of authority brought to the mountains by "General Tecumseh Sherman and some of his lieutenants" (17). Harris notes that "the truth is, the Poteets and the Pringles and the Hightowers of Hog Mountain had their own notions of what constituted Union men. They desired to stay in the United States on their own terms. If nobody pestered them, they pestered nobody" (17). As Harris shows, the backcountry mountain community's resistance to the war is not a matter of politics, but rather of defending and maintaining their tenacious commitment to their notion of liberty.

Harris depicts a similar attitude regarding the war in "A Conscript's Christmas." The story is set in 1863 and depicts two Confederate soldiers,

Captain Dick Moseley and Private Bill Chadwick, who have been sent into the mountains to retrieve Israel Sprulock, an army conscript who had been "yerked" into the army, but who had "yerked himself out" (49). Harris notes: "They were not in a friendly region. There were bushwhackers in the mountains . . . . They had that day ridden past the house of the only member of the Georgia State convention who had refused to affix his signature to the ordinance of secession, and the woods, to use the provincial phrase, were full of Union men" (46). As the men ride on, Chadwick complains, "'When I j'ined the army I thought I was goin' to fight the Yankees, but they slapped me in the camp of instruction over there at Adairsville, an' now here we are fightin' our own folks. If we ain't fightin' 'em, we are pursuin' after 'em, an' runnin' 'em into the woods an' up the mountains'" (48). When they encounter a mountain minister, Uncle Billy, they are given a chilly and critical reception. He lectures them: "'I've had Israel Spurlock in my min' off an' on' ev'ry since they run him down an' kotch him an' drug 'im off to war. He was weakly like from the time he was a boy . . . . He knowed that he was drug off right spang at the time he wanted to be getherin in his craps, an' savin' his ruffage, an' one thing an' another bekaze his ole mammy din't have a soul to help her but 'im'" (54–55). The humor throughout the story derives from the mountain community's defiance of authority. Uncle Billy goads the men: "'You thought that while your Uncle Billy was a-moonin' aroun' down the hill yander you'd steal a march on your Aunt Crissy, an' maybe come a-*conscriptin' of her* into the army" (60, my emphasis). In another scene, a former colonel during the Mexican War, Dick Watson, lectures them "'that this hain't Mexico, an' that they hain't no war gwine on on this 'ere hill. You know that mighty well'" (67). As Watson's comment suggests, the mountaineers are not opposed to war—as evidenced by Watson's role in the Mexican War—but are opposed to a war that is dividing the Union.

While issues of war, conscription, and deserters are serious subjects, they are treated with playful humor. Yet the community's very serious commitment to protect one of their own is a persistent theme throughout the tale. The united community repeatedly undermines the outsiders' mission, and the soldiers begin to sense the impotence of their authority. Chadwick confides his misgivings to Moseley: "'It's my belief that we are gwine on a fool's errand'" (83). His suspicion is confirmed when, after resting by a tree, he wakes to find himself "dragged backward from the log by strong hands . . . lying flat on his back, with his hands tied, and as helpless as an infant. He looked up and discovered that his captor was Israel Spurlock" (91). Moseley is also captured, and the men are held prisoner in the hope that the man who sent them on the mission, Adjutant Lovejoy, "would come in search of them" (101). Lovejoy takes the bait, and he and his men are also captured. Yet in spite of the prisoners' status as captives, they are treated to plain folk hospitality, invited by Danny Lemmon's to "'stay over an' take Christmas wi' us, sech ez we'll have'" (100). During the Christmas festivities, they also attend Spurlock's wedding, officiated by Uncle Billy. Harris notes that the sermon "was not the less meaty and sincere, not the less wise and powerful, because the English was ungrammatical and the rhetoric uncouth," an observation reminiscent of North Carolina frontier humorist Hardin E. Taliaferro's mountain preachers (103). But Harris's tale takes a decidedly serious turn when one of the "prisoner/guests" "seized a musket," yet "before he could raise his gun a streak of fire shot forth into his face, and he fell and rolled to the side of the road" (112). The story presents the cultural ethos of the mountaineers, who treat outside interference with good-natured humor—which will, however, stretch only so far.

In one of his most interesting but largely overlooked stories, "Blue Dave," Harris demonstrates his signifying skills, playing on the plantation tradition, the slave narrative, and featuring trickster figures from both black trickster tales and frontier humor. Lucinda MacKethan notes, "[T]he Southwestern humorists used the trickster figure to highlight class differences and satirize the rudeness of frontier life. The most important characters of this genre are Simon Suggs and Sut Lovingood" (914). The presentation of the frontier trickster figure, typically a conman, is further complicated by a more complex example of the con game, which is, Michael Oriard points out, in "tales of cheating the cheater, a local variation of the folklore tradition of tricking the trickster" (14). Oriard notes that "the best example of the former appears in Longstreet's *Georgia Scenes*, in the story 'The Horse-Swap'" (14). Similarly, Mel Watkins observes of African American folklore, "in the animal tales, the rabbit or hare, who could be mischievous, even arrogant and malicious, was occasionally tricked by weaker animals. This counter theme, which [Charles] Joyner designates as the 'trickster out-tricked,' accentuated another aspect of slave morality" (73).

The trickster tales that were "told night after night at the slaves quarters" featured distinct types of trickster figures: the animal trickster, most notably Brer Rabbit, and the slave trickster featured in the John and Ole Massa tales (Thomas 81). Lawrence Levine notes that the animal tales operated to

> effect a rough sort of justice, and to protect themselves from some of the worst features of the slave system, slaves translated many of the tactics of their animal trickster tales into their own lives. Like Brer Rabbit, slaves learned to *maneuver* as well as they could from their position of weakness. (121, my emphasis)

Gibert Osofsky notes that "in the rich folklore of Old John, the symbolic slave hero who mastered the art of tricking," was engaged in the strategy of "'putting on Ole Massa'" (21). But what these trickster tales share at their "most elemental" level is "a confrontation in which the weak use their wits to evade the strong" (Levine 106). Harris is best known for his animal tale collections featuring Uncle Remus, yet his negotiation with antebellum tricksters, black and white, suggests he was uniquely familiar with a variety of trickster figures. Furthermore, the tricksters featured in frontier humor and black folktale traditions share many characteristics, most notably verbal dexterity and an emphasis on wit as a weapon in a contest of intellect. Victory is measured by their ability to outsmart their opponents.

Harris's short story "Blue Dave" begins in 1850 during the funeral of one of the town's most prominent citizens, Felix Kendrick. As Harris provides Kendrick's personal history, he demonstrates the fluid nature of the southern social hierarchy by depicting Kendrick's father as a man of humble origins who was a "hatter by trade, who had come to Georgia in search of a precarious livelihood" (52). The elder Kendrick, "shrewd, close-fisted, and industrious," "became an overseer" (52). Due to his success, "he commanded a large salary, and saved money. This money he invested in negroes, buying one at a time and hiring them out. He finally came to be the owner of seven or eight stout field hands; whereupon he bought two hundred acres of choice land and set himself up as a patriarch" (52). This character portrait is reminiscent of Longstreet's narrator Baldwin, who also came from a plain farming community and rose into the upper ranks of Savannah society. Furthermore, while the elder Kendrick has no regard for the social distinction his hard-earned wealth makes possible, Kendrick's son is more class-conscious. In order to demonstrate the family's rise in social status, the son builds a house with a double veranda, tall chimneys, and a collection of gables "to show that 'some folks was as good as other folks'" (52).

The entire community turns out for Felix Kendrick's funeral, and Harris features two local farmers in attendance discussing the events of the day. Class distinctions are indicated by language, with plain folk farmers using backcountry vernacular that is set in contrast with the speech of characters like George Denham, who uses standard English that displays his formal education. In addition to evidencing the fluid nature of the social structure, this sketch also shows that while there were certainly instances of clashes between planter and plain folk, interaction between classes was customary. Indeed, the narrative frame of the frontier humorists depended on sustained relationships and verbal exchanges between characters of different classes, such as: Alexander G. McNutt's Jim and Chunkey and their relationship with the Governor, George Washington Harris's George and Sut, and Augustus Baldwin Longstreet's Baldwin and Hall and their interaction with a wide array of plain folk characters.

Harris also introduces a unique narrative element in his characterization of Blue Dave, drawing this portrait from the hero featured in slave narratives, the escaped slave. As Susan Tracy notes, "the runaway represented the assertion of their humanity, and, if male, of black masculinity" (147). John Blassingame observes that "the ubiquitous runaway defied all the odds. Sometimes he stayed away until his anger or that of his master subsided. Cold and hungry, he frequently returned after a few days . . . on other occasions, however, the runaway eluded his pursuers for weeks, months, or even years, safe in his bailiwick near the plantation" (110). While slave narratives focused on permanent escape into the North or Canada, and were a crucial component of the abolitionist press, temporary escape was far more common. Moreover, temporary flight demonstrated a psychological independence that the institution of slavery was structured to deny, and by running, slaves were able to assert more control over their lives, often choosing when to return and on what terms.

The runaway also represented the appealing quality of simply defying authority and exasperating masters. William Tynes Cowan notes that "the planter's sense of himself was to a large degree dependent upon his conception of his slaves. Not only did his ownership of slaves signify his class status, but signs of happiness among his slaves were indicative of his quality as a patriarch: a good master would have happy slaves . . . . It was that knowledge of runaways, defiant in the wilderness that threatened the planter's conception of his slaves, and therefore his self-concept"—and, it is important to point out, his reputation in the community could be a source of keen embarrassment (22–23). Indeed, rumors about this slave are widespread in the community. During the funeral, Brother Roach spots a "powerfully built negro" hiding behind "one of the gables on the roof" and immediately recognizes Dave (55). Roach tells Brannum, "'That nigger, roosting up there so slick and cool, is Bledser's Blue Dave. Nuther more, nuther less'" (55). Blue Dave had run away seven years ago, and his "success in eluding pursuit caused the ignorant minded of both races to attribute to him the possession of some mysterious power. He grew into a legend; he became a part of the folk-lore of the section. According to popular belief, he possessed strange powers and great courage; he became a giant, a spirit of evil . . . . *The negroes had many stories to tell of him*" (56, my emphasis). Early in the narrative, "stories" about Dave suggest that he is feared by "both black and white" (56), but as the narrative develops, it becomes apparent that the slaves' stories operate covertly to protect him, generating fear in the white community. The black community seemingly employs trickster wisdom to signify on the white community and enable Dave's unique form of freedom.

Dave is also a particularly bold and independent individual, qualities undermining nineteenth-century essentialist racial ideology, as well as demeaning black literary figures. Osofsky notes that "even to conceive the possibility of escape required a special quality of mind: imagination, independence, cunning, daring, and a sense of self-pride . . . . It called for the use of subtle psychological weapons" (20–21). Harris endows Blue Dave with these qualities and notes that little was known of the history of Blue Dave before

> he was brought to the little village of Rockville in chains in a speculator's train, —the train consisting of two Conestoga wagons and thirty or forty forlorn-looking negroes. The speculator explained that he had manacled Blue Dave because he was unmanageable; and

> he put him on the block to sell him after making it perfectly clear to everybody that whoever bought the negro would get a bad bargain. Nevertheless Blue Dave was a magnificent specimen of manhood, straight as an arrow, as muscular as Hercules, and with a countenance as open and as pleasant as one would wish to see. He was bought by General Alfred Bledser, and put on his River Place. He worked well for a few weeks, but got into trouble with the overseer, and finally compromised matters by taking to the woods. He seemed born for this particular business; for the track dogs failed to find him, and all the arts and artifices employed for capturing and reclaiming runaways failed in his case. It was a desperate form of freedom he enjoyed; but he seemed suited to it, and he made the most of it. (57)

In this narrative, Harris deviates dramatically from the characteristics of traditional plantation fiction with which he is commonly associated, not only featuring a fugitive slave, but noting that "it was a common thing to hear of fugitive negroes" (56). Susan Tracy explains that in the antebellum plantation tradition, "recalcitrant or rebellious blacks are rarely portrayed, and those that are, are treated as exceptions. In fact, there are only three rebellious black men in all of the literature" (146). And this type of omission is not limited to fiction. In his book *Who Speaks for Margaret Garner*, Mark Reinhardt points out that while the Margaret Garner case was covered extensively in the northern press throughout the course of capture and trial, the South responded largely with silence or extreme "censorship" (207). Moreover, Harris endows this character with qualities of manhood that directly undermine antebellum and postbellum stereotypes of black masculinity. Blue Dave's flight challenges the "happy darky" image of the antebellum era, and his intellect, sense of self, and compassion undermine the postbellum "degeneration" theorists who characterize free black men as reverting to bestial savagery, preying on vulnerable white women.

Blue Dave is also a man of courage and risks his liberty by revealing himself to Kitty Kendrick so she can warn George Denham that he should not attempt to cross the river owing to the flood. When she asks him to identify himself, he replies, "'I mos' fear'd, Miss Kitty'" (58). As Harris notes, "the tone of his voice was something more than humble. There was an appeal in it for mercy" (58). To alleviate her fear of him, Dave tells her to "'des ax yo' little br'er. Little Mars. Felix, he knows I ain't no bad nigger'" (58). Dave's statement insinuates that the child has been aiding this runaway. Dave has been at large for seven years, and Felix is an eight-year-old and could, therefore, only have become familiar with Dave during his life as a fugitive. It is interesting to note that Harris also features a young boy, Joe Maxwell, in his semibiographical *On the Plantation*, showing Joe Maxwell assisting the fugitive slave Mink (40). Yet in spite of the risk Dave takes on Kitty's behalf, she lacks her brother's compassion and is more concerned with appearances. Kitty chastises her brother: "'You've disgraced us all. You knew Blue Dave was hiding on top of the house all the while. What would be done with us if people found out we had been harboring a runaway negro?'" (58). Young Felix, however, "had views of his own," and replies, "'I don't care if I did. If you tell anybody, I'll never run up the road to see if Mr. George is coming as long as I live; I won't ever do anything for you'" (59). Felix adds defensively, "'He's the best nigger man I ever saw, less'n it's old Uncle Manuel when he gets that old, 'cause Uncle Manuel said so'" (59). The information the boy inadvertently shares suggests that old Uncle Manuel is also in contact with Dave.

The implication of Manuel's involvement with Dave is verified when Kitty, relaxing her "principles" a bit after Dave has rescued George, visits Manuel's cabin. Harris describes Manuel as "old, wise, and cunning," as well as distrustful of her, a white woman. When Kitty asks him to deliver food to Dave, Manuel "hesitated a moment before replying; and even then his caution would not allow him to commit himself" (64). Lawrence Levine notes that throughout the trickster stories, an important message was repeated "over and over: 'It's bad to talk too much . . . don't tell all you see.' There is abundant evidence that the slaves thoroughly assimilated this lesson. Even their friends and defenders testified to the slaves' duplicity and secretiveness" (99–100). Indeed, while collecting folktales in 1880s Joel Chandler Harris commented on the cautious distrust among African Americans. In the introduction to his first collection of Uncle Remus stories, he writes: "I have found few negroes who will acknowledge to a stranger that they know anything of these legends; and yet to relate one of the stories is the surest road to their confidence and esteem. In this way, and in this way only, I have been enabled to collect and verify the folklore in this volume" (xxv). The slaves' vigilant distrust of the white community is a common element in Harris's narratives of the Old South and undermines "the myth of the contented slave" (Turner 29).

Manuel's prayer of gratitude for Kitty's offering, however, confirms his access to Dave. Moreover, when Dave approaches the Denham Plantation to tell Mrs. Denham about her son's accident, Harris notes that "he was well acquainted with the surroundings at the Denham Plantation, having been fed many a time by the well-cared-for negroes" (65). The detail of the slave community's involvement with a runaway offers a unique glimpse behind the mask. Moreover, Dave functions as a slave trickster, exercising full control over his life—with the added benefit of exasperating his master, "bidding defiance to the law of the State and Bill Brand's track dogs," as well evading the patrollers for years (56). Levine notes that the trickster "could outwit his master again and again, but his primary satisfaction would be in making his master look foolish and thus exposing the myth of white omniscience and omnipotence" (132). Indeed, the longevity of Dave's evasion suggests he is not only physically strong, but also intellectually sharp, outwitting and outmaneuvering the white community with the covert assistance of the black community.

Dave is, however, supremely cautious and demonstrates an important lesson circulated in the folktales. Lawrence Levine notes:

> While each tale may bring the satisfaction of the weak triumphing over the strong, the cycle itself has a more complicated message: Rabbits may win battles but they don't win wars. Rabbits don't replace foxes and wolves; they're rabbits! They have to use their wits all the time. They're always in danger. They never become secure. They're never on top. That was the lesson being taught to the young; not some simple fantasy of victory, but what you needed to *survive* in this world. (xviii, my emphasis)

Harris suggests that Dave's rescue of George Denham is motivated by sincerity and compassion, but also—more subversively—by his savvy understanding that the Denhams promise to be advantageous allies.

Dave's assessment proves accurate and introduces another feature common to southern folktales, the trickster-tricked motif. Harris concludes the tale by again featuring a discussion between Brother Roach and Brother Brannum. Roach recounts events from the previous Saturday when he ran into General Bledser, who boasted that he had made a trade that made him "'particular proud'" (69). Bledser bragged that he "'sold Blue Dave'" and believed he duped Mrs. Denham by selling her a fugitive slave who has proven impossible to catch(69). His delight is undermined, however, when the Denham carriage approaches. Roach had asked Bledser to "'look clost at that nigger on the carriage,—look clost at him'" (69). Roach explains that when Bledser saw Dave driving the carriage, he exclaimed, "'Why, what the thunderation!'" And as the carriage passed, Mrs. Denham called out, "'Good-morning, Giner'l, good-morning! David is a most excellent driver'" (69). Brother Roach tells Brother Brannum:

> The Giner'l managed for to take off his hat, but he was in-about the worst whipped-out white man I ever see. And arter the carriage got out of hearing, sir, he stood in that there door there and cussed plump tell he couldn't cuss. "When a man's been to Congress and back, he's liable for to know how to take the name of the Lord in vain. But don't tell em about the wimmen, Brother Brannum. Don't!" (69)

Bledser is embarrassed and loses his temper, and the conversation between the farmers suggests that they, too, enjoy this planter's besting. Indeed, Roach is described as "laughing until he began to wheeze" (69) while telling Brannum the story.

While Darwin T. Turner asserts that the Denhams' purchase of Dave undermines the story's subversive potential, in the context of Georgia's slave codes, manumission was possible only by special legislative act and tended to be approved only "as long as local opinion supported manumission" (Ford 295). Given Dave's reputation as an elusive fugitive, legislative permission granting his manumission would have been highly unlikely. Moreover, Dave was at large for over seven years, indicating that he had a compelling reason to remain in the area—most likely ties to family and friends. Had the Denhams successfully manumitted him, he would have lost access to his community because, as Lacy K. Ford notes, "in 1826, Georgia mandated that all newly manumitted slaves be removed from the state" (295). The scene described by the farmers thus suggests that Dave and Mrs. Denham negotiated a deal that satisfied both parties and simultaneously getting the best of Bledser. Lewis Hyde points out that most tricksters "are male," but adds, "there may be female tricksters who have simply been ignored" (335). In this tale, Mrs. Denham and Dave are depicted as a team featuring a white woman as tricky and enigmatic as her black trickster partner.

Another trickster duo is depicted in "Balaam and his Master." In his portrait of William Cozart, Harris draws on the cultural ideal of the traditional Virginia gentleman. Before the mid-eighteenth century, Virginia maintained a fairly tightknit gentry class that wielded extensive power. Webb notes that in the colonial era, the

> Virginia colony had evolved into a rigid, three-tiered society. At the top was a landed English-American aristocracy whose wealth and holdings owed much to the patronage of the ruling royalty in the mother country. Contrary to the prevailing mythology of a ruggedly competitive, rags-to-riches ethos among those who had braved the Atlantic to come to America, the majority of this privileged class was originally granted huge tracts of land by royal decree. Family names and quasi-royal prerogatives were taken seriously, and as the generations unfolded, this "Cavalier aristocracy" took great pains to protect and advance their own interests as well as those of others in their small circle of elites. (2141)

But by the early 1760s, as Isaac Rhys demonstrates, the gentry's hegemony was weakened by a popular evangelical movement that conflicted with Anglican authority. Further deterioration of power occurred in the post-Revolutionary era with the triumph of "republicanism," resulting in changes "to the traditional forms" that were replaced with "an ideology in which 'the individual' was the legitimating metaphor" (314). Rhys notes:

> [T]he old order had induced a sense of obligation to public service among those whose family and fortune had set them over their neighbors in parish and county. Within the new framework of contractual association the local units seemed to be less like patriarchal protectorates and more like outlets for the electoral ambitions of individuals. An acute sense of lost public spirit resulted. (314)

By the late eighteenth century, the decline of the Virginia tobacco economy compelled many members of these formerly powerful families to seek new opportunities in the Southwest, particularly after the Louisiana Purchase and Eli Whitney's invention of the cotton gin. These two developments combined to create a new market in cotton production, as well as a revived market in the domestic slave trade. While Virginia's patrician families transported rigid notions of class distinctions tied to lineage and bloodlines rather than wealth alone, the ideology of "the individual" replaced the aristocracy's sense of social responsibility with a more opportunistic sensibility. Furthermore, the upper class's hierarchical worldview often clashed with the backcountry ethos of independence and "lack of subservience to outsiders or outside forces" (Hahn 45).

As Harris notes, William Cozart represents "the Old Virginia fashion," yet he exhibits greater personal ambition than that inherent in traditional protectorate ideology, and with his "wagons and his negroes," he settles in middle Georgia, where he "bought hundreds of acres of land" and thus became "the leading citizen of the place" (8–9). This "thrifty village" grew into "a flourishing town," and the "Cozarts remained the leading family, socially, politically, and financially" (9). The family's peace is disturbed, however, by the birth in the 1830s of Berrien Cozart, who grew to become "a thorn in the side of those who loved him best" (10). Harris undermines FFV ideology with Berrien Cozart, who had "a temper of extreme violence and an obstinacy that had no bounds," characteristics suggesting that the Cozarts' class status is simply a matter of wealth rather than inherently superior bloodlines (12).

Harris introduces another interesting feature in this character portrait through Berrien Cozart's relationship with his body servant, Balaam. While Berrien's father lacks the ability to exert control over his rebellious son, "only one person in the world had any real influence over him—a negro named Balaam" (10). Balaam is introduced as a "negro with an independence and a fearlessness extremely rare among slaves" and is the only character in the text able to exercise any influence on Berrien (12). Furthermore, owing to Balaam's limitations as a slave with no legal or social rights, his power derives from the only resource available to him: his intelligence, which Harris emphasizes throughout the narrative. For example, Berrien's father hires a tutor to educate him, but the tutor "was not very much to Berrien's taste" (13), and he insults and assaults the young teacher. Balaam then enters the room, "closing the door carefully behind him, and almost immediately the tumult ceased. Then the negro appeared leading his young master by the arm . . . . The negro, with his hand on the boy's shoulder, was saying something unpleasant, for the tutor observed one or two fierce gestures of protest. But these soon ceased" (14). Harris does not recount what Balaam says to subdue Berrien, but the slave is depicted as the only person able to control this "sensual, cruel, impetuous, and implacable" young man (15). Indeed, Balaam is repeatedly described giving the impression of "leading his young master" through influence and intelligence.

Balaam's sway over Berrien also functions to undermine William Cozart's role as a patriarch. David Hackett Fischer notes that in the Virginia tradition, childrearing was geared toward preparing "the child to take its proper place in the social hierarchy. The child's will was not broken, but in a phrase that Virginians like to use, it was 'severely bent against itself.' This end was accomplished primarily by requiring children to observe elaborate rituals of self-restraint" (313). In spite of William Cozart's social, economic, and political power, he is unable to bend the will of his rebellious son. Yet his slave, Balaam, possesses an influence and authority the elder Cozart lacks.

As the narrative progresses, Harris draws on frontier and slave trickster traits in developing the character portraits of this unique duo. After Berrien is expelled from college and disinherited by his father, he tells Balaam: "'You belong to me, but I'll give you your choice; you can go with me, or you can stay. If you go, I'll probably get into a tight place and sell you; if you stay, Pap will make a pet of you for my sake" (19). Balaam chooses to stay with Berrien because the alternative is to "go to the overseer and tell him to put you to work'" (20), which means picking "five hundred pounds of cotton every day" (18). Berrien sets out to make his way in the world as a con man and seems to live by Simon Suggs's credo: "[I]t's good to be shifty in a new country." Balaam, however, lives by African American folk wisdom, which, as Nigel Thomas notes, taught that "to be black in America and survive necessitates being a trickster" (81). Winifred Morgan points out that "southwestern tricksters struggle to win; African-American tricksters struggle to *survive*," a perspective especially relevant to this unique story (212).

Berrien Cozart is particularly well suited to the frontier trickster lifestyle and embraces the con game as a livelihood. Harris notes that "there were few games of chance in which he was not an adept. No conjurer was so adroit with the cards or the dice" (25). But like other frontier tricksters,

Berrien eventually becomes a trickster-tricked when "one fine day luck turned her back on him, and he paraded on fine afternoons in front of Lloyd's Hotel a penniless man" (25). Furthermore, when Balaam discovers that Berrien "had made up his mind to sell him," he draws on black trickster wisdom for his own protection: "'Well, suh,' said Balaam, brushing his master's coat carefully, 'you kin sell me, but de man dat buys Balaam will git a mighty bad bargain'" (25). Berrien asks what he means, and Balaam replies, "'You kin sell me, suh, but I ain't gwine stay wid um' . . . . 'I got legs, Marse Berry. You know dat yo'se'f'" (26). The two then embark on a scheme to sell Balaam, who will run "armed with a 'pass' which formally set forth to all to whom it might concern that the boy David had express permission to join his master in Nashville, and this 'pass' bore the signature of Elmore Avery, a gentleman who existed only in the imagination of Mr. Berrien Cozart" (30). During Balaam's journey, he uses trickster wit on a number of occasions to evade trouble. For example, he is asked by a white man who his master is, and having forgotten the name on his pass, Balaam explains,

> "I runned my han' und' de lindin' er my hat an' pulled out de pass, an' say, 'Boss, dis piece er paper kin talk losts better dan I kin.' De man look at me right hard, an' den he tuck de pass an' read it out loud. Well, suh, w'en he come ter de name I des grabbed holt un it wid my mi,' an' I ain't never turned it loose tell yit." (31)

Berrien Cozart is eventually arrested and jailed, and Balaam is captured during a rather perplexing escape attempt. Harris notes that the jailer discovers Berrien dead, "and crouching beside him was Balaam. How the negro had managed to make his way through the masonry of the dungeon without discovery is still one of the mysteries of Billville" (43).

While Balaam superficially appears to conform to the literary and cultural stereotype of devoted servant, as Darwin T. Turner contends, his trickster traits suggest loyalty to a lifestyle rather than to a master. His situation is preferable to the alternative, common condition of most slaves working from sun to sun in a cotton field. Ultimately, the narrative device again draws on the frontier humor trickster-tricked motif, but the black trickster featured in this story demonstrates the trickster's most important message—survival.

In the story "Where's Duncan?" Harris introduces a character representing a unique amalgam of southwest humor and African American folktale trickster traits. The tale is particularly compelling because of its implicitly subversive content, which addresses the taboo topic of "the forbidden theme of black/white miscegenation," as well as the implied sexual exploitation of a female slave (Kinney 45). James Kinney notes that in the antebellum era, "the nearly two-century struggle to contain miscegenation amounted to this—they prohibited legal intermarriage, punished illicit unions between black men and white women, but tolerated those between white men and black women as long as the mulatto children followed the condition of their slave mothers" (6). Harris establishes his narrative structure by using the common frontier humor frame technique, opening the sketch with "old man Isaiah Winchell a-gabling about old times" (149). And like the frontier humorists, Harris also utilizes a narratee, a character who functions as the listener in the tale, a role that becomes evident when Winchell uses the second person "you" in telling what he calls not a story, but "a happening" (149).

Winchell notes that in 1826, he was a young man of eighteen put in charge of "ginning and packing cotton" after the overseer left. After preparing the cotton for market, Winchell and Crooked-leg Jake load the wagon and start for Augusta, but when Winchell learns that Jake is drunk, he is compelled "to drive six mules, and there was only one rein to drive them with" (151). During the trip, "there came out of the woods a thick-set, dark-featured, black-bearded man with a bag slung across his shoulder" (152). This man helps with the team and joins Winchell in his journey. Harris introduces a particularly intriguing element when Jake wakes up and asks who is driving. After Winchell recounts the stranger's arrival, Jake asks, "Is he a sho' 'nuff w'ite man? (153). Winchell replies, "'Well, he looks like he is,' said I; 'but I'm not certain about that'" (154). The element of confusion regarding the stranger's racial identity complicates the racial binary of black and white, a particularly important distinction in an era of slavery, and later, segregation—the era in which the story is set and the era in which it was published.

Jake's question also implies that a black character is privy to information about this "stranger" that his master lacks. His master is thus not equipped to understand the full implications of the stranger's behavior or figurative speech. Toward the end of their journey, the character identifies himself as "Willis Featherstone" and claims, "'I am simply a vagabond.'" But he adds, "'I have a rich daddy hereabouts, and I'm on my way to see how he is getting along'" (157). Before his departure, Featherstone poses a "riddle" but advises, "'If you can't unriddle it, it will unriddle itself'" (157). He tells Winchell, "'A father had a son. He sent him to school in Augusta, until he was fifteen. By that time, the father grew to hate the son, and one day, in a fit of anger, sold him to a nigger speculator'" (157). Unable to "unriddle" the riddle, Winchell simply shrugs off the odd exchange.

Another strange encounter occurs later that evening when "a tall mulatto woman" approaches the camp and relays an invitation from her master, Giles Featherstone, to join him for dinner. While Winchell does not appear to notice that the stranger and the woman's master share the same surname, the stranger's question to the woman shows this is not simply coincidence. He asks her, "'Where's Duncan?'" (163). Her reaction indicates that the question is a source of intense pain. The woman "stood like one paralyzed. She gasped for breath, her arms jerked convulsively, and there was a twitching of the muscles of her face pitiful to behold" (163). When Featherstone repeats the question, she rose and "ran off into the darkness, screaming;—'He sold 'im!—he sold Duncan! He sold my onlyiest boy!'" (164). As the narrative events unfold, so too does the riddle. During the night, Jake wakes Winchell to tell him about a "'mighty rippit up dar at dat house on de hill'" (164). Jake urges Winchell to take action, declaring, "'Dey gwine ter be trouble up dar, sho ez you er born'" (165). His insistence suggests he possesses disturbing insight regarding the potential for further "trouble," but Winchell ignores Jake's appeal and returns to sleep. Jake again awakens Winchell, as the trouble escalates and the house becomes engulfed in flames. Winchell rushes to the house, and through a window, witnesses the mulatto woman "engaged in an encounter with a gray-haired white man . . . like two bull-dogs fighting. The woman had a carving-knife in her right hand, and she was endeavoring to push the white man against the wall" (166). During the fight, Winchell notes, "Once, and only once, did I catch the sound of a voice; it was the voice of the nigger woman; she had her carving-knife raised in the air in one hand, and with the other she had the white man by the throat. 'Where's Duncan?' she shrieked" (168). After the woman "plunged the carving-knife into his body, not only once, but twice," the house collapses in flames (168). Winchell concludes the story by noting that "Crooked-leg

Jake insisted to the day of his death that the man who had driven our team sat in a chair in the corner of the dining-room, while the woman and the man were fighting, and seemed to be enjoying the spectacle" (169).

While Harris presents Winchell as the narrator of the story, Crooked-leg Jake provides key elements necessary to "unriddle" the riddle, and it becomes clear that the woman is the stranger's mother and that he is the son referenced in the riddle. Moreover, the riddle implies that sexual exploitation of a female slave resulted in a son whose father (and master) sold him to a slave speculator and therefore profited from the separation of a mother and her child. The stranger's amalgam of black and white trickster traits are evident in his "vagabond" freedom, which would have involved some form of escape from the slavery his father sold him into, as well as the use of wit to survive. His frontier trickster traits are suggested by his mission to see "how his father is getting along," indicating he is carrying out a plan (157). Lucinda MacKethan identifies Simon Suggs and Sut Lovingood as two examples of frontier humor trickster figures, but these characters are driven by distinctly different motives. Suggs is notorious for being "shifty," an opportunist, but Sut Lovingood is more often driven by an important backcountry attitude toward justice. David Hackett Fischer notes that "backsettlers shared an idea of order as a system of retributive justice. The prevailing principle was *lex talionis,* the rule of retaliation. It held that a good man must seek to do right in the world, but when wrong was done to him he must punish the wrongdoer himself by an act of retribution that restored order and justice in the world" (765). Many of Sut's antics are motivated by retaliation; indeed, the sketch "Parson Bullen's Lizards" is subtitled "retribution." As the story of the stranger concludes, it becomes evident that retaliation is also the motivating force behind the son's "visit" to his father. Harris's narrative also strategically integrates controversial elements rarely featured in nineteenth-century fiction, such as the issue of miscegenation—particularly sexual exploitation of a slave woman—as well as a chronicle of the long-lasting devastation resulting from the separation of a mother from her child. The story is ultimately an example of intertextual signifying at its most poignant.

Darwin T. Turner justifiably chastises Harris for his metaphorical reference to slavery as a university, but in the context of an era reneging on the social and civil rights of black Americans, this figurative device suggests that Harris was again signifying. Harris writes, "Here is a university of slavery that shall lead the savage to citizenship" (7). While use of the word "savage" has understandably outraged a number of readers, the word was also commonly employed during the post-Reconstruction era by radical racists perpetuating the theory that once free of the "civilizing" influence of slavery, black Americans were reverting to bestial "savagery." Harris's use of the word "savage" undermines the connotation it had for his contemporaries by relegating the word to an era that has passed. Harris thus indicates a transitional phase has resulted in citizenship, which, he suggests, African Americans have earned are therefore entitled to. Harris expresses similar sentiments in his non-fiction, as Jeremy Wells points out, and "was insistent in several essays published during his lifetime that African Americans had not yet been given the chance to show whether they could contribute to U.S. civil society and that they deserved the opportunity" (54). Furthermore, by engaging in signifying systems of the antebellum era, Harris celebrates the rich artistry of written and oral folktales featuring the cultural, social, and community values of non-elite southerners, highlighted by frontier humor and African American folktale traditions.

WORKS CITED

Barthes, Roland. "From Work to Text." *The Norton Anthology of Theory & Criticism*. 2nd ed. Ed. Vincent B. Leitch. New York: Norton, 2010. 1326–31. Print.

Blassingame, John W. *The Slave Community: Plantation Life in the Ante-bellum South*. New York: Oxford University Press, 1972. Print.

Cochran, Robert. "Black Father: The Subversive Achievement of Joel Chandler Harris." *African American Review* 38.1 (2004): 21–34. Print.

Cowan, William Tynes. *The Slave in the Swamp: Disrupting the Plantation Narrative*. New York: Routledge, 2005. Print.

Fischer, David Hackett. *Albion's Seed: Four British Folkways in America*. New York: Oxford University Press, 1989. Print.

Ford, Lacy K. *Deliver Us From Evil: The Slavery Question in the Old South*. New York: Oxford University Press, 2009. Print.

Gates, Henry Louis, Jr. *The Signifying Monkey: A Theory of African-American Literary Criticism*. New York: Oxford University Press, 1988. Print.

Hahn, Steven. "The Yeomanry of the Nonplantation South: Upper Piedmont Georgia, 1850–1860." *Class, Conflict, and Consensus: Antebellum Southern Community Studies*. Eds. Orville Vernon Burton and Robert C. McMath Jr. Westport, CT: Greenwood Press, 1982. 29–56. Print.

Harris, Ashleigh. "Speaking the 'Truth by Dissembling': Necessary Ambiguities in the Tar Baby Tale." *Journal of Literary Studies* 16.3-4 (2000): 58–75. Print.

Harris, George Washington. *Sut Lovingood Yarns Spun by a 'Nat'ral Born Durn'd Fool'*. New York: Dick & Fitzgerald, 1867. Print.

Harris, Joel Chandler. *Balaam and His Master and Other Sketches and Stories*. New York: Freeport Press, 1891. Print.

———. "Introduction." *The Complete Tales of Uncle Remus*. Ed. Richard Chase. Boston: Houghton Mifflin, 1983. Print.

———. *Mingo, and Other Sketches in Black and White*. Boston: J. R. Osgood, 1884. Print.

———. *Stories of Georgia*. New York: American Book Co., 1896. Print.

Hemenway, Robert. "Introduction." *Uncle Remus, His Songs and Sayings*. New York: Penguin, 1982. 7–31. Print.

Hyde, Lewis. "Where Are the Women Tricksters?" *Trickster Lives: Culture and Myth in American Fiction*. Ed. Jeanne Campbell Reesman. Athens: University of Georgia Press, 2001. 185–93. Print.

Inge, M. Thomas, and Ed Piacentino. "Introduction: The Humor of the Old South; or, Transgression *He* Wrote." *Southern Frontier Humor: An Anthology*. Eds. M. Thomas Inge and Ed Piacentino. Columbia: University of Missouri Press, 2010. 1–23. Print.

Kinney, James. *Amalgamation! Race, Sex, and Rhetoric in the Nineteenth-Century American Novel*. Westport, CT: Greenwood Press, 1985. Print.

Kristeva, Julia. *Revolution in Poetic Language*. Trans. Margaret Waller. New York: Columbia University Press, 1984. Print.

Lee, Julia Sun-Joo. "Knucklebones and Knocking-bones: The Accidental Trickster in Ellison's *Invisible Man*." *African American Review* 40.3 (2006): 461–73. Print.

Levine, Lawrence W. *Black Culture and Black Consciousness: Afro-American Folk Thought From Slavery to Freedom*. 30th Anniversary Ed. New York: Oxford University Press, 2007. Print.

Longstreet, Augustus B. *Georgia Scenes: Characters, Incidents, &c. in the First Half-Century of the Republic*. 1835. Savannah, GA: Beehive, 1975. Print.

Lynn, Kenneth S. *Mark Twain and Southwestern Humor*. Boston: Little, Brown, 1958. Print.

MacKethan, Lucinda H. "Plantation Fiction." *The Companion to Southern Literature: Themes, Genres, Places, People, Movements, and Motifs*. Eds. Joseph M. Flora and Lucinda MacKethan. Baton Rouge: Louisiana State University Press, 2002. 650–52. Print.

———. "Trickster." *The Companion to Southern Literature: Themes, Genres, Places, People, Movements, and Motifs*. Eds. Joseph M. Flora and Lucinda MacKethan. Baton Rouge: Louisiana State University Press, 2002. 913–15. Print.

Morgan, Winifred. "Signifying: The African-American Trickster and the Humor of the Old Southwest." *The Enduring Legacy of Old Southwest Humor*. Ed. Ed Piacentino. Baton Rouge: Louisiana State University Press, 2006. 210–26. Print.

Oriard, Michael. "Shifty in a New Country: Games in Southwestern Humor." *Southern Literary Journal* 12.2 (1980): 1–28. Print.

Osofsky, Gilbert. *Puttin' On Ole Massa*. New York: Harper & Row, 1969. Print.

Reinhardt, Mark. *Who Speaks for Margaret Garner?* Minneapolis: University of Minnesota Press, 2010. Print.

Rhys, Isaac. *The Transformation of Virginia 1740–1790*. Chapel Hill: University of North Carolina Press, 1982. Print.

Taliaferro, Hardin E. *Fisher's River (North Carolina) Scenes and Characters*. New York: Harper & Brothers, 1859. Print.

Thomas, Nigel H. *From Folklore to Fiction: A Study of Folk Heroes and Rituals in the Black American Novel*. New York: Greenwood Press, 1988. Print.

Tracy, Susan J. *In the Master's Eye: Representations of Women, Blacks, and Poor Whites in Antebellum Southern Literature*. Amherst: University of Massachusetts Press, 1995. Print.

Turner, Darwin T. "Daddy Joel Harris and His Old-Time Darkies." *Southern Literary Journal* 1.1 (1968): 20–41. Print.

Watkins, Mel. *On the Real Side: Laughing, Lying, and Signifying*. New York: Simon & Schuster, 1994. Print.

Webb, James. *Born Fighting: How the Scots-Irish Shaped America*. New York: Broadway Books, 2004. Print.

Wells, Jeremy. *Romances of the White Man's Burden: Race, Empire, and the Plantation in American Literature, 1880–1936*. Nashville, TN: Vanderbilt University Press, 2011. Print.

FROM SWAMP DOCTOR TO CONJURE WOMAN

Exploring "Science" and Race in Nineteenth-Century America

BRUCE BLANSETT

In his collection of dialect tales published in *The Conjure Woman and Other Conjure Tales*, Charles Chesnutt challenges a wide range of social and scientific prescriptions of racial difference that pervaded the culture surrounding the Civil War. Working against the popular tradition of plantation fiction, Chesnutt's *Conjure Tales* disrupts the traditional narrative of black inferiority and presents a counter-narrative steeped in conjure, signifying, and a healthy trickster tradition. To do so, Chesnutt's work denaturalizes the unexamined scientific theories of race that girded pro-slavery arguments during the Civil War, justifying the severe racism of post-Reconstruction America. Chesnutt, though revolutionary in his subversive techniques and highly respected as one of the first prominent African American authors, reworks various techniques, forms, and subversive strategies already employed by a southwest humor antecedent, Henry Clay Lewis, whose sketches in *Odd Leaves from the Life of a Louisiana Swamp Doctor* (1850) highlight many of the ideological tensions of the nineteenth century.

Lewis, a practicing physician and humorist, disrupts traditional scientific and medical discourse by juxtaposing the compassionate swamp doctor with the posturing professional man, the city physician. Similarly, Chesnutt describes conjure men and women whose roles within their communities often parallel those of swamp doctors and provide a telling juxtaposition to what was then considered legitimate medicine. In *Shared Traditions: Southern History and Folk Culture*, Charles Joyner describes the nature of professional medicine in the South as juxtaposed to popularity of folk medicine: "Southern folk medicine embodies a cultural system centering around a broad spectrum of vernacular healers from midwives and herbalists to conjurers, root doctors, and faith healers. Southern women often play crucial roles as healers who reassure their patients by embodying traditional concepts of health and illness even as they modernize traditional healing practices with elements of scientific medicine" (17). Joyner's discussion demonstrates that Lewis and Chesnutt were not drawing up arbitrary comparisons. A strong culture of folk and alternative medicine supplemented, replaced, and added value to professional medicine. Lewis and Chesnutt exploited professional medicine's relationship with folk medicine in order defamiliarize and denaturalize the often dubious authority of professional medical discourse.

The link between Lewis and Chesnutt is not only thematic, but also functional and stylistic. Among the most overt links between them is the episodic nature of each of their respective works and the storytelling devices that link these various installments. The distinct, yet interrelated incidents of each work function as representative cross sections of contemporary life. Lewis's work, using the reflective voice of Madison Tensas, boasts the authenticity of an experienced physician reflecting on a colorful personal past, while Chesnutt's two storytellers—John as framer and Julius as narrator of the embedded tales—represent divergent cultural perspectives that draw readers into this conversation. Storytelling thus becomes an important trope for each of the pieces. In fact, many scholars have focused on the frame narrative and storytelling aspects of Chesnutt's work[1], and these tropes often become contextualized as chief points of control and resistance within the text.[2] Scholars of Lewis have also focused on narrative technique and its particular influence in his work. In his book *Counterfeit Gentlemen: Manhood and Humor in the Old South*, John Mayfield asserts, "more than any other humorist before George Washington Harris, Lewis adopted the pose of the 'obsessive confessor.' It is a pose *un*-Southern and manipulative, and it adds to the audaciousness of Lewis's art" (87). Unifying the many interpretations of storytelling in the two works are the ways in which the technique functions to create intimacy with the reader. In the same way that John and Annie often occupy the role of listener (or narratee), readers of these two works necessarily take on this role and become part of the story being told—or at least a part of the world in which the story is situated.

Beyond the similarities in the structure of the two works, Chesnutt's reliance on wordplay and multiple meanings—though certainly a product of the trickster tradition—also has an early exemplar in Lewis's sketches. In "'Aesculapius in Buckskin': The Swamp Doctor as Satirist in Henry

Clay Lewis's *Odd Leaves*," Mark A. Keller examines Lewis's reliance upon verbal play: "Lewis reinforces this concept of the ambiguity of words in an organic way in *Odd Leaves*—through his employment of puns and similar forms of wordplay. Indeed, Henry Clay Lewis ranks as the most skillfull [*sic*] punster among the humorists of the Old Southwest" (439). According to Keller, "Lewis's favorite type of wordplay in *Odd Leaves* is *syllepsis*, a figure of speech occurring when a single word is employed that will yield more than one meaning, usually because of the context in which it appears or because of its phonetic association with another word not present in the structure" (440). Keller points to the words Lewis employs in "The Curious Widow" as the doctor considers playing a prank on his landlady to remedy her curiosity: "I almost relented of my purpose, but my love letters read, my duns made evident, my poetry criticized by eyes to which Love would not lend his blindness to make perfect; and then—she is a widow! My heart, at this last reflection, became immediately barred to the softening influence of forgiveness, and I determined in all hostility to *face* her" (qtd. in Keller 440–41). This type of punning is typically employed by Lewis as a comic device, though still often tied to his frequent use of the grotesque.

For Chesnutt, syllepsis is an equally useful and relied upon form of wordplay, often employed to achieve the same comedic, grotesque—sometimes tragic—effect. In her article "A Mind Enslaved?: The Interaction of Metaphor, Cognitive Distance, and Narrative Framing in Chesnutt's 'Dave's Neckliss,'" Jennifer Riddle Harding deals with the ways in which Chesnutt employs metaphor as a subversive technique:

> For example, "Dave's Neckliss" blends a representation of a slave named Dave with the concept of ham; the working mental spaces that represent these domains align metaphorically along several counterpart relations, such as Dave's body aligned with a pig's body, and Dave's role in the world aligned with a pig's role in the world; when these aligned elements are brought together and emphasized in a metaphorical blend, properties that emerge include absurdity and humor. (429)

According to Harding, one of the chief ways in which this blending and resultant "absurdity and humor" come about is through punning. Harding points to an example of this punning in "Dave's Neckliss": "Julius eventually finds Dave hanging in the smokehouse: 'he des got ter b'lievin' he was all done turnt ter a ham; en den he had gone en built a fier, and tied a rope roun' his neck, des lack de hams wuz tied, en had hung hisse'f up in the smoke-'ouse fer ter kyo'" (435). "Curing" in this passage melds Dave's identity with the essence of a ham by signifying both a means of preserving food and the pathologizing of African Americans by the scientific and medical communities during this time period. Chesnutt, though often using wordplay as a means through which to mask a subversive covert meaning,[3] employs the same techniques as Henry Clay Lewis and other southwest humor antecedents to enrich and add humor to his dialect tales.

Throughout Chesnutt's other tales, as in the "curing" of Dave in "Dave's Neckliss," punning and other types of wordplay frequently align with medical scenes or the language of medical discourse. These moments of duality often characterize the gap between the white community's understanding of medicine and the black community's lack of faith in this system. Since black individuals so often became the target of scientific experiments and medical conjecture during this time, medical languages often connoted pain or prejudice to black persons, while simultaneously signifying progress and enlightenment to the white population. A second example of this type of signifying occurs in "Mars Jeems's Nightmare." When Ole Nick, the plantation's overseer and slave breaker, encounters a willful new slave (who the tale suggests is the conjured plantation owner), his solution to the problem is to tie up the new slave and give him "fo'ty wid a dozen er so th'owed in fer good measure" (Chesnutt 62). This act is characterized as a cure for "laziness and impidence" and is specifically referred to as such: "De nigger went on at a tarrable rate, des lack a wil' man, but co'se he wuz bleedzd ter take his med'cine, fer he wuz tied up en couldn' he'p hisse'f" (62). The use of the word "med'cine," in this instance, highlights one of the goals of science for the white community: defining and controlling the black population (62). The scene also makes it clear that for the black population this term indicates the source of pain, not a respite from it.

Similar to the subjective meanings brought to bear in "Mars Jeems's Nightmare," the use of medical jargon in both Chesnutt and Lewis becomes a locus of misunderstanding or a point of humor for the characters. For example, in a chapter of Lewis's book titularly described as

"Getting Acquainted with the Medicines," the student Tensas disastrously misinterprets his mentor's instructions to "take it down and digest" as a directive to *in*gest the contents of the dispensary, rather than his actual instruction to writing down and summarizing information (36). This potentially lethal misinterpretation occurs because of linguistic differences between student and teacher. Tensas values the instructions in the most medical way possible, though doing so seems both wildly undesirable and dangerous: "By the father of physic, thought I, this study of medicine is not the pleasant task I anticipated—rather arduous in the long run for the stomach, I should judge, to swallow and digest all the medicines, from Abracadabra to Zinzibar" (36). This statement, accompanied by Tensas's continued willingness to do what it takes to become a doctor, demonstrates the mysteriousness and inscrutability of nineteenth-century medicine to those outside the profession and points to language as one of the causes of this misunderstanding. Lewis, through his verbal play on this disparity, satirizes the pretensions of the medical profession—especially of the city doctors.

Chesnutt provides a similar moment of departure in "A Deep Sleeper." In this instance, instead of being the root of an entire drama, the lapse in apprehension remains unacknowledged and occurs in the narration rather than in the specific action of the imbedded tale. After the doctors examine Skundus, they tell the plantation owner that he had experienced a "catacornered fit" (Chesnutt 144). Here, the inability to translate medical jargon into common language becomes a point of humor and gives this moment special significance. In fact, the absurd presence of the wrong word—"catacornered" instead of "catatonic"—becomes even more complicated by the fact that it is unclear how the mistake originated. The various possibilities, then, all reinforce the divide between the white scientific community and the black community of (often unwilling) patients. One explanation for the error could be that medical terminology, and the medical profession more broadly, are both inadequate and counterfeit, relying on complicated language to obscure an absence of actual legitimacy. The second feasible explanation, though more subtle as a critique, proves just as damning: The error could lie in either the original mishearing of the phrase during the time of the story, or else be a fault of Julius's creation. This misinterpretation draws attention to the separation between white medical mythology and the beliefs of the black population. The mainstream white physicians are neither legitimized nor understood by the black community, and this passage, as a result of Chesnutt's play on words, exemplifies this complication.

In addition to revisiting stylistic choices made earlier by Henry Clay Lewis, Charles Chesnutt also reworks modes of subversiveness akin to those in Lewis's work—especially in each author's treatment of the black population and resistance to the medical status quo. Chesnutt, as a major African American writer, has long been lauded for his opposition to the rampant mistreatment and misrepresentation of black figures. Lewis, especially for the time and atmosphere in which he was writing—and notably for a white author—challenges many of the same prescriptions that Chesnutt would later take on. In his article "The Image of the Negro in the Writings of Henry Clay Lewis," Alan Rose describes the culture that dominated during Lewis's lifetime:

> One of the most striking characteristics of pre-Civil War Southern literature is the virtual absence of explicit images of two of the basic forces of this pre-secessionist and slaveholding society: the rebellion against authority and the fear of Negro violence. The literature abounds with images of good-natured and utterly harmless house servants, but one rarely sees the opposite image, the demonic Negro, whose entire goal is to destroy the white Southerner. (255)

Henry Clay Lewis, however, chooses to ignore these precedents and depicts this very fear. Rose suggests that he may have, in fact, "identified with the Negro as a fellow minority-figure, while at the same time sharing the fear of Negro violence (but not the inhibitions against expressing it) that pervaded the South" (257). This tension is easily observable in both "The Curious Widow" and "A Struggle for Life," in which he simultaneously demonizes and identifies with black figures. Though depicting black characters in a less-than-favorable light—and despite the likelihood that Lewis, too, was impacted by the ubiquitous racism of the antebellum South—his treatment of black figures in this way actually sheds light on the flaws of the racist system, instead of ignoring and covering up these issues like so many other authors were willing to do during this period.

Throughout his lifetime, Chesnutt struggled against the same type of tradition in works of plantation fiction. Richard Brodhead describes this trend in his introduction to *The Conjure Woman and Other Conjure Tales*:

> With the official end of Reconstruction in 1877, southern regionalism spawned a specialized subgenre, a form with the more or less overt function of excusing the North's withdrawal from the plight of the freed southern slave. This subgenre, prefigured in Joel Chandler Harris's *Uncle Remus: His Songs and His Sayings* (1880) and perfected in Thomas Nelson Page's *In Ole Virginia* (1887), deployed a black rustic figure, an ex-slave but still-faithful retainer to testify to his love of the old days and his lack of desire for equal social rights. (5)

Just as many authors during Lewis's time portrayed a harmless, positive racial relationship, writers during Chesnutt's career also lauded an idealized version of the institution of slavery. Though perhaps challenging these prescriptions in a more direct and deliberate way, Chesnutt still approximates the action taken by Henry Clay Lewis decades earlier. Chesnutt, keeping its genre conventions intact, erodes the idealized image put forth in plantation fiction by illustrating a much more horrific and realistic version of slavery in his tales. In fact, heartbreak and barbarism feature prominently throughout *The Conjure Woman and Other Conjure Tales*. These instances are frequently seen in both the threats by slave owners and overseers and in slaves' quality of life on the plantations. In fact, in almost all of Chesnutt's stories a slave is either threatened with or punished with "fo'ty," and there are some instances where the brutality is even more pronounced. In "Mars Jeems's Nightmare," for instance, Chesnutt shows the extent to which slave owners were capable of inflicting abuse upon their human property. Julius explains:

> W'en his daddy, ole Mars John McLean, died, de plantation en all de niggers fell ter young Mars Jeems. He had be'n bad 'nuff befo,' but it wa'n't long atterwa'ds 'tel he got so dey wuz no use in libbin' at all ef you ha' ter lib roun' Mars Jeems. His niggers wuz bleedzd ter slabe fum daylight ter da'k, w'les yuther folks's didn' hafter wuk 'cep'n' fum sun ter sun; en dey didn' git no mo' ter eat dan dey oughter, en dat de coa'ses' kin.' (57–58)

Here, Chesnutt shows the misery of plantation life for slaves. Not only were they forced to work impossible hours, they were only given the meanest sustenance, and their only respite is death: "[D]ey wuz no use in libb'in at all ef you ha' ter lib roun' Mars Jeems" (57). They were, in effect, completely defenseless. And while this treatment is depicted as more extreme than the norm, it both demonstrates the capacity of slave owners to be capricious and cruel and shows that the norm was for slaves to work "fum sun ter sun" (58). This hopeless situation is again underscored in "The Dumb Witness." After the slave Viney has ruined her master's chance to marry (presumably by exposing a sexual relationship between them), her master Malcolm displays the extent of his power over her: "'I will teach you,' he said to his housekeeper, who quailed before him, 'to tell tales about your master. I will put it out of your power to dip your tongue in where you are not concerned'" (165). Not only is Viney severely punished for what she has done, but there is no hope of salvation: "There was no one to say him nay. The law made her his. It was a lonely house, and no angel of mercy stayed his hand" (165). This combination of helplessness and cruelty is virtually ubiquitous throughout Chesnutt's tales, as slaves are beaten, lent out, sold, starved, and humiliated. Instead of apologizing for slavery or depicting nostalgic reminiscences of earlier times, as many other authors chose to do, Chesnutt illustrates the "darker side of slavery" in his conjure tales (46).

Perhaps the most significant precedent Henry Clay Lewis established is the way in which he challenges, through satire, many aspects of the scientific and medical communities. According to John Mayfield in *Counterfeit Gentlemen,* Lewis "uses medicine as a metaphor to explore the corruptions and purgations that he must endure to succeed" (85). As Lewis's main character and alias, Madison Tensas, trains to become a physician, he defamiliarizes and barbarizes many of the prevailing medical techniques and attitudes of this elite culture. In the same episode about his medical training that highlights Lewis's humorous use of wordplay, "Getting Acquainted with the Medicines", Tensas's reaction to the unhappy task of sampling the entire dispensary adds a darker perspective to the otherwise comic scene. Though ready to advance his education, Tensas is not too keen on the idea of drinking arsenic and considers allowing "Old Tubba, the Indian," to test it instead. Tensas's internal monologue in this scene provides insight into the approach to life and medicine taught aspiring physicians: "This Indian, he is of no earthly account or any use to any one; science often has demanded sacrifices, and he would be a willing one; but—it may kill him; I can't do it; to kill a man before I get my diploma will be murder; a jury might not so pronounce it, but conscience would" (Lewis 38). This moment of reflection highlights several issues that would have been so accepted they would not normally have even been examined. For example, Lewis draws attention to the dogma that sacrifice in the name of science is categorically for the greater good. At the same time, he points specifically to the people who are forced to make these sacrifices: not the well-to-do white men, but the disenfranchised groups that "Tubba the Indian" represents. Lewis also suggests that the status conferred on medical practitioners is artificial; in the mind of Madison Tensas, a medical diploma stands in as justification for murder. With this arbitrary signifier comes the license to perform the role of God, with the ability to exploit human life as needed for scientific progress.

This equation of medical learning with scientific absolutism becomes even more tenuous in the obvious posturing of medical students and of city doctors generally throughout Lewis's work. In saving Tubba's life, the medical students invoke the "array of medical lore" with which they have been indoctrinated. However, the shouts of "sulphas zinci—stomach, arteri, pump, otomy—must—legs—hot-toddy—to bleed him—lectricity—hot blister—flat-irons—open his—windpipe," are characterized by Tensas as "the jargon of voices" (Lewis 39). Medical treatment, then, becomes less about diagnosing and treating than about the pretense of medical expertise. Tensas highlights this tendency in his differentiation between swamp doctor and city doctor:

> The city physician has soft hands, soft skin, and soft clothes: we have soft hearts but hard hands; we are rough in our phrases, but true in our natures; our words do not speak one language and our actions another . . . our characters, when not original, are impressed upon us by the people we practice among and associate with, for such is the character of the pioneers and pre-emptionists of the swamp. (24)

Tensas, all the while identifying with swamp doctors himself, clearly defines the insincerity of city doctors and their ineffectuality in understanding and treating their patients.

It is this type of hollow knowledge that Chesnutt works to undermine in his *Conjure Tales*. During the nineteenth century, the leading scientific thinkers, mostly prominent physicians, categorically attributed characteristics to entire races of people. In an effort to justify slavery before the war and to reaffirm notions of white racial superiority during the post-Reconstruction period, race theorists described and rationalized—using highly scientific jargon—what they saw as the innate inferiority of all black people. In *Race in North America,* Audrey Smedley traces the course of racism and scientific racial studies through the history of North America, and explains some of the theories involving African Americans that were used to reinforce racist ideologies and as justifications for slavery. Smedley contends that during the nineteenth century, "[S]cientists constructed definitions and characterizations of each racial population, focusing especially on the identification of 'the Negro' in the context of what had come to be defined as white civilization" (235). These scientific hypotheses, which not only separated black individuals from the white population, but also professed that blacks were far inferior to whites, were then commonly accepted as truths.

Two of the leading hypotheses regarding the origin of races, though necessarily in opposition to one another, both proposed that persons of African descent were biologically inferior to those of European descent. The hypothesis that dominated before Charles Darwin's 1859 publication of *The Origin of Species* was known as monogenesis and posited that individuals were produced by a single act of creation, then diverged through time from their common ancestor (Smedley 238). In this scientific hypothesis, according to Smedley, scientists had "long accepted the fall from grace and subsequent 'degeneration' as sufficient explication for the dehumanized status of the Negro" (240). This notion suggests that Africans were less highly evolved than Europeans intellectually, culturally, and socially. The other hypothesis of creation, known as polygenesis, was conceived in 1799 by Dr. Charles White, an English physician who suggested that blacks were "an intermediate form between true human beings (white Europeans) and apes" (Smedley 236). White formed this hypothesis based on his studies of anatomy, in which he compared traits of blacks, white Europeans, and apes (Smedley 237). Despite the contrary nature of the two hypotheses, each reinforced racial theories asserting even more firmly the already widespread belief in black inferiority.

Slaveholders clearly had a vested interest in accepting the idea of black inferiority. This assertion would allow individuals to rationalize and justify their enslavement of an entire race of people. According to Smedley, this idea was also endorsed by the white population after the Civil War. Smedley states:

> One inescapable fact of the nineteenth century was that many whites profited in a great many ways, from economic opportunities to psychic satisfaction, from the seemingly indelible barrier that had been erected between blacks and whites. This was especially true after the Civil War and Reconstruction, when blacks were systematically eliminated from skilled, and unskilled, employment to make room for white labor. (254)

Thus, scientific corroborations of racism informed not only antebellum attitudes toward African Americans, but continued with renewed vigor after the end of the Civil War. Black persons, according to views popular in both periods, were mentally inadequate, naturally idle, and possessing a child-like inadequacy when it came to acting, thinking, or surviving independently. Charles Chesnutt, in *The Conjure Woman and Other Conjure Tales*, subverts these scientifically supported racist ideas and debunks the many justifications that arose during the antebellum and postbellum periods for of slavery and bigotry.

One of the chief medical theorists of racial difference, Samuel Cartwright, a medical doctor from Louisiana, was chosen by the Medical Association of Louisiana to describe "the Diseases and Physical Peculiarities of the Negro Race." In his compilation of scientific conclusions, Cartwright imposes several physical and mental characteristics upon blacks and feeds commonly held perceptions with what was then seen as hard science. Cartwright states:

> When left to himself, the negro indulges in his natural disposition to idleness and sloth, and does not take exercise enough to expand his lungs and to vitalize his blood but dozes out a miserable existence . . . being too indolent and having too little energy of mind to provide for himself proper food and comfortable lodging and clothing. The consequence is, that the blood becomes so highly carbonized and deprived of oxygen, that it not only becomes unfit to stimulate the brain to energy, but unfit to stimulate the nerves of sensation distributed to the body. (rpt. in Hammonds and Herzig 82)

Thus, according to Cartwright, the naturally lazy black person is prone to a condition in which inactivity leads to buildup of one gas and shortage of another, and results in what he calls "*Dysæsthesia Æthiopis*," a condition characterized by "so great a hebetude of the intellectual faculties as to be like a person half asleep, that is with difficulty aroused and kept awake" (82). Cartwright then suggests that this condition can only be remedied by exercise that "is expended in cultivating those burning fields in cotton, sugar, rice and tobacco" (84).

Chesnutt signifies on this notion of blacks' "natural disposition to idleness and sloth" and the "sleepy indolence" that Cartwright describes. The dialect tale "A Deep Sleeper" is an overt satire of both *Dysæsthesia Æthiopis* and of the belief in black persons' propensity for sloth. In this tale, one of Master Dugal's slaves, Skundus, goes missing from the plantation for a month, and when he eventually comes back to the field to work, he explains that he had been asleep in the barn. Master Dugal's reaction to Skundus's return provides a telling look at the white point of view. Master Dugal rages at Skundus: "'Whar yer be'n run erway ter, yer good-fer-nuthin', lazy, black nigger . . . I'm gwine ter gib yer fo' hundred lashes. . . I'm gwine ter hang yer up by yer thumbs en' take ev'y bit er yer black hide off'n yer, en' den I'm gwine ter sell yer ter de fus' specilater w'at comes' long buyin' niggers fer ter take down ter Alabam'" (Chesnutt 143). Master Dugal's tirade suggests that the commonly held belief was that blacks were naturally lazy and that, as a result, they were always trying to get out of doing their work—just as Cartwright predicted. The end of this tale, however, satirizes the science Cartwright uses to support his assertions. After making a public spectacle of questioning and threatening Skundus, Master Dugal sends for his slave to come to the big house. Julius reports that:

> Skundus went up 'spect'n' fer ter ketch forty. But w'en he got dere, Marse Dugal' had fetched up old Doctor Leach fum down on Rockfish, 'en another young doctor fum town, en' dey looked at Skundus's eyes en' felt of his wris' en' pulled out his tong, en' hit 'im in de chis', en' put dey yeahs ter his side fer ter heah 'is heart beat; en' den dey up 'n made Skundus tell how he felt w'en 'e went ter sleep en' how he felt w'en 'e woke up . . . dey tole Marse Dugal' Skundus had had a catacornered fit, en' had be'n in a trance fer fo' weeks. (Chesnutt 144)

The combination of Master Dugal's sending for two doctors and the spectacle of these two giving Skundus a check-up, drawing a medical conclusion based upon Skundus's story, suggests that the white community did think black people were, in fact, susceptible to a peculiar type of illness. The conclusion of this tale, however, suggests the folly of this perspective. The doctors tell Master Dugal that since Skundus's fit occurred around the same time that his girlfriend, Cindy, was sent away from the plantation and that his return coincided with hers, this event was likely the episode's trigger. Master Dugal, therefore, should allow the two to get married if he wants to prevent any reoccurrences of this sort of incident. So, as the story ends, the reader observes a married Skundus and Cindy, and Julius adds that Skundus was never known to have another episode. By not only demonstrating a slave's capacity for subversiveness, but also showing how the white master's belief in the science of the day makes him more susceptible to this type of deception, this entire tale functions as a satire on the science of the white community.

Another racist belief of the white community—one endorsed scientifically by Samuel Cartwright, and one extensively satirized by Chesnutt—is that African Americans are, because of their weak minds, predisposed to superstition. According to the highly respected physician Cartwright:

> On almost every large plantation, there are one or more negroes, who are ambitious of being considered in the character of conjurers—in order to gain influence, and to make the others fear and obey them. The influence that these pretended conjurers exercise over their fellow servants, would not be credited by persons unacquainted with the superstitious mind of the negro. (rpt. in Hammonds and Herzig 78)

Cartwright makes the specious claim that all blacks have impressionable minds and points to this attribute as a major failing in their community (even though conjurers played a practical role in nineteenth-century society and were widely recognized even among the white population).[4] Chesnutt, though his work relies heavily upon conjuring, conjure men, and conjure women, critiques this view of the undiscerning, superstitious African American. One of the most powerful, yet subtle ways in which Chesnutt is able to refute this viewpoint is by drawing several parallels between conjuring and medical practices of the day, and between conjure people and physicians. Richard Brodhead, the editor of *The Conjure Woman and Other Conjure Tales*, also recognizes this parallel. Brodhead asserts in the introduction to Chesnutt's work, "Julius has his own system of medical expertise, administered not by professional men but by conjure women" (7). In "The Goophered Grapevine," Chesnutt places conjuring and medicine on the same plane, and although depicting them in opposition in this tale, he demonstrates that they are equivalent forces. According to Julius, the conjure woman in the tale could "wuk de mos' powerfulles' kin' er goopher,—could make people hab fits, er rheumatiz, er make 'em des dwinel away en die; en dey say she went out ridin' de niggers at night, fer she wuz a witch 'sides bein' a conjuh 'oman" (Chesnutt 36). The suggestion here is that the conjure woman has a mastery of the human body, just like a medical doctor supposedly has. In "The Goophered Grapevine," Julius tells of Master Dugal, who cannot keep his slaves from eating the grapes on his vineyard. Dugal then decides to make a visit to a conjure woman, Aunt Peggy. Just as one would pay a doctor for his medical expertise, Dugal gives Aunt Peggy ten dollars to work her magic on the grapevines, so as to keep his slaves from eating his profits. A new slave, Henry, who does not know anything about the goopher, eats some of the grapes and falls ill. Afterwards, Master Dugal "sent fer a mighty fine doctor, but de med'cine didn' 'pear ter do no good; de goopher hada good holt. Henry tole de doctor 'bout de goopher, but de doctor des laff at 'im" (Chesnutt 40). The fact that the doctor's medicine was completely ineffectual against the conjuring levies a pretty strong critique of medicine, at the same time placing the two forces in the same social arena. Not only does medicine fail to work against the goopher—which according to white society is mere superstition—but the reader also observes the pretensions of this learned individual, who scoffs at the notion of a goopher, even though his expertise proves no more effective than he would expect conjuring to be. Henry, the goophered slave, eventually dies in this episode—at the same time as the grapevines.

Chesnutt, in a further critique of the science of medicine, again equates this discipline with conjuring. By showing the similar foci of conjuring and medicine, and through his demonstration of the parallel vocations of a conjure woman and a licensed physician, each collecting payment for specialized skills and knowledge, Chesnutt is able to disrupt the rhetoric lauding formal medicine as strictly factual and conjuring as mere superstition. One example of Chesnutt's performance of this debunking occurs in his description of a conjure woman's concoction, a remedy that strongly resembles both the medicine described in scientific literature and the flighty suggestions of Henry Clay Lewis's posturing medical students. In "The Goophered Grapevine," Julius describes the process by which Aunt Peggy works her conjure magic. Julius states that "she sa'ntered 'roun' 'mongs' de vimes, en tuk a leaf fum dis one, en a grape-hull fum dat one, en a grape-seed fum anudder one; en den a little twig fum here, en a little pinch er dirt fum dere,—en put it all in a big black bottle, wid a snake's toof en a speckle' hen's gall en some ha'rs fum a black cat's tail, en den fill' de bottle wid suppernon' wine" (Chesnutt 36–37). Chesnutt employs this image as well as the mention of "roots en yarbs" to satirize the ingredients used by doctors to cure patients' ailments (Chesnutt 98). The parallel becomes more evident when judged alongside a description of a physician's prescription, such as Dr. Cartwright's remedy for a fever common to African Americans. Cartwright recommends:

> A combination of ipecacuanha, rhubarb and cream of tartar, each half a drachm, and a tea-spoonful of paregoric, in ginger or pepper tea, is a very safe and effectual medicine. It will vomit, if there be bile or much mucosity, and will afterwards act on the bowels, promote secretion of urine, and determine to the surface; after which, a dose or two of quinine will generally effect a cure. (rpt. in Hammonds and Herzig 74)

This prescription is almost identical to Aunt Peggy's directions in "Mars Jeems's Nightmare," in which she advises Solomon, "'You take dis home, en gin it ter de cook, ef you kin trus' her, en tell her fer ter put it in yoo' marster's soup de fus' cloudy day he hab okra soup fer dinnah. Min' you follers de d'rections'" (Chesnutt 60). These directions and the okra soup, as well as the ingredients in "The Goophered Grapevine," function as satire of a doctor's prescription and instructions to his patient. By drawing a parallel between medicine and conjuring, Chesnutt is able to demonstrate that the white population's faith in medicine is as questionable—and may be as ill informed—as the conjuring superstitions Cartwright contends are so prevalent in the black population. In fact, Elliot J. Gorn discusses the similarities between medicine and magic in his article "Black Magic: Folk Beliefs of the Slave Community." Gorn argues:

> We must resist the tendency to dichotomize "primitive" superstition and "modern" science, for magical and scientific thinking are not as different as they first appear. Both are singularly empirical in that they match cause and effect through observation; both find pattern, regularity, and order where the untrained eye sees only random events; and both prescribe means of controlling the environment. (295–96)

This type of reasoning[5] aligns well with Chesnutt's parallel of conjure woman and professional man, despite Cartwright's ignorance of these similarities. Cartwright, oblivious to the scope of his characterization, comments, "[T]hese imposters [conjurers], like all other impostors, take advantage of circumstances to swell their importance, and . . . inculcate a belief in their miraculous powers to bring good or evil upon those they like or dislike" (rpt. in Hammonds and Herzig 78). While this disparagement was aimed at conjure men and conjure women, the passage equally well to scientists who took similar advantage of the white population and its overwhelming desire to prove the worth of whites over blacks. These scientists and physicians could forge a reputation while satisfying the need of the public to have scientific rationalizations for their long-standing beliefs.

Thus, Charles Chesnutt takes up the mantle of Henry Clay Lewis's previous work in order to disrupt an unchallenged but largely imperfect discourse. Lewis, by calling attention to medical atrocities and by confronting a normalized view of the medical profession, lays the groundwork for Chesnutt's questioning of normative discourse. Each author questions the status quo, disquieting audiences and interrupting their ability to take traditional beliefs for granted or accept unquestioningly the dominant discourse. For Chesnutt, normative did not mean natural, and his *Conjure Tales* follow the lead of Henry Clay Lewis's *Odd Leaves* in rewriting and reexamining traditional narratives. From his use of humor and language, to the ways in which he denaturalizes unexamined discourse, Henry Clay Lewis serves as an appropriate forbearer of the important work espoused by Charles Chesnutt, who extended, reappropriated, and reemphasized many Southwest humor tropes to combat traditional discourses decrying African American legitimacy.

NOTES

1. For an overview of storytelling and framing in African American literature, see Bertram D. Ashe's book, *From within the Frame: Storytelling in African American Studies*. For a specific focus on the ways in which these tropes function in Chesnutt's work, see Robert B. Stepto's "'The Simple but Intensely Human Inner Life of Slavery': Storytelling, Fiction, and the Revision of History in Charles W. Chesnutt's 'Uncle Julius Stories.'"
2. In "Command Performances: Black Storytellers in Stuart's 'Blink' and Chesnutt's 'The Dumb Witness,'" Peter Schmidt characterizes a tendency by white figures to demand and thrive upon the performances (typically storytelling) of black individuals. Similarly, Jennifer Riddle Harding, in "A Mind Enslaved? The Interaction of Metaphor, Cognitive Distance, and Narrative Framing in Chesnutt's 'Dave's Neckliss,'" discusses the ways in which John and Annie attempt to control Julius's tales through interpretation, and the ways in which Julius's heavy reliance on metaphor functions as a source of resistance against this tendency.
3. In her article, "Overfamiliariz[a]tion as Subversive Plantation Critique in Charles W. Chesnutt's *The Conjure Woman & Other Conjure Tales*," Gretchen Martin provides a cogent discussion of the tension between overt and covert content in Chesnutt's work and the cultural milieu he was challenging.
4. In *Conjure in African American Society*, Jeffrey E. Anderson disrupts the suggestion that conjure was merely a charade for the superstitious. He explains that though much of their power did come from the community's buy-in, conjurers still affected real change within in their communities—as spiritualists, yes, but also with practical medicines and poisons. Anderson also points to various accounts suggesting the white community's belief in conjure.
5. Steven M. Stowe, in *Doctoring the South*, also describes a southern approach to health that aligns with the conjurer's approach: "Prevention of disease called for commonsense caution regardless of class or race: bundle up at night; stay out of drafts; get enough sleep; be careful about getting wet; do not sneeze on your sister. Personal rituals of cleanliness and diet, charms worn on the body or spoken, and well-timed doses of potent mixtures . . . were daily things one could do to avoid sickness" (6). Stowe also describes nineteenth-century medical practice as experiential, regional, and dependent upon patients' trust, all qualities that overlap with the role of the conjurer during this time.

WORKS CITED

Anderson, Jeffrey E. *Conjure in African American Society*. Baton Rouge: Louisiana State University Press, 2005. Print.

Ashe, Bertram D. *From within the Frame: Storytelling in African American Studies*. New York: Routledge, 2002. Print.

Brodhead, Richard. Introduction. *The Conjure Woman and Other Conjure Tales*. Durham, NC: Duke University Press, 1993. 1–21. Print.

Cartwright, Samuel. "Report on the Diseases and Physical Peculiarities of the Negro Race." 1851. Rpt. in Evelynn Hammonds and Rebecca Herzig, *Nature of Difference: Sciences of Race in the United States from Jefferson to Genomics*. Cambridge, MA: MIT Press, 2008. 67–86. Print.

Chesnutt, Charles. *The Conjure Woman and Other Conjure Tales*. Ed. Richard Brodhead. Durham, NC: Duke University Press, 1993. Print.

Gorn, Elliott J. "Black Magic: Folk Beliefs of the Slave Community." In *Science and Medicine in the Old South*. Ed. Ronald L. Numbers and Todd L. Savitt, 295–326. Baton Rouge: Louisiana State University Press, 1989. Print.

Harding, Jennifer Riddle. "A Mind Enslaved? The Interaction of Metaphor, Cognitive Distance, and Narrative Framing in Chesnutt's 'Dave's Neckliss.'" *Style* 42.4 (2008): 425–47. Print.

Israel, Charles. "Henry Clay Lewis's *Odd Leaves*: Studies in the Surreal and Grotesque." *Mississippi Quarterly* 28 (1975): 61–69. Print.

Joyner, Charles W. *Shared Traditions: Southern History and Folk Culture*. Urbana: University of Illinois Press, 1999. Print.

Keller, Mark A. "'Aesculapius in Buckskin': The Swamp Doctor as Satirist in Henry Clay Lewis's *Odd Leaves*." *Southern Studies: An Interdisciplinary Journal of the South*. 18 (1979): 425–28. Print.

Lewis, Henry Clay. *Odd Leaves from the Life of a Louisiana Swamp Doctor*. Baton Rouge: Louisiana State University Press, 1997. Print.

Martin, Gretchen. "Overfamiliariz[a]tion as Subversive Plantation Critique in Charles W. Chesnutt's *The Conjure Woman & Other Conjure Tales*." *South Atlantic Review* 74.1 (2009): 65–86. Print.

Mayfield, John. *Counterfeit Gentlemen: Manhood and Humor in the Old South*. Gainesville: University Press of Florida, 2009. Print.

Rose, Alan H. "The Image of the Negro in the Writings of Henry Clay Lewis." *American Literature* 41.2 (1969): 255–63. Web. 30 October 2010.

Schmidt, Peter. "Command Performances: Black Storytellers in Stuart's 'Blink' and Chesnutt's 'The Dumb Witness.'" *Southern Literary Journal* 35.1 (2002): 70–96. Print.

Smedley, Audrey. *Race in North America*. Boulder, CO: Westview Press, 2007. Print.

Stepto, Robert B. "'The Simple but Intensely Human Inner Life of Slavery': Storytelling, Fiction, and the Revision of History in Charles W. Chesnutt's 'Uncle Julius Stories.'" *History and Tradition in Afro-American Culture*. Ed. H. Günter Lenz. Frankfort, Germany; New York: Campus, 1984. 29–55. Print.

Stowe, Steven M. *Doctoring the South: Southern Physicians and Everyday Medicine in the Mid-Nineteenth Century*. Chapel Hill: University of North Carolina Press, 2004. Print.

SHERWOOD BONNER AND THE POSTBELLUM LEGACY OF SOUTHWESTERN HUMOR

KATHRYN McKEE

THIS ESSAY BETRAYS TRADITIONAL EXPECTATIONS FOR SOUTHwestern humor in two signal ways: It focuses on four stories written, not in the antebellum period, but in the postbellum one—all authored by a woman. My purpose is not to argue with the useful and largely accurate characterizations of the genre that have held sway, or with the trajectory of the form's prevalence.[1] Rather, my goal is to suggest that the eclectic writer Sherwood Bonner (Katherine Sherwood Bonner McDowell [1849–83]) is one of the earliest postbellum writers directly indebted to the genre, not in a diluted, "feminized" form, but in a manner that clearly recalls the spirit of antebellum humor and what Inge and Piacentino have calculated as its potentially "transgressive" nature (*Southern Frontier Humor* 6). Four of the stories collected in Bonner's *Dialect Tales* (1883)—"Hieronymus Pop and the Baby," "Dr Jex's Predicament," "Aunt Anniky's Teeth," and "The Gentlemen of Sarsar"—share a reliance on the strategies and sensibilities of southwestern humor. Demonstrating that Bonner was actively imitating the form is secondary to recognizing an overarching commonality uniting her with her antebellum precursors; Bonner's humor exposes the fault lines of southern culture—in her case as they destabilized expectations for both race and gender in an uncertain postbellum world. In this group of stories, Bonner explores not only changing roles for black and white men and women, but also humor as a means of resisting the simultaneous instantiation of restrictively contoured white womanhood at the center of nascent "lost cause" ideology.

The notion that there is a dearth of women writers among the practitioners of southwest humor seems to rest on generally received understandings of the humor itself—how it was created and how it was received. In addition to being generally thought "unfunny," women have seemed unlikely to create sport at the expense of someone else, an unkindness ill-suited to the expectations of either the antebellum cult of domesticity or the Victorian associations of womanhood with rigorous self-control.[2] In contrast, southwestern humor, with its penchant for violence and obsession with the physical body, frequently embeds moments of callous, unsympathetic laughter and regularly depicts the comeuppance of characters who roundly deserve (or do not deserve) to be mocked by means that are anything but genteel. In his introduction to *The Humor of the Old South*, James Justus maintains that the southwest humorists belong to "a vital, if narrow, room in the house of fiction," for "[w]ithin a generation, purged of their more barbarous inelegancies, the linguistic scofflaws of A. B. Longstreet, Johnson Jones Hooper, and George Washington Harris modulate into the better-behaved colloquialists of Sherwood Bonner, Mary Noailles Murfree, and Joel Chandler Harris, who endearingly violate the rules with dignity and homespun fluency" (3). This essay adopts a different position, suggesting that it is precisely because Sherwood Bonner extends the conventions of southwestern humor into a new frontier—the world of the post–Civil War South—that she is an awkward fit with prevailing expectations for both women's writing and regional writing of the time. Hers is an unladylike landscape shot through with violence, ranging from the seemingly harmless stuffing of Uncle Brimmer's misshapen body through the opening to the loft ("Dr. Jex's Predicament") to the bloody extraction of Aunt Anniky's teeth, to the celebrated hanging that leaves Hieronymus Pop to babysit his infant brother, right through to the "nigger hunt" that pulls the gentlemen of Sarsar out of bed on a frosty morning. This is a world littered with bodies that constantly demand our attention—with their color variation, with their physical comedy, with their pain—and our sympathies drift, when they are activated at all, uncertain where the author is aligning them. Only when we stop to look closely at who laughs in Bonner's tales, and who is being laughed at, do we unlock the transgressive power of her latter-day southwest humor and the new frontier it simultaneously reflects and disrupt.

Born in 1849 in Holly Springs, Mississippi, Katherine Sherwood Bonner led an unconventional life before and after the Civil War. Her father was a medical doctor, and she was born into a world of some privilege that included the African American slave on whom her later series of "Granmammy" sketches was based. Educated first at the Holly Springs

Female Academy, later at Hamner Hall in Alabama, and finally back in Holly Springs at the Select School for Young Ladies, Bonner harbored a desire to write from an early age. Her marriage to Edward McDowell in 1871 was ill starred; they divorced in 1881 but had lived together only fitfully during the previous decade. In 1873, Katherine McDowell left her young daughter in the care of her family in Mississippi and went to Boston to seek further education and opportunities as a writer. She found both, and by the time of her premature death from breast cancer in 1883, she was the author of numerous stories, sketches, and travel letters, in addition to the novel *Like Unto Like* (1878) and two collections of short fiction, *Dialect Tales* (1883) and the posthumously published *Suwanee River Tales* (1884).

Her writing varied in quality—sometimes verging on hackwork—because she needed to sell material in order to support herself. Yet despite the uneven quality of her output, Bonner emerges as a writer of considerable skill who unflinchingly confronted the changing nature of her southern landscape. She ardently hated Yankees in her strongly sectional reminiscence of Holly Springs, "From '60 to '65," but in *Like Unto Like*, her portrait of an embittered grandmother's violent sleepwalking episodes to the graveyard Bonner suggests that gall cannot sustain life indefinitely in the New South. *Like Unto Like* is, finally, an anti-reconciliation novel in which the marriage orchestrated to model national healing does not materialize. But in the novel's central character, Blythe Herndon, Bonner creates an anti-belle who insists on charting her own course past the institution of marriage altogether and into the sort of independent womanhood Bonner sought for herself. Like many of her stories, the novel features a range of characters beyond the young white southern women at its center, including lower-class white characters, a northern reformer, and Civil Rights Bill, the African American man with whom Blythe, finally, cannot bring herself to share a meal. Cognizant, then, of the tensions shaping her South, Bonner wrote into her texts the central dilemma of her position: how to be a white southern woman at a time when the power of whiteness threatened to diminish and the strictures of womanhood threatened to squeeze out her own ambitions. In the travel columns she sent back to the *Memphis Daily Avalanche* from various locations in the Northeast, Bonner indirectly and often humorously ponders reconciliation and the relation of region to nation. In her controversial poetic satire, "The

Radical Club," she deploys humor to mock the staid conventions of the New England reform movement. And in her short fiction she persistently locates women at the center of her storytelling, probing their experiences with an interest in both what gender constructions made possible and what they denied. Her dialect tales in the southwestern tradition, then, are consistent with the larger themes and tone of her work, even as they confront an anxiety less plain in her other writing: the relationship of black to white in the unstable atmosphere of the postbellum South.[3]

Bonner's four stories share various affinities with antebellum humor that facilitate reading them as an extension of the earlier form. They all rely on dialect to create humor, for instance, and in all four cases, Bonner structures her tale as a frame narrative that quickly exposes the narrator's supposition that he or she is superior to the less polished characters being described, often following the gentlemen/yahoo formula. The stories likewise depend to some degree on bodily humor ("hanging" babies, rotting teeth, fat bodies and dead ones), aligning themselves with Stephen Railton's argument about southwestern humor: The body is at the center of the genre (92). Further, all of Bonner's tales in the southwest genre contain moments of violence or implied violence casually recalled and darkly humorous. Overall, these four stories are playful, populated by pranksters and tricksters who create comedy through incongruity.

A less frequently discussed dimension of southwest humor—the presence of African American characters—further unites these four tales. Although not staples of the antebellum genre, black characters do appear, most often "in a demeaning and dehumanizing manner" (Inge and Piacentino, *Southern Frontier Humor* 15), but occasionally with an agency that is startling for the period and ultimately rendered non-threatening by the comic situation and dialogue that come with it.[4] In "The Comic Voice of James Edward Henry," for example, Ed Piacentino focuses on a little-known practitioner of the genre, in whose 1837 sketch, "My Man Dick," we encounter what "may be the earliest work in the southwestern humor tradition to feature an African American slave who comically challenges and defies the racial hierarchies of the time" (53–54). In fact, Dick emerges as a far more likeable character than his master, so that, perhaps unintentionally, Henry "seems to have enlarged the slave's identity, interjecting into his character several admirable traits that illustrate multiple facets of his person and that show him to be superior to his master" (56–57).

Piacentino wagers that Henry, publicly a pro-slavery advocate, is himself alarmed by the emergence of Dick's humanity, reducing his creation back to "a familiar role, the all-too-readily-recognizable stereotype of the cheerful, contented, and dutiful body servant" (57) via humor, a tool that ultimately masks Dick's transgressive potential. Henry's humor, writes Piacentino, is "a conciliatory medium" (63).

Scott Romine's argument in "Darkness Visible" explores more fully the cultural work performed in a series of texts that include African American characters. He examines "the genre's conflation of racial blackness and tropes of pollution, contamination, and abjection" (72) in order to suggest that racial attitudes are explicit in southwestern humor only lurk beneath the surface of other antebellum southern writing. Using anthropologist Mary Douglas's *Purity and Danger*, Romine suggests that blackness in stories by Robb, Field, and Lewis, among others, is consistently linked to contamination and must be purged—although allowing that blackness does not equate always or only with skin color. White men, for instance, who threaten the sexual purity of white women, or white women who fail to perform their prescribed roles can "absorb . . . themes of contamination and pollution" (75). The genre's overwhelming concern with boundaries—those between narrator and character, between reader and writer, North and South, male and female, black and white—means that ultimately "Southwestern humor offers insight into a culture whose conception of blackness went well beyond contented Sambos to a nightmarish reality lurking beneath" (81).

Bonner adopts a similar strategy in all four of her dialect tales, cloaking the disruptive with laughter and resorting to familiar stereotypes that contain her characters and help them retain their legibility for readers. Yet in other ways, Bonner's tales open beyond the characteristics of antebellum humor to make meaning in their own specifically postbellum context. Her stories emphasize, for example, the element of masquerade and performance. Minstrelsy maintained its popularity after the Civil War, and Bonner, too, turned to stereotyped images of blackness—faithful male retainers and jovial mammies. But periodically she upsets the balance of power that should have characterized relations between black and white. In each of these stories—with the exception of "Hieronymus Pop and the Baby," which includes no white characters but clearly implies the existence of a white audience—African American characters slip out of their assigned roles and actively league themselves against the white authority that believes it controls the narrative, much in the spirit of Charles Chesnutt's later Uncle Julius. When at the end of "The Gentlemen of Sarsar" the narrator confesses he does not know "just where truth ended and imposture began" (36), readers might be similarly befuddled. Bonner herself, perhaps startled by the humanity her black characters seem periodically to threaten, often shoves them back into assigned roles, but only after the damage has been done and the specter of postwar racial reorganization introduced.

Bonner's work persistently undermines all white male authority, offered up, not just in traditional gentleman characters, but also in consistently emasculated members of the medical profession. Certainly doctors figure prominently in southwestern humor,[5] but more often as tellers of tales than as dupes within them. Bonner's undercutting of white male medical authority in her presentation of Dr. Jex and Dr. Babb ("Aunt Anniky") is particularly intriguing, because Bonner's own father was a doctor. Although by all accounts her relationship with him was largely positive, their association undoubtedly bore the strains of her controversial choices—to divorce, to leave her child, and to pursue her ambitions as a writer in the Northeast. In undercutting the authority of the medical profession, Bonner likewise took aim at the southern patriarchy's more generalized expectations for white womanhood and resisted through her humor the roles predetermined for her. Unsettling the boundaries of race is not Bonner's only transgression. In using humor to resist well-defined gender boundaries, she illustrates Romine's point about the antebellum genre: "Where there is racial disorder, gender trouble is likely to be found in close proximity" (76). Bonner disrupts the shared bonds of masculinity that Inge and Piacentino, as well as Gretchen Martin, find uniting male characters in activities central to southwestern humor. Even when characters appear to have regained equitable footing, as at the end of "The Gentlemen of Sarsar," they have in fact only acceded to her narrative authority and to the power exerted by the female characters of the tale.

Finally, several of Bonner's tales, written as the nation reassembled itself and contemplated its status as a global power, are marked by interlocality, that is, awareness of another geographical location as a useful reference point in describing one's own situatedness. In subtle but surprising and recurrent ways, Bonner turns her eyes outward to people and places that transcend the boundaries of the South just as the "lost cause" is energizing the rhetoric of southern exceptionalism. From the Middle Passage to the Middle East, Bonner's imagination surges toward other geographies for help in mapping her own. As Jennifer Greeson points out in her provocative new study, *Our South: Geographic Fantasy and the Rise of National Literature* (2010), prior to the twentieth century—and particularly in the closing years of the nineteenth—the region emerges as "a domestic site upon which the racialist, civilizing power of U.S. continental expansion and empire abroad may be rehearsed and projected." As such, "the South always points beyond the national borders" (4). What Bonner finds repeatedly, however, in her outward, rather than backward, glances are images of disorder and disruption that mirror her own anxiety about the relationship of blackness to whiteness, and masculinity to femininity in the new world of the New South.

"Hieronymous Pop and the Baby," first published in June 1880 in *Harper's New Monthly Magazine*, initiates Bonner's merger of her earlier African American dialect sketches with humor.[6] The story opens with a mother instructing her son on the care of his baby brother, while she and the rest of the family, including the twins Savannah and Weekly, hurry off to watch a hanging. When Tiddlekins becomes inconsolably fussy, Hieronymus determines the child has a heat rash and decides he will be more comfortable if cooler. The coolest place Hieronymus can think of is down in the family's well, so he rigs up a method for the day's second hanging—this time of a baby fastened to a well bucket. His charge occupied, Hieronymus forgets all about Tiddlekins until his parents return and begin looking for the infant. Upon hearing Tiddlekins's cries, they reel him up and restore him with a whiskey bath—most of which his father consumes. When Hieronymus reappears, his father escorts him to the woodshed, at which point the narrator discreetly "draw[s] a veil" (248).[7]

Several elements of "Hieronymus Pop and the Baby" tie it to southwestern humor. Violence, or implied violence, pervades nearly every moment of the story, yet the narrator's dispassionate tone overlays that violence with a kind of callous detachment that allows the reader to experience the cruelty as part of a comic text. The hanging, for example, is a family affair. We have the sense that Tiddlekins and his caregiver. Hieronymus, are being left at home primarily because they might disrupt the group's enjoyment. Thus "his mother and the rest of them trotted off, gay as larks, to see a man hanged" (244), leaving Hieronymus to seek solace in "the contemplation of a bloody picture pasted on the wall, cut from the weekly paper of a wicked city" (245). Hi forgets that he has suspended his baby brother down the well because his friend entices the boy away to watch a dog fight, and when the rest of the family returns, Weekly proposes that Tiddlekins is missing because Hi has murdered him, a theory explained by the fact that Weekly can read and "was much addicted to gory tales of thunder and blood" (246). Hanging, in fact, provides the controlling and repeated imagery of the story: The family attends one as if it were a picnic, Tiddlekins is "hanged" down the well, and Hi's siblings darkly hint that "'Dar'll be anudder hangin' in town befo' long, and Hi won't miss dat hangin'" (247). Bonner layers potentially comic irony here. An African American family attendance at the lynching of a member of its own race (is this a legal execution or an extralegal lynching?) seems impossibly cruel and tasteless, yet Bonner does nothing to dissuade the reader from this interpretation.

In the most casual invocation of a link between blackness and violence in "Hieronymus Pop and the Baby," Bonner actually calls forth the genocide of the transatlantic slave trade. Upon learning that Tiddlekins is in the well, Mother Pop shrieks, "tumbling down all in a heap, and looking somehow like Turner's 'Slave-Ship,' as one stumpy leg protruded from the wreck of red flannel and petticoats" (247). Bonner refers here to Joseph Mallord William Turner's popular nineteenth-century painting, "The Slave Ship: Slavers Throwing overboard the Dead and Dying—Typhoon Coming On," first exhibited in England in 1840 ("Turner's 'The Slave Ship'"). Turner's depiction of a slave ship about to be overtaken by a powerful storm at sea portends the abolition of the international slave trade, already outlawed since 1833 in the British Empire. But the painting is linked to history—the real-life *Zong* Incident from 1781, in which a British slaver captain, en route from Africa to Jamaica, elected to discard the bodies of 132 dead and dying slaves into the ocean. What Bonner calls forth in this moment is, in fact, a host of restless black bodies, represented by Turner as floating human parts about to be devoured by sinister sea creatures. The painting pushes shackled arms out of the bloody waves in its lower right quadrant, so that Mother Pop's "one stumpy leg" in Bonner's story, emerging from "red flannel," mimics Turner's disembodied chaos at sea. Weekly speculates that the wailing they hear from the well is

Tiddlekins's ghost, but there are other haunted presences in this story: the violence of slavery, the unarticulated terror of the Middle Passage, and the inexorable communion of slavery and capitalism.[8]

Bonner surely knew what Turner's "Slave-Ship" depicted, and in her casual conjoining of its bloody chaos and Mother Pop's comic collapse, she registers a level of racial anxiety and a preoccupation with black bodies that the story struggles to contain at various other moments. Patricia Yaeger's study of twentieth-century women writers from the South, *Dirt and Desire: Reconstructing Southern Women's Writing, 1930–1990*, is instructive here. Particularly apt is Yaeger's attention to gargantuan bodies, the stark juxtapositions of black and white, and the gaping holes of texts into which disappear the black "throwaway" bodies she reads as indices of women writers' uneasiness with the contested racial divides they confronted in their own experiences as white southerners, but wrote about obliquely. We find many of these same elements and anxieties reflected much earlier in Bonner's work, where they similarly threaten to disrupt the text. "Hieronymous Pop and the Baby" opens with Mother Pop's admonition to her son not to leave the house "on no account, not if de skies fall an' de earth opens ter swaller yer" (244). Yet this is just what happens—the earth does swallow Tiddlekins. Clearly Bonner's landscape is filled with holes capable of swallowing bodies thrown away by the culture inhabiting it. Her description of Tiddlekins's body makes it a grotesque, comically dehumanized object: "But as it still fretted and tossed, he let it severely alone, and the flies settled on the little black thing as if it had been a licorice stick" (245). Bonner's story "is fully consonant with a sporadic pattern of imagery found throughout Southwestern humor in which black bodies are rendered grotesque and bodily contact is rendered disgusting" (Romine 78). If, as Yaeger maintains, "the grotesque can be understood as a prose technique for moving background information into the foreground of a novel or story" (25), then Bonner has placed Tiddlekins's repellant body at the very center of her narrative—and with it a tacit acknowledgment that his is a body out of place, a signal of racial disorder and a marker of white anxiety.[9] What is more, in using Turner's painting to weave the transatlantic slave trade into her story, Bonner locates Hieronymous Pop within a voracious global network of exchange that swallowed countless throwaway bodies, resurfacing in the 1880s to disrupt the hierarchies of postbellum life.

All of that is not to say that Bonner was an abolitionist or in any way an advocate for increased rights for African Americans. Despite the feminist bent of her views, Bonner's attitude toward race appears in most ways to have been conventional for its time. Yet repeatedly in her work, black characters trouble the waters of white-dominated power structures, suggesting at a minimum that Bonner was a keen observer of her culture who used her humorous sketches to reflect the issues of her day. A second tale flavored with the traits of southwest humor, "Dr. Jex's Predicament," originally published in *Harper's Weekly* on December 18, 1880, ultimately portrays blackness and whiteness as inextricably bound together. The story opens with the unannounced arrival of Uncle Brimmer, presumably a former slave, who has walked from Mississippi to Kentucky to offer his services to the narrator's sister-in-law, Mabel, who has only recently set up housekeeping as a newlywed. In response to Mabel's protests that they have no room for Uncle Brimmer, the household cook, Aunt Patsey, offers the loft above the detached kitchen as his residence. Debate ensues about whether the substantial body of Uncle Brimmer can actually fit into the constrained space of the kitchen loft. But Uncle Brimmer manages to squeeze through the window entrance and set up housekeeping, happily settled until he falls ill. The family summons the local physician, Dr. Trattles Jex, a slight man who nonetheless "was as pompous and self-important as though he had found the place to stand on, and could move the world with his little lever" (112). In repeated instances of physical comedy, Bonner emphasizes the incongruity of Uncle Brimmer's sloppy girth and Dr. Jex's pristinely diminutive self. The two meet when Uncle Brimmer forces his body partway out of the loft opening, as Dr. Jex stations himself halfway up the ladder to commence his examination of the patient—beginning with the tongue Uncle Brimmer sticks out, unsolicited. When the neighbor's bull breaks loose and charges at the sight of Dr. Jex's red handkerchief, it knocks the ladder out from beneath the esteemed physician, leaving him clinging to Uncle Brimmer's neck. And because Uncle Brimmer's girth has caused him to become stuck in the window, the pair remains suspended in this mutually dependent position.

From the moment she introduces Dr. Jex, Bonner encourages the audience to laugh at him and at his compromised manhood: "Dr. Trattles Jex . . . lived in Middleburn, seven miles away, and he came trotting over on a great bay horse, with a pair of saddle bags hanging like Gilpin's bottles,

"HOLD ME!" CRIED THE DOCTOR.

Figure 2: Bonner, "Dr. Jex's Predicament," Dialect Tales (1883).

one on either side. He looked as diminutive as a monkey perched on a tall horse's back" (112). Bonner sets the story's tone by invoking William Cowper's comic 1782 poem, "The Diverting History of John Gilpin," a lengthy, rollicking verse in which the title character bypasses his intended destinations because of his wayward horse, in the process breaking the bottles of wine he has secreted beneath his cloak and strapped on either side of his mount. Cowper depends upon conjuring a physically incongruous, comic image of Gilpin (he loses two different wigs and cloaks and runs through the laundry), just as Bonner paints a strikingly visual image of Dr. Jex. Bonner further undermines the doctor's authority by linking him to primitiveness and blackness via her reference to the monkey, long a reference point in derogatory assessments of black intellect. What is more, from Dr. Jex's "pink and beardless face" (112) issues a cracking voice that the narrator is unsure whether to associate with youthfulness or "'nature,'" concluding only "what a treasure it would have been could he let it out to masqueraders!" (113), the implication being that Dr. Jex's sexual identity is not clear. Dr. Jex panics when the bull, a certain sign of virile, hypersexualized masculinity, knocks the loft ladder out from under him, an emasculation underscored by the fact that he must cling to Uncle Brimmer, shouting "'*Hold me* UP! . . . SEND FOR *help*!'" (115). The tools of his questionable expertise go clattering to the ground: "[A] cloud of quinine, calomel, Dover's and divers other powders and pills, broke in blinding confusion" (115).[10] Some days after the crisis has been averted and the good doctor saved by the narrator's brother and his farm hands, Uncle Brimmer "got well, and went in to see the doctor," returning with a stylish new wardrobe, which the narrator speculates were promised "inducements for him to hold fast" (118). When quizzed about his gifts, Uncle Brimmer archly returns, "'Master Dr. Jex is a gentleman; starch in or starch out, he's de gentleman straight'" (118), thus reinforcing the notion that Dr. Jex is an unstarched male, a feminized man. Surely Dr. Jex has done more than thank Uncle Brimmer. The doctor must also have encouraged Brimmer to forget his unseemly panic and his womanly pleas for help. At the very least, the two men have shared a moment of mutual dependence and great embarrassment—particularly the white doctor, who is saved by a black man with the sort of embrace more traditionally left to lovers of different sexes. But lest there be any residual authority left in Dr. Jex, we need only consult the name Bonner gives him: "Trattles," a term meaning "the rounded droppings" of sheep and rabbits (*Oxford English Dictionary* 3376). Dr. Trattles Jex is not just feminized, then, he is blackened as well, and although white patriarchy eventually restores order in the form of the narrator's brother, Sherwood Bonner has dealt white masculine authority a significant blow and presented blackness uncomfortably out of place in her seemingly harmless and comical tale.

Elsewhere Bonner turns to black female characters as sources of power and knowledge and as the most agile creators of humor. "Aunt Anniky's Teeth," originally published on June 3, 1882, in *Harper's Weekly*, relies on various elements of southwestern humor to create a comedy in which the title character manages to slip the stereotype of good-natured mammy in favor of an empowering performance as a trickster figure. Aunt Anniky nurses the narrator's mother back to health and when invited to name her reward, requests "'a han'sum chany set o' teef'" to replace her five remaining natural ones (249). Anniky wears her new teeth with pride, until they are destroyed in a comic misunderstanding. Anniky, whose healing power extends to black and white patients, is nursing Uncle Ned. Overtaken by thirst in the night, Ned snatches up a glass of what he assumes to be ice cubes and crunches them, only to discover that he is munching on the sleeping Anniky's false teeth. His violent reaction awakens her: "'[S]omebody's sheizin' me by de head, a-jammin' it up 'gin de wall, a-jawin' at me like de angel Gabriel at de rish ole sinners in de bad plashe'" (252). The two bring their dispute to the narrator's father. Ned believes Anniky cruelly tricked him, and so he refuses to pay her the pig he had promised for her nursing services, while Anniky maintains that his debt is outstanding because his consternation about the ice mix-up actually broke his fever. Unable to arrive at a solution acceptable to both parties, the narrator's father proposes the pair conjoin their interests through marriage, an overture each party initially opposes but finally concedes to try. The narrator's father, foreseeing a lifetime of quarreling for the pair, promises to make Anniky a wedding present of another set of dentures. Ned gets a case of cold feet and summons the narrator to write his dictated farewell note, confessing the existence of another wife while simultaneously proclaiming, "'I wuz born a bachelor, an' a bachelor will I represent myself befo' de judgement seat'" (254). The narrator delivers the note as instructed, and Anniky immediately dispatches a message meant to ascertain the status of the promised teeth. Assured that she can still have them, Anniky laughs at the idea that she will mourn Ned's departure, confiding in the narrator, "'Bless you, chile, it was de teef I wanted, not de man!'" (255).

From the beginning of the story, Bonner takes pains to circumscribe white male authority—not just in the form of the narrator's father, but particularly in the form of the dentist, Dr. Alonzo Babb—in a manner reminiscent of her treatment of Dr. Jex. Yet Dr. Babb is physically the opposite of the earlier physician. Where Bonner depicts Jex as emasculated and under-sized, she makes Babb large and overbearing, loud and violent. The narrator recalls him as "the odd fish of our village. He beams in my memory as a big round man, with hair and smiles all over his face, who talked incessantly" (250), thus suggesting a correlation between his name and "babble." No one can wholly tune him out, though, because his stories are so horrifically riveting. Pointing to a gold ring he wears that is "the size of a dog collar," Dr. Babb explains that he made it by fusing "old fillings—plugs, you know—that I saved and had made into this shape . . . . Sometimes a eye, oftener a jaw, occasionally a front . . . . Often, as I sit in the twilight, I twirl it around and around, a-thinking of the wagon-loads of food it has masticated, the blood that has flowed over it, the groans that it has cost . . ." (250). In the midst of his storytelling, Aunt Anniky mercifully slips under the influence of Dr. Babb's laughing gas. She must have heard some of his babbling, however, because as she emerges from her stupor, she embarrasses the narrator by "winking at Dr. Babb in the most confidential manner, and repeating over and over again, 'Honey, yer ain't harf as smart as yer thinks yer is!'" (251). We are, of course, invited to explain away her forthrightness as a result of the laughing gas, but the narrator pointed out during an earlier, gas-free exchange with the dentist that Anniky's "head was as flat as the floor where her reverence bump should have been" (250). In fact, the narrator reveals in the tale's opening that her father gives equal credit to the family doctor and to Aunt Anniky for his wife's recovery, thus endowing Anniky with a certain level of power that the tale thereafter struggles to contain.

Aunt Anniky resists her stereotypical role as benignly good-humored mammy, naming the dentist's inflated sense of self, outwitting the physically stronger Uncle Ned, and manipulating "Mars' Charles" to accomplish her own objectives. Yet Bonner's creation of this figure is not an uncomplicated endorsement of black female power. The narrator's extended description of Anniky reveals the play between black and white that Yaeger finds a useful index to white female anxiety:

> The effect was certainly funny. In the first place, blackness itself was not so black as Aunt Anniky. She looked as if she had been dipped in ink and polished off with lamp-black. Her very eyes showed but the faintest rim of white. But those teeth were white enough to make up for everything. She had selected them herself, and the little ridiculous milk-white things were more fitted for the mouth of a Titania than for the great cavern in which Aunt Anniky's tongue moved and had its being. The gums above them were black, and when she spread her wide mouth in a laugh, it always reminded me of a piano lid opening suddenly and showing all the black and white ivories at a glance. Aunt Anniky laughed a good deal too, after getting her teeth in. (251)

This focus on the gaping hole that is Anniky's mouth, then, concentrates the narrator's focus—not just on the opening and the words that come out of it, but on the laughter that spills forth as well. Anniky has the power to disrupt, not just by what she says, but most pointedly by what she chooses to mock. It is ultimately Anniky's laughter that echoes through the text and points to its unsuccessful effort to contain the blackness at its core. Significantly, Bonner resists slipping into this darkness suggested by Anniky's mouth.

"The Gentlemen of Sarsar," first published in the December 16, 1882, issue of *Harper's Weekly*, is the final southwestern humor sketch published during Bonner's lifetime and the most overtly transgressive in its treatment of both gender roles and racial hierarchy. Told in the first person by Ned Merewether, the tale recounts his adventures as he travels to a backwoods community to collect an outstanding debt on behalf of his father. The debtor is a man called Andy Rucker, the ringleader of a local band nicknamed " the Gentlemen of Sarsar." Ned is immediately absorbed into their midst and swept up in participating in an idiosyncratic local practice—a "nigger hunt," in which he appears mistakenly to kill the quarry, a young African American man named Bud Kane, who dies after the fact, Rucker explains, of "traumatic tetanus" (28). Ned is approached thereafter by a series of people—Ned's mother, his fiancée, his minister, his wife, and finally the doctor who treated him—seeking financial recompense for their loss or services. In desperation, Ned barely escapes town with his life and without the payback he himself was seeking, twice that sum having been allegedly paid out by Andy Rucker in posting Ned's bond. After returning to civilization, Ned is surprised Christmas morning to find none other than Bud Kane on his doorstep, bearing puppies as a reconciliatory present, and bringing the news that all had been a ruse carried out at Ned's quite literal expense. The puppies, however, so delight Ned's fiancée, Angie Bell, that she agrees to marry him. The concluding line, a conciliatory one, belongs to Ned: "I loved all the world; I blessed Andy Rucker; and I forgave the Gentlemen of Sarsar!" (37)

From the tale's beginning, Bonner paints Sarsar as a place completely foreign to Ned. Clearly intent upon unsettling the hierarchy of power that has engendered Merewether's comical sense of entitlement, Bonner renders this gentleman a buffoon who conducts himself "with what malicious friends called my 'prize-poem manner'" (9). Perhaps even his own father is finally in on the comic juxtaposition of his dandified son and the backwoods king, acknowledging, "Old Ruck is as saucy and rough a tonic as any man could swallow. You will need all your mother-wit in dealing with him'" (11). And he warns, "'[T]here are people up among those hills who actually try to vote for General Jackson to-day!'" (11). Depicting Sarsar as a place both out of step with the contemporary moment and populated by common, uneducated white men, the narrator's father sets the stage for his son's dislocation. "'If courage is needed,'" proclaims the narrator, "'I am the son of my State—the State that does not know how to surrender!'" (9). But this sectional rhetoric rings hollow in 1882 when pronounced by a man too young to have fought in the Civil War, and the words do nothing to bolster the reader's confidence in Ned. In fact, Ned struggles to find Sarsar at all, stopping several times to ask directions from people who "looked on me as a stranger from a far-off land" (13). Offended when he is offered oysters from a can, Ned invokes a topsy-turvy world of wonder when he compares his guide, "a bright mulatto boy" named Dee Jay, who works at the Widow Joplin's "place of entertainment" (12), to an "innocent Yahoo," escorting him, "a returned Gulliver" (13). By story's end, Ned seeks any means of escaping this "accursed place" (32), not so much because of its lack of civility as its complete reversal of any power structure he can recognize.[11]

In fact, those typically disenfranchised in Ned's more comfortable world best him at every turn, repeatedly exceeding the authority he should wield as a landed gentleman. Ned longs to make Rucker's acquaintance, a wish that is quickly granted, but he is unsettled after a few drinks by "a laughing devil in Mr. Rucker's eye." Determined "not to seem unsophisticated" (15), Ned unaccountably enters a discussion with Rucker concerning "negro chase[s]," and although Ned sensed "I was the butt of a joke, and secretly resented it" (16), he cannot ferret out the contours of the humor. Instead, Ned rises repeatedly to Andy Rucker's subtle assaults on his gentlemanly masculinity, which contrasts with the backwoodsmen's virility. When Rucker speculates that Merewether's riding skills may not be sufficient for participation in the "negro hunt," Ned confesses " . . . I was really piqued, and thought I should like to show this rough man of Sarsar whether I could ride or not" (19). Once the chase commences, Ned is possessed by it: "[A]ll is confusion in my memory. Wild, wild riding I recall, and a sense of reckless delight that vented itself in shrill cries to my horse . . . . [T]he very drops of blood in my veins seemed to dance like the pine needles in the wind. What we pursued I no longer knew. I was beside myself with the passion of the chase" (21–22). Enveloped at last in an activity that will yield an unquestioned display of his masculinity, Ned thunders orgiastically toward Andy Rucker's punch line. Having flung himself headlong into proving his masculinity to a crowd of backwoods boasters, Ned Merewether, the gentleman who should have remained the gauge of decorum, becomes an object of derision.

Yet a great deal of the story's comic power erupts through the roles played by its African American characters, signaling a further reversal of power that intensifies both the story's humor and its subversive potential. Almost immediately, Rucker takes Merewether with him to deliver the news of Bud's accident to his mother, Aunt Diana, who, upon its receipt,

> sprung to her feet. Anything more uncanny and witch-like than her appearance cannot be imagined. On one side of her head her hair stood out like an electrified mane, evidently fresh from a vigorous carding; on the other it lay flat in little snaky cotton twists. Her eyes rolled till they seemed all white. One hand was on her hip; the other stretched toward us with a clinched fist. (24)

Bonner retools Diana here into a modern-day black Medusa, who exercises undue power over both of the story's white men. At the same time, her name recalls Diana, the goddess of hunting and protector of women. She first reveals the intricacies of Rucker's sport with Ned, explaining how he paid an unwilling Bud to act as quarry—then she threatens Ned with the law and pronounces him a murderer. In a culture that would during the Jim Crow era resort to extralegal lynching as a regular means of enforcing segregation, Aunt Diana's threatening a white man with the law sounds an extraordinary note, further indicating the unusual arrangement of power in Sarsar. Her extended fist becomes an upturned palm when she becomes the first in a series to demand monetary recompense for Ned's act. She cuts off his stumbling apology with the pronouncement, "'Sorrow don't butter no corn-pone'" (24).

Later Ned has another visitor, Bud's mixed race fiancée. She rebuffs Ned's clucking overtures in a manner reminiscent of Bud's mother, returning "'I'm jest as free as anybody, and I don't want no foolin' nor soft talk from you nor no other white gentleman!'" (30). What she wants is money, and money she gets. She intends to swap the items she has collected for her wedding for her first husband's tombstone, inscribed with a clue to the proceedings:

"He wus too bright fur earth,
He wus taken from our hearth.
Of angels ther wus a dearth,
So they welcomed him with mirth (30).

The mirth here occurs at the expense of Ned Merewether, yet so submerged has he become in Andy Rucker's narrative, Ned is oblivious to the comic role he has been assigned in the unfolding drama. Perhaps most startling is the visit Ned receives from the pastor of "'de Fust Methodis' Church, limited,'" who calls to collect the sum Bud had promised to donate for a new church. He laments that Bud met his end "'as so many of our color loses der manly sperrit—by submittin' to de white folks as if dey was monkeys instid o' men'" (31). As Heidi Hanrahan points out, "[e]ven the eventual revelation that Bud Kane is alive cannot erase the power of these words" (55). They are uttered by a black man about the plight of black men in the postwar South, but put in his mouth by a white female author whose body of work tantalizingly argues for black humanity, even as the stories cloak with humor their most transgressive moments. The minister's equation of monkeys with black playacting and performance recalls the narrator's earlier description of Dr. Jex, further signaling the fluidity of racial classification in Bonner's uncertain world, as well as the susceptibility of all characters to the roving power of humorous caricature.

The story's gentleman figure pays money rather than collects it and relinquishes power rather than asserts it. The backwoods Andy Rucker, in order to accomplish this derisive unseating of the patriarchy, has to league a number of constituencies, and therein lays the tale's most unusual element. Without the performance of Bud Kane and those connected to him, Rucker does not have a scheme at all; he has only the looming obligation of unnamed debt. And while Rucker may be growing out his gray curls as a sign of solidarity with the defeated Old South (he has not cut his hair since Vicksburg), he uses every opportunity to signal to Ned Merewether that they are living in a changed world. Yoked to the humor that rollicks

"DIS AIN'T NUTHIN' SHORT OF MURDER, IT AIN'T."

Figure 3: Bonner, "The Gentlemen of Sarsar," *Dialect Tales* (1883).

through Sarsar, however, is an uneasiness with the shifting balance of racial power. Twice, Rucker hints darkly at the specter of a race riot caused by Ned's accidental shooting of Bud. "'The negroes here are a wild lot, and, backed by certain lawless white men I could mention, would just as soon lynch you as not'" (28), Rucker cautions as they ride away from Aunt Diana's cabin. The tables are turned: Black lynch mobs hunt down white men, and black women demand and receive money from gentlemen. Here the mob is only imagined. Later, however, Ned observes outside the magistrate's office a "mob of negroes [who] had collected, and muttered threats made my blood run cold" (31). And while the mob may admittedly be in the pay of Rucker, the story elsewhere outlines the limitations of his power. In the note Bud Kane delivers explaining the farce and returning Ned's money, Andy confesses "'I had nothing to do with Mother Kane's onslaught, that was unpremeditated and original'" (36). Thus even Rucker's choreographed humor cannot fully contain the power of black womanhood and its disruptive potential.

Yet at the same time Bonner comments on a reconfigured South, she positions it ambivalently, plotting the region both within an imaginative landscape and on a world map. First invoking Swift's far-removed world, the narrator later signals that he finds Sarsar not just fantastical, but truly foreign, describing the morning of the hunt by remarking, "I must say I felt uncommonly ticklish—as much so as if I had been in Arabia with a set of Bedouins inviting me for 'sport' to plunder one of the desert caravans" (20). Equating the gentlemen of Sarsar with wandering Bedouins does little to anchor them to any distinctly southern hierarchy of power. Instead, doing so looses them to define themselves outside of those structures. "Sarsar" is more than a nonsense word, made up to accentuate the distance between that place and the reader's "real" world. Bonner refers to a passage from Thomas DeQuincey's *Autobiographic Sketches* (1853) in which he recounts the passing of his sister when he was a child. Remarking upon the contrast between the hot summer wind and "the frost which overspread my sister's face," DeQuincey feels transported into some revelation born of the moment: "Frost gathering frost, some Sarsar wind of death, seemed to repel me; some mighty relation between God and death dimly struggled to evolve itself from the dreadful antagonism between them" (43).[12]

As a term, "Sarsar" means a "northwest wind of Iran," with its connotation being an "'icy wind of death'" (*Glossary of Meteorology*). Certainly the winds of change, if not of death, swept through nineteenth-century Persia [present-day Iran], the area a shifting colonial spoil traded between Great Britain and Russia in what Patrick Clawson and Michael Rubin characterize as a "joust for political control . . . in a diplomatic, political, and military competition that became known as the Great Game" (32), culminating in the country's being division in 1907 into two spheres of influence (46). What precisely Bonner intends by blowing an icy Iranian wind of death through her story is not clear, but it seems unlikely that "Sarsar" is a random choice. The consequences of her using the name may be tied more closely to DeQuincey's musings than to Iranian weather patterns, but in positioning her Sarsar as a jumbled reflection of relations in a postbellum South, Bonner, like DeQuincey, dwells on a moment of transition—hers occurring between the end of the antebellum South and the establishment of a region fully governed by Jim Crow segregation. James Justus finds that "one of the strengths of the [southwest] humorists' moment is its *in-betweenness*," "[t]heir time is a transitional one of remaking, reformulating, repossessing; their place is a transitional territory of mobile boundaries and shifting landmarks in which the making, formulating, and possessing are still provisional attempts" (9). As the antebellum humorists thrust their identities into an area still settling into its national role, so Bonner navigates a similarly imprecise moment—but this time as a region fits itself back into a nation populated by freed people who will eventually insist on narrating their own stories. Uncertain of her position, Bonner orientalizes this South, linking it to another turbulent region. Her bold move signals yet again the death of conventional white male authority. If anyone is chilled by Bonner's Sarsar wind, it is the gentleman narrator who has lost his ability to discern truth from imposture in a shape-shifting world he can no longer decode, much less direct.[13]

Bonner's final test of southwestern humor's transgressive power comes in her characterization of Bud Kane himself, the quarry of the gentlemen's hunt and the character who reveals to Ned the extent of the latter's deception. The narrator describes Bud as "a flying figure—a male Atalanta bounding over the ground with splendid speed" (22). The reference is to the mythological account of Atalanta, who outran all of her suitors because she had been warned by an oracle not to marry. From the beginning of Bulfinch's mythological account, the Atalanta figure is a shape-shifter—and certainly a worthy inhabitant of Bonner's Sarsar. Atalanta, described as "a maiden whose face you might truly say was boyish for a girl, yet too girlish for a boy" (Bulfinch 141), immediately slips the yoke of easy gender definition. While the narrator clearly defines Bud Kane as male—"a man—a muscular, finely-shaped young negro, entirely nude but for a fox-skin thrown over this shoulders" (22), knowing that the Atalanta figure of mythology ends up wedded to one of her pursuers adds a sexualized dimension to Ned's appraisal of Bud's body. Thus Bonner further emphasizes the confused nature of life in Sarsar, where appearances cannot be trusted, and where roles rooted in race and gender are fluid rather than fixed. After he has shot his "quarry," the narrator describes the horrific scene that greets his eyes: "[T]here lay the poor wretch bleeding, like Marco Bozzaris, and not a man among them all spoke a word of comfort" (22). In comparing Bud Kane to Bozzaris, a central figure in the early nineteenth-century Greek fight for independence from Turkey, Bonner clearly intends to create a comic dislocation between a recognized war hero and the participants in a backwoods ruse. That goal accomplished, Bonner's allusion still tantalizes. Bozzaris (perhaps more accurately spelled Markos

Botsaris [1790–1823]) was a trickster figure in his own right. According to Jacqueline Petropoulos, the military leader participated in a series of meetings with Turkish officials at which he pretended to negotiate for surrender, all the while simply buying time for his forces to mass (246). Even after he was killed in battle, his fellow soldiers recognized the importance of his physical presence to their cause; they covered his body and kept it on the battlefield in order to conceal his death from both their comrades and their enemies (Petropoulos 246–47).

Bonner surely knew the story of Bozzaris through Fitz-Greene Halleck's famous poem, "Marco Bozzaris" (1825), written only two years after its subject's death, when the Greek struggle for independence would have undoubtedly struck an empathetic chord in a fledgling United States. Figuring "Death" as a male come to Bozzaris's "bridal chamber," the poet extends in this verse what John W. M. Hallock in *The American Byron* figures as a central theme in much of Halleck's life and work: same-sex desire (97–98). The body of Bozzaris—and by extension the body of Bud Kane—becomes not just admired and sacrificed, but fetishized and yearned for, ultimately uncontainable by either Halleck's verse or Bonner's narrative of hypersexualized white male authority, persistently undermined.

In comparing Bud Kane to Marco Bozzaris, it seems unlikely that Sherwood Bonner was thinking about all of these associations. But it does seem clear that Bud Kane is a black man out of place, doing the "master's" bidding at the same time he is outwitting the master and embodying a desired object of manliness. Bonner scuttles back inside the boundaries of humor and stereotypic blackness by story's end, when another body, like that of the real-life Botsaris, wields power even after its supposed death. "The Gentlemen of Sarsar," then, illustrates most plainly a series of constant features in Bonner's work: her use of dark humor, her willingness to challenge conventions rooted in raced and gendered hierarchies, and her awareness of her time and place as transitional and thus particularly imbued with the anxieties of the moment. Plotting Bonner and her largely forgotten stories on the map of United States literature muddles the coordinates of antebellum southwestern humor, postbellum regional writing, and imprecisely articulated expectations for writing by women. Yet the playful intricacies of her storytelling demand our attention because unwinding them reveals much about our literary legacy, the post–Civil War South, and the nation that was to come.

NOTES

1. The introduction to Hennig Cohen and William B. Dillingham's anthology, *Humor of the Old Southwest* (1964; 1975; 1994), remains a staple in defining the genre. "Seldom has a literary movement or school of writers of any time or place reflected more unanimity in background, temperament, literary expression, aims, and beliefs," they conclude (xx). That gender unified the group is clear: "The Southern frontier was a man's world. The essentially masculine emphasis of the frontier allowed and even encouraged the kind of writing that this group produced" (xxxix). *Southern Frontier Humor: An Anthology* (2010), edited by M. Thomas Inge and Ed Piacentino, significantly expands the list of writers grouped under the genre's heading. See the introduction to that volume for a useful critical history of southwestern humor and for a recent overview of the genre's defining themes and strategies.
2. In *A Very Serious Thing*, Nancy Walker specifically explains that women experienced the antebellum frontier in very different ways than did men, and thus seldom contributed to the genre of raucous tall tales that depended on exaggerated physical prowess. She also points out that expectations for how women would use language—delicately—differed from men's license to be bawdy. The study of American humor, and the premise that men and women have created it differently, has occupied considerable critical attention. In 1885, Kate Sanborn edited *The Wit of Women*, an intentional refutation to the commonplace that women had none. She included Sherwood Bonner's "The Radical Club." For more recent literary discussions of women and humor, see Barreca, Walker and Dresner, Camfield, Bennett, and Zwagerman. My goal is not to demonstrate that men's humor and women's humor are different categories, but rather to suggest that Bonner appropriated particular strategies for creating humor that were, in the nineteenth century—and have consistently been since then—linked with the male-dominated genre of southwestern humor.
3. For additional biographical information about Bonner and a more comprehensive critical treatment of her work, see McAlexander. Anne Razey Gowdy's *A Sherwood Bonner Sampler, 1869–1884* (2000), contains a valuable introduction to the author's life and works and reprints, for the first time, a broad selection of Bonner's travel letters, sketches, and short stories, including "Hieronymus Pop and the Baby" and "Aunt Anniky's Teeth." In 1997, the University of South Carolina Press reprinted *Like Unto Like* with an extended critical introduction by Jane Turner Censer.
4. Inge and Piacentino list Hardin E. Taliaferro, John S. Robb, James Edward Henry, Francis James Robinson, and Henry Clay Lewis as among the southwestern humorists who at least experimented in their tales with "resisting, contesting, and reconfiguring character portraiture influenced by biased racial attitudes and racist ideologies" (16). In his "Contesting the Boundaries of Race and Gender in Old Southwestern Humor," Piacentino closely reads a series of stories that bestow humanity on African American characters—only to revoke it through humor that diffuses the tales' subversive potential.
5. Doctors are central, for example, in Henry Clay Lewis's *Odd Leaves of a Louisiana Swamp Doctor* (1850) and in Marcus Lafayette Byrn's *The Life and Adventures of an Arkansaw Doctor* (1851), although in both cases the doctor figure is the primary narrator

of the tales. Orlando Benedict Mayer was himself a doctor in South Carolina, but medical antics are not the focus of his stories.

6. For an earlier treatment of this story and "Aunt Anniky's Teeth," see McKee. My emphasis there is on Bonner's use of African American characters in these two pieces, as well as in her Gran'mammy tales, but does not extend to an examination of her strategies in the context of southwestern humor.
7. Page numbers for "Hieronymus Pop and the Baby" and "Aunt Anniky's Teeth" refer to Gowdy's *A Sherwood Bonner Sampler*, rather than to Bonner's original edition, because the former is more readily available to readers of this essay. Page numbers for "Dr. Jex's Predicament" and "The Gentlemen of Sarsar" refer to the 1883 *Dialect Tales*. These stories have not been reprinted, but they are available in *A Digitalized Library of Southern Literature*, http://docsouth.unc.edu/southlit/.
8. The *Zong* case, known in legal terms as *Gregson v. Gilbert* (1783), is particularly notorious because it instigated changes in the practice of insuring slave ships. The owners of the *Zong* successfully sued for compensation for commodities lost at sea, although the decision was later overturned on the basis that slaves were humans, not animals, and so could not be legally disposed of to safeguard the ship. The ship's captain's explanation for his decision—that water supplies were dangerously low—was also found to be suspect. Public outcry against such blatant inhumanity significantly bolstered the cause of British abolitionists. For additional information, see Burnside, Bailey, and Walvin.
9. Bonner's description echoes, in both content and tone, the depiction of an African American infant in Henry Clay Lewis's "Stealing a Baby," collected in his 1850 volume of southwestern humor, *Odd Leaves from the Life of a Louisiana Swamp Doctor*, and explored at length by Romine in "Darkness Visible." In the morgue, the tale's narrator, a medical student, happens upon a mother and infant "both so black in the face that I would have suspected foul play, had it not been accounted for by the fact that they were negroes" (134). Finding himself "riveted" by the baby, the narrator stashes the infant's body under his coat, stealing it to use as an object for private dissection. Unfortunately, the narrator meets with a dog who perhaps mistakes his hidden package for something edible: "My cloak flew open as I fell, and the force of the fall bursting its envelope, out, in all its hideous realities, rolled the infernal imp of darkness upon the gaze of the laughing, but now horrified spectators" (137). This merger of the comic with the revolting ends Lewis's tale, the story having served, by its final paragraph, to explain both why the narrator is but a swamp doctor and yet a bachelor. He encounters his beloved shortly before he is bereft of his cadaverous package, leading Romine to conclude that "black and female bodies similarly gravitate toward a condition of corruption" that ultimately testifies to the need to keep the boundaries of race and gender intact (79).
10. "Dover's" likely refers to Dover's powder, developed by Thomas Dover (1660–1742) and described as "a mixture of opium and ipecacuanha, formerly much used as an anodyne and diaphoretic" (*Oxford English Dictionary* 736), that is, as an aid to induce sweating. In this case, Dr. Jex undoubtedly does not need a dose of his own medicine.
11. In her recent article, "'Kiss my foot! Here's whar I wuz bred an' born': Wags in Sherwood Bonner's Short Fiction," Heidi Hanrahan offers for the first time the extended critical treatment of "The Gentlemen of Sarsar" that the story deserves. She points up Ned's

abysmal inability to read and interpret the situation in which he finds himself—particularly as it relates to race—equating him to a northern readership, equally befuddled by life in the postbellum South, and more than willing to accept an account suggesting order had been restored via a comic ending. As Hanrahan argues, Bonner's story, in fact, does just the opposite, suggesting that "the people of Sarsar are far from rehabilitated and chastened members of the healed nation" (50), with Andy Rucker operating as a particularly unsettling trickster figure.

12. Bonner writes, "Who does not remember DeQuincey's 'Sarsar wind of desolation,' and the chill shudder that quivered through the soul as the harsh adjective came blowing like a discord into the music of that incomparable writing?" (9) She misquotes the passage, though; DeQuincey refers to "some Sarsar wind of death" (43).
13. An Internet search for "sarsar" today takes one to Sarsar & Co., founded in 1979 in Damascus and advertising itself as "the first company in Syria to produce and deliver the Nitrous Oxide Gas to all private and public hospitals, for anesthesia purposes." At least metaphorically, the icy wind still blows, but it is—at least I hope—not always linked to death. http://www.sarsar.com/ (accessed 05/17/11).

WORKS CITED

Bailey, Anne C. *African Voices of the Atlantic Slave Trade: Beyond the Silence and the Shame.* Boston: Beacon Press, 2005. Print.

Barreca, Regina, ed. *New Perspectives on Women and Comedy.* Philadelphia: Gordon and Breach, 1992. Print.

Bennett, Barbara. *Comic Visions, Female Voices: Contemporary Women Novelists and Southern Humor.* Baton Rouge: Louisiana State University Press, 1998. Print

Bonner, Sherwood. *Dialect Tales.* New York: Harper & Brothers, 1883.

———. *Dialect Tales.* New York: Harper & Brothers, 1883. *A Digitalized Library of Southern Literature.* http://docsouth.unc.edu/southlit/. 17 May 2011.

———. *Like Unto Like.* 1878. Columbia: University of South Carolina Press, 1997. Print.

———. *Suwanee River Tales.* Boston: Roberts Brothers, 1884. Print.

Bulfinch, Thomas. *Bulfinch's Mythology.* New York: Crown, 1979. Print.

Burnside, Madeleine. *Spirits of the Passage: The Transatlantic Slave Trade in the Seventeenth Century.* New York: Simon & Schuster, 1997. Print.

Camfield, Gregg. *Necessary Madness: The Humor of Domesticity in Nineteenth Century American Literature.* New York: Oxford University Press, 1997. Print.

Clawson, Patrick, and Michael Rubin. *Eternal Iran: Continuity and Chaos.* Vol. 3 of The Middle East in Focus, edited by Barry Rubin. New York: Palgrave Macmillan, 2005. Print.

Cohen, Hennig, and William B. Dillingham, eds. 1964. *Humor of the Old Southwest.* Athens: University of Georgia Press, 1994. Print.

Cowper, William. *The Poetical Works of William Cowper.* 2 vols. Ed. Rev. George Gilfillan. Edinburgh: James Nichol, 1854. Print.

DeQuincey, Thomas. *Autobiographic Sketches.* Boston: Ticknor and Fields, 1853. Print.

"Dover's powder." *The New Shorter Oxford English Dictionary.* New York: Oxford University Press, 1993. Print.

Gowdy, Anne Razey. *A Sherwood Bonner Sampler, 1869–1884: What a Bright, Educated, Witty, Lively, Snappy Young Woman Can Say on a Variety of Topics*. Knoxville: University of Tennessee Press, 2000. Print.

Greeson, Jennifer. *Our South: Geographic Fantasy and the Rise of National Literature*. Cambridge, MA: Harvard University Press, 2010. Print.

Halleck, Fitz-Greene. "Marco Bozzaris." *Poems*. New York: Hurst, n.d. 70–73. Print.

Hallock, John W. M. *The American Byron: Homosexuality and the Fall of Fitz-Greene Halleck*. Madison: University of Wisconsin Press, 2000. Print.

Hanrahan, Heidi. "'Kiss my foot! Here's whar I wuz bred an' born': Wags in Sherwood Bonner's Short Fiction." *Studies in American Humor* 3.19 (2009): 45–61. Print.

Inge, M. Thomas, and Ed Piacentino, eds. *The Humor of the Old South*. Lexington: University Press of Kentucky, 2001. Print.

———, eds. *Southern Frontier Humor: An Anthology*. Columbia: U of Missouri Press, 2010. Print.

Justus, James H. *Fetching the Old Southwest: Humorous Writing from Longstreet to Twain*. Columbia: University of Missouri Press, 2004. Print.

———. "Introduction." *The Humor of the Old South*. Eds. M. Thomas Inge and Edward J. Piacentino. Lexington: University Press of Kentucky, 2001. 1–10. Print.

Lewis, Henry Clay. *Odd Leaves from the Life of a Louisiana Swamp Doctor*. 1850. Baton Rouge: Louisiana State University Press, 1997. Print.

McAlexander, Hubert H. *The Prodigal Daughter: A Biography of Sherwood Bonner*. 1981. Knoxville: University of Tennessee Press, 1999. Print.

McKee, Kathryn. "'Honey, Yer Ain't Harf as Smart as Yer Thinks Yer Is!': Race and Humor in Sherwood Bonner's Short Fiction." *Southern Literary Journal* 35.1 (2002): 28–46. Print.

Martin, Gretchen. *The Frontier Roots of American Realism*. New York: Peter Lang, 2007. Print.

Petropoulos, Jacqueline. "Botsaris, Markos 1790–1823." *Encyclopedia of Greece and the Hellenic Tradition*. Ed. Graham Speake. London: Fitzroy Dearborn, 2000. Print.

Piacentino, Ed. "The Comic Voice of James Edward Henry: Reclaiming Another Writer for the Tradition of Old Southwestern Humor. *Studies in American Humor* 3.10 (2003): 51–64. Print.

———. "Contesting the Boundaries of Race and Gender in Old Southwestern Humor." Inge and Piacentino, *The Humor of the Old South* 52–71. Rpt. from *Southern Literary Journal* 32.2 (2000): 116–40. Print.

Railton, Stephen. *Authorship and Audience: Literary Performance in the American Renaissance*. Princeton, NJ: Princeton University Press, 1991. Print.

Romine, Scott. "Darkness Visible: Race and Pollution in Southwestern Humor." Inge and Piacentino, *The Humor of the Old South* 72–83. Print.

Sanborn, Kate. *The Wit of Women*. 3rd ed. New York: Funk & Wagnalls, 1886. Print.

"Sarsar." *Glossary of Meteorology*. http://amsglossary.allenpress.com/glossary/search?id =sansar1. 17 May 2011.

"Sarsar & Co." http://www.sarsar.com/. 17 May 2011.

"Turner's 'The Slave Ship." *Museum of Fine Arts, Boston*. http://www.mfa.org/collections/ object/slave-ship-slavers-throwing-overboard-the-dead-and-dying-typhoon-coming. 20 May 2011.

"Trattles." *The New Shorter Oxford English Dictionary*. New York: Oxford University Press, 1993. Print.

Walker, Nancy. *A Very Serious Thing: Women's Humor and American Culture*. Minneapolis: University of Minnesota Press, 1988. Print.

———, and Zita Dresner, eds. *Redressing the Balance: American Women's Literary Humor from Colonial Times to the 1980s*. Jackson: University Press of Mississippi, 1988. Print.

Walvin, James. *The Zong: A Massacre, the Law and the End of Slavery*. New Haven, CT: Yale University Press, forthcoming 2011. Print.

Yaeger, Patricia. *Dirt and Desire: Reconstructing Southern Women's Writing, 1930–1990*. Chicago: University of Chicago Press, 2000. Print.

Zwagerman, Sean. *Wit's End: Women's Humor as Rhetorical and Performative Strategy*. Pittsburgh: University of Pittsburgh Press, 2010. Print.

"I WA' N'T BAWN IN DE MASH TO BE FOOL' BY TRASH!"

Mark Twain's "A True Story" and the Culmination of Southern Frontier Humor

TRACY WUSTER

I

MARK TWAIN'S STORIES HAVE BEEN ANTHOLOGIZED FREquently in collections of Southwest humor. Cohen and Dillingham included several sketches by Twain in the 1964 and 1975 editions of their foundational anthology, *Humor of the Old Southwest.* In their 1994 revision, they removed Twain, arguing that "Mark Twain is now recognized as the culmination of Old Southwestern Humor," and that his inclusion was no longer necessary to prove that point (ix). In *Southern Frontier Humor: An Anthology* (2010), M. Thomas Inge and Ed Piacentino include Mark Twain as "the only major American author to contribute to and emerge from the movement" and frame him as "its primary American literary heir" (xi, 4). While Mark Twain made use of the genre of southern frontier humor artistically, I would argue that his professional and cultural links are tenuous and call into question the easy linkage of Twain and the southern frontier tradition.

In scholarship that seeks to trace the relationship between Mark Twain and southern frontier humor, a common trope has been use of the idea of "culmination." In these critical formulations, it would seem that scholars are vacillating between two meanings of that word: the more precise sense of the highest point, consummation, or crowning achievement, and the more common, but lexically incorrect, usage of end point or conclusion. One might trace this "culmination" to Bernard DeVoto's argument in *Mark Twain's America* (1932), which posited a teleological line from frontier humor to Mark Twain's best writings: "In them an American civilization sums up its experience; they are the climax of a literary tradition. But from the laughter of anonymous frontier storytellers to the figure of Huckleberry Finn a clearly traced line exists, and Huckleberry Finn could have been arrived at along no other path" (240–41).[1] More recently, James Atkins Shackford argued that southern frontier humor "developed through a long line of humorists, and finally culminated in Mark Twain. The original strain at last petered out as the primitive conditions of life out of which it had grown disappeared" (qtd. in Inge, 209). Here and elsewhere, scholars have framed the issue of the connection between the genre of southern frontier humor and Mark Twain's works as being some combination of high point and end point.

In what seems a telling omission, few scholars have discussed Mark Twain's "A True Story, Repeated Word for Word as I Heard It" (1874) in relation to southern frontier humor.[2] The story is not mentioned in Kenneth Lynn's comprehensive *Mark Twain and Southwestern Humor* (1959), in James H. Justus's *Fetching the Old Southwest* (2004), or in Inge and Piacentino's *The Humor of the Old South* (2001). This lack of critical attention is curious. Formally, "A True Story" fits within the southwestern tradition of the frame tale, in which an educated narrator introduces a humorous vernacular speaker, whose story focuses on the "brutal and mean nature of existence at the bottom of society" (Inge and Piacentino, *Southern Frontier Humor* 171). However, the story does not clearly fit into the southern frontier tradition in thematic ways: the location is geographically unspecified, the story addresses the inhumanity of slavery directly, and the vernacular storyteller is a former slave (Aunt Rachel), a drastic departure from the southern frontier tradition of featuring few black characters, fewer black speakers, and even fewer black women. Furthermore, in "A True Story" the frame narrator, Misto C-----, does not return at the end of the story, allowing Rachel to have the powerful last word, one which turns the punch line of southwestern humor back on the implied audience for antebellum humor—white readers.

My goal in this essay is not to prove or disprove a linkage between Mark Twain and southern frontier humor, or to weigh the relative importance of the genre to Mark Twain's career. Instead, I want to focus on how the classification of certain of Mark Twain's works as "culminations" of southern frontier humor might obscure key aspects of Twain's career, of the relationship between antebellum and postbellum southern writing, and of the representation of American culture in humor. Central to my examination is the place of Mark Twain's "A True Story" as a key transition point, both artistically and professionally, in his career as a humorist. The story employs certain formal aspects of southern frontier humor and a southern subject matter, but Twain published the story in the prestigious *Atlantic Monthly*, a distinctly northern periodical with the distinct aim of representing a national literary culture. Twain's story was his first work published in the *Atlantic Monthly*, where it fit the magazine's goal of creating a distinctly American literature through local color fiction. Because of promotion by the magazine's editor, William Dean Howells, Mark Twain was increasingly discussed as a humorist who might be worthy of inclusion in the company of quality American authors. "A True Story" symbolizes a key episode in Mark Twain's career, in which North and South, West and East were linked in complicated artistic, professional, and cultural ways.

Due to both its continuities with and departures from southern frontier humor, "A True Story" marks a central transition point in Twain's oeuvre and in the transition from antebellum to Gilded Age representations of race in local color fiction. Examination of the story in relation to the genre of southern frontier humor, as well as within Mark Twain's career as a humorist, raises questions about the categorization of literary genres, the representation of race and gender in American literature, and the continuities and disjunctions between southern frontier humor of the antebellum period and postbellum southern local color writing.

Local color fiction, like southern frontier humor, most often focused on the cultural friction between educated elites and groups with increasing political power: poor whites in the Jacksonian era and African Americans during Reconstruction and Jim Crow. Whereas the antebellum humor of the South focused on relationships between a Whig elite and the rising Jacksonian masses, the postbellum writing of the South focuses largely on questions of black-white relationships within the domestic sphere. Twain's story concentrates on a domestic scene—one of home and family, one in which domestic servants are included. Shifting from the largely masculine public scenes of much southwestern humor, Mark Twain's story signals a shift in local color writing to the home and the family—a realm largely framed as feminine. Twain's story "domesticates" southern humor in the word's national sense, one that links ideas of family to the nation state. Instead of masculine endeavors of comic violence or feminine scenes of domestic tranquility, Rachel's story narrates a history of the domestic violence of slavery, in which the humor is combined with a vernacular power over both her employer and, possibly, her former masters.

In turning to the South as a subject for fiction, Twain drew on the central formal characteristics of southern frontier humor—the frame tale and the vernacular speaker—but used them to address questions of race and gender in ways that more closely linked him with northern traditions that linked artistic work with moral aims. Adopting a formal hallmark of the frame tale, and taking on a distinctly southern topic, Mark Twain placed his story in conversation with southern literature—including southwestern humor—but the story challenged the underlying cultural work of the genre through its reversal of narrative power. As a vernacular narrator, Rachel is both humorous in her use of dialect and powerful—thematically and physically—in her narrative. In presenting her story, Twain moved beyond the cruelty inherent in much southern frontier humor and presented a human and humane character in Rachel.

Formally, southern frontier humor is marked by the use of the vernacular narrator within a frame tale narrated by, in Kenneth Lynn's terms, a "Self-controlled Gentlemen" (64–65). As M. Thomas Inge argues, this formal convention, while not applicable in every case, is the most common narrative structure of the genre, and it creates important incongruities between the grammatical and the vernacular, between the time of the story and the time of action, and between the realistic frame and the fantastic story (*The Frontier Humorists* 6). Use of the frame tale, especially in "The Celebrated Jumping Frog of Calaveras County," is the most direct link between Twain and Old Southwest humor.[3] The key linkages between southern frontier humor and "A True Story" are use of the frame narrative and the vernacular speaker. Twain's story weds the frame tale of southwestern humor with the domestic scene of the plantation novel, but thematically the story combines the traditions into something new.

Thematically, the genre of southern frontier humor is more varied. The main characters are largely white, poor, and male, and the situations often involve physical actions (fights, hunts, pranks, hoaxes, weddings, funerals, and other local customs). As Inge has succinctly noted, the best adjective to define the genre is "masculine" (*The Frontier Humorists* 5). James Justus explains that most of the tales are set in a non-specific south, in which the main features of the geography are the people inhabiting the land (8–9). Justus argues that in southwestern humor the question of the racial other—both Native American and African American—was largely evaded, with slavery largely framed as natural. He writes:

> Although their world was a de facto biracial society, the humorists rarely identified slavery as an institution either to be defended or criticized. In the same era that the minstrel show flourished, real African-Americans in the Old Southwest are seldom sources of ethnic humor in the newspaper sketches. Slaves appear as part of a social matrix, another condition of the authors' world, like climate and geography." (208)

As Ed Piacentino has shown, even the most subversive instances of racial or gender transgression in this tradition were almost entirely contained within a "non-controversial framework," in which the white male author reinforced the cultural views of the presumably white male audience of the stories ("Contesting the Boundaries" 137–38). While Twain takes up some of the thematics of this humor in certain pieces, it remains open to question how much these formal and/or thematic influences are unique to southwestern humor, and how much they might also be found in the regional humor of Down East, New England, New York, midwestern, or western humor.

Culturally, the humor of the southern frontier genre functioned as commentary on political, social, and economic changes. While the cultural significance of the genre has long been debated, critics have focused on the frame tale and the subsequent relationship between gentleman narrator and vernacular narrator as the locus of cultural meaning.[4] According to this view, the violent and unruly characters of the stories were meant to be laughed at, a form of cultural superiority that contained the tribulations of the vernacular characters in the narrative frame. James Justus and other scholars have subsequently argued that the politics of the humor were not as clearly anti-Jacksonian as Kenneth Lynn asserted. Rather, the authors were more or less ambivalent to the growing influence of the masses. The range and scope of southern frontier humor offered a range of commentary on the development of southern society, especially in terms of the relationship most often dramatized in the narratives—that between educated white narrators and uneducated, mostly poor, white speakers.

While the dramatization of whiteness in these stories remains complicated, the representation of blackness in the bulk of southern frontier humor is more clearly defined. In this genre, slavery is framed as a natural state. Black characters are largely portrayed as subsidiary, to be laughed at because of their "natural," uneducated, and comical position in society. The role of African American characters was limited in southern frontier humor, but the characterization of the slave shifted as the question of slavery became increasingly national in the decades leading up to the Civil War. In the works of Longstreet, Thompson, and other earlier writers, the slave was largely contained in the stereotype of the "happy darky" character—a common image in the humor of both North and South, in plantation novels and on the minstrel stage. With the rise of abolition and sectional crisis, the treatment of slavery in southwestern humor reached what Kenneth Lynn called "an apotheosis of fury" toward threats of blackness, especially in the treatment of African Americans in the work of George Washington Harris and Henry Clay Lewis (104). The cultural threat of abolition and of slave revolt was increasingly met with portrayals of blackness as polluted, inhuman, or bestial. As Scott Romine has argued, southwestern humor relied on codes linking "racial pollution" to both social disorder and gender trouble, reflecting a deeper tradition of racial abjection in American literature (qtd. in Inge and Piacentino, *The Humor of the Old South*, 80–81). With the coming of the Civil War and emancipation, the question of social order and its links to racial politics was radically transformed, and the genre of southwestern humor is normally thought to conclude with the war—with the exception of certain of Mark Twain's stories.

II

The use of a frame narrative is one of the key aspects of southern frontier humor because it places the relationship between educated narrator and uneducated speaker at the center of both the production of humor and the cultural work of that humor. The relationship between author, narrator, vernacular speaker, and reader is never simple in southwestern humor, and variation does exist, but the cultural question of class—and later race—dynamics largely flows from the positioning of narrative voices. In postbellum writing, white authors were forced to account for African American characters as human because the political, economic, and social facts of emancipation and Reconstruction asked white Americans to recognize African Americans as human beings, rather than property. Instead of a regional literature concerned with class conflict, the local color fiction of the South was a national genre connected to a complicated set of national questions about race and reconciliation.

Pascal Covici, in *Mark Twain's Humor: The Image of the World* (1962), holds that the proposition that southwestern humor was part of Twain's heritage was axiomatic, but that the scope of Twain's humor transcended the limitations of the genre and "enlarged their usefulness for literary art" (qtd. in Inge, 257). Covici writes that southwestern humorists were "pre-Howellsian realists," who focused on action and dialogue, largely eliding internal human feelings: "If a reader is asked to respond to victimized protagonists, or to a protagonist's victims, as though they were of the same flesh and spirit as himself, he is not going to laugh as he watches their cruel and exaggerated suffering" (qtd. in Inge, 235). In other words, if we see the slaves assembled to worship in George Washington Harris's "Sut at a Negro Night Meeting" as human beings with emotions—or even physical feeling—then Sut's "assisting" them with noxious gas and hornet stings ceases to be funny. Aimed at modern readers who are more sensitive to the dehumanization of slavery, the humorous climax of the story—as the hornets Sut has unleashed cause the maddened insects to sweep through the meeting—becomes merely cruel:

> "Wun yoke ove steers wif a big sled cum tarin heds down, an' tails strait up, rite thru the shed, an' I think they mus hev swep' out ni ontu thuty niggers, big an' littil, an' a few bainches, intu the woods wif em, a-stickin ontu thar ho'ns, ontu the yoke, on thar backs, an' on the stakes ove the sled. Yere cum a big gray hoss, like a streak, draggin a buggy ontu hits side wif the top up. His eyes wer red, an' his years laid back; he scoop'd up his buggy plum full, an' jis' kep on. I observed Pimpil-face tangled up in the runnin gear, an' true tu the

> suckit rider's instink, he wer climbin powful fur a inside seat. He run a-pas' a postes what hed a ole tin pan atop ove hit full ove rich pine knots a burnin: he scoop'd that in amung his cargo ove niggers tu warm em on thar thorny way, an' then he jis' run by the lite ove hit." (Harris 168–69)

Covici argues that Mark Twain adapted certain formal and thematic aspects of southwestern humor and applied them to new purposes, shifting away from an eighteenth-century view of satire focused on laughing at ridiculous characters to a nineteenth-century view of the contingency of knowledge. By making the frame narrator part of the joke—if not the butt of it—Mark Twain's use of the frame story reframed the narrative relationship between narrator and vernacular speaker, and between author and reader.

When Mark Twain created a frame narrative in which an educated, presumably white, narrator retold that story of a black vernacular narrator, the narrative relationship went beyond storytelling to questions of representations of race and gender in the politically charged era of Reconstruction. In giving voice to Rachel, Misto C----- and Mark Twain first raised the question of race and then presented a new version of the frame tale, one in which the vernacular narrator physically and morally reverses the stereotyped position she is given. Through the narrative relationship established between the story's characters, Rachel's humanity shows the stereotype presented by Misto C----- to be the real joke.

Formally, "A True Story" begins with a conventional frame story. The narrator describes the scene: the porch of a farmhouse on a hill, an evening in summer. The most obvious difference between Mark Twain's "A True Story" and southwestern humor—and the reason it may not have been considered in the southern frontier genre—is the domestic setting and characters of the story. Although the conceit that the story is "true" would place it at Quarry Farm in Elmira, New York, and link the narrative to the story of "Auntie Cord," "A True Story" has no specific geographical setting, and its subject is definitely southern. To a reader of the *Atlantic Monthly*, the story could be set in the Old Southwest or in upstate New York. That "A True Story" is presented as "true" does not necessarily make it more factual than fictional for readers, irrespective of the historical precedents associated with the tale.[5]

More importantly, the narrator establishes a human geography that reflects common tropes of southern fiction. Aunt Rachel is described as "sitting respectfully below our level, on the steps,—for she was our servant, and colored" (Twain 591). The development of character is entirely focused on Rachel, who is framed as a stereotypical contented "Mammy":

> She was a cheerful, hearty soul, and it was no more trouble for her to laugh than it is for a bird to sing. She was under fire, now, as usual when the day was done. That is to say, she was being chafed without mercy, and was enjoying it. She would let off peal after peal of laughter, and then sit with her face in her hands and shake with throes of enjoyment which she could no longer get breath enough to express. (591)

Rachel is established as lower than the narrator and his family—both physically and socially—and enjoying a "chafing" so much as to be able to express her enjoyment only in laughter. The transition to Rachel's story turns on the narrator's acceptance of her laughter as an indication of her essential character, an acceptance reflective of the literary and cultural stereotype of the essential nature of black characters.

The frame story thus replicates a conventional southwestern humorist's approach to a vernacular speaker, describing Aunt Rachel according to literary and social conventions. However, the story introduces a character seldom seen in southern frontier humor: the mammy. Beginning roughly in the 1820s, the mammy character was prominent in debates over slavery and the portrayal of the South in fiction. As Kimberly Wallace-Sanders argues, the mammy, and specifically the mammy's body, "is the site where fiction, history, autobiography, memoir, and popular culture meet in a battle over the dominant representation of African American womanhood, and African American motherhood more specifically" (3). Aunt Rachel embodies the mammy stereotype in her "mighty frame and stature" (591) and in her subservient laughter, an image reinforced by an illustration of her in *Mark Twain's Sketches, New and Old* (1875), in which the story was republished (see fig. 4).

The transition from frame narrator to vernacular narrator is based on the narrator's racial assumptions. Rachel's laughter inspires a question that exposes the narrator's (and possibly the reader's) assumptions: "At

Figure 4: "I's one o'de ole Blue Hen's Chickens, *I* is." (From *Mark Twain's Sketches, New and Old* [1875]).

such a moment as this a thought occurred to me, and I said: 'Aunt Rachel, how is it that you've lived sixty years and never had any trouble?'" (591). The question causes an immediate shift in mood and in physical action, setting Rachel's story in motion and highlighting the importance of the act of storytelling. The story continues:

> She stopped quaking. She paused, and there was a moment of silence. She turned her face over her shoulder toward me, and said, without even a smile in her voice:— "Misto C-----, is you in 'arnest?"
>
> It surprised me a good deal; and it sobered my manner and my speech, too. I said:—
>
> "Why, I thought—that is, I meant—why, you *can't* have had any trouble. I've never heard you sigh, and never seen your eye when there wasn't a laugh in it" (591).

The shift from laughter to earnestness is accompanied by a physical change in the voice and manner of both Rachel and Misto C-----, the narrator readers may identify as "Mr. Clemens." The narrator's question, and his stammering response to Rachel's earnest reply, highlight the assumptions underlying the stereotype of the jolly mammy. Misto C----- assumes that actions portray emotions and that countenance is only skin deep—at least if that skin is "colored." The question betrays a basic ignorance of Rachel as a person with a history, as well as a broader, and possibly willful, ignorance of the history of African Americans, as individuals and as a people.

If the frame sets up a relationship of narrative and personal superiority of the narrator over Rachel, then Aunt Rachel's vernacular tale reverses both through the physical and psychological power of her tale. As she begins her tale, Rachel shifts physically, and her story raises issues concerning slavery almost unheard of in southern writing:

> She faced fairly around, now, and was full of earnestness.
>
> "Has I had any trouble? Misto C-----, I's gwyne to tell you, den I leave it to you. I was bawn down 'mongst de slaves; I knows all 'bout slavery, 'case I ben one of 'em my own se'f. Well, sah, my ole man—dat's my husban'—he was lovin' and' kind to me, jist as kind as you is to yo' own wife. An' we had chil'en—seven chil'en—an we loved dem chil'en jist the same as you loves yo' chil'en" (591).

Informing Misto C----- of her history, Rachel creates an equivalency that points out a common humanity—her love for her husband and children is just the same as his. This evocation of the common humanity of black and white as "jist the same" repeats at key moments in her story, challenging many previous portrayals of African American family life.

On the surface, Rachel's vernacular dialect may threaten to consign her to a merely humorous status, especially in her repeated use of her mother's statement of superiority: "I want you to understan' dat I wa'nt bawn in the mash to be fool' by trash! I's one o' de ole Blue Hen's Chickens, *I* is!" (592). Rachel's superiority over her fellow slaves, and after her emancipation over both white officers and black soldiers, is based on her control of the domestic space of the kitchen. Rachel's power is reinforced by her physical presence as a storyteller. As she narrates her former owner's decision to sell her and her family, the narrator breaks in to describe the changing scene: "Aunt Rachel had gradually risen, while she warmed to her subject, and now she towered above us, black against the stars" (592). Her subsequent narration of the slave auction in which she and her family were parted is powerfully tragic, and the violence of the scene is unmitigated by humor. As her youngest child is physically torn from her arms, Rachel (who must be imagined by the reader as looming over her auditors) states: "But dey got him, de men did; but I took and tear de clo'es mos' off of 'em an' beat 'em over de head wid my chain; an *dey* give it to *me*, too, but I didn't mine dat" (592). In the shift from laughter to earnestness, Aunt Rachel's vernacular narrative has humanized her through two of the most powerful of abolitionist images: the slave auction and the breakup of slave families. Giving voice to Rachel, the narrative attacks stereotypes of African American character by forcing the audience—Misto C----- and the readers—to listen to one incident in the tragic history of slavery.

After her emancipation, Rachel is asked to cook for Union officers, and she proudly relates the honor given her by a general, who tells her, "'If anybody come meddlin' with you, you jist make 'em walk chalk; don't be afeared,' he say; 'you's 'mong frens, now'" (592). Once again, Rachel marks the equivalence of black and white when she narrates how she asked the officers if they knew of her youngest son and listened "to my troubles jist de same as if I was white folks" (592). The climax of the story, when Rachel tells of being reunited with her son, links Rachel's developing narrative power with the her physical presence. While narrating the story of a dance of black troops, in which her repeated statement of pride leads to her son's recognition of his mother, she acts out the scene: "I jist straightened myself up, so, —jist as I is now, plum up to de celin', mos', —an' I digs my fists into my hips, an' I says, 'Look-a-heah!' I says, 'I want you niggers to understan' dat I wa'nt bawn in de mash to be fool' by trash! I's one o' de ole Blue Hen's Chickens, *I* is!'" (593). Her evocation of her superior status, reenacted for Misto C----- and his family, both literally and figuratively places her above her audience.

The active nature of Rachel's storytelling is heightened in the final paragraph, in which she tells of being reunited with her son Henry. Note the highly physical implications of the storytelling, in which Misto C----- stands in for Henry in the reenactment.

> I was a-stoopin' down by de stove jist so, same as if yo' foot was de stove—an' I'd opened de stove do' wid my right han'—so, pushin' it

> back, jist as I pushes yo' foot—an' I'd jist got de pan o' hot biscuits in my han' an' was 'bout to raise up, when I see a black face come aroun' under mine, an' de eyes a-lookin' up into mine, jist as I's a-lookin' up clost under yo' face now; an' I jist stopped right dah, an' never budged! jist gazed an' gazed so; an' de pan begin to tremble, an' all of a sudden I knowed! De pan drop' on de flo' an' I grab his lef' han' an' shove back his sleeve—jist so, as I's doin' to you—an' den I goes for his forehead an' push de hair back so . . . (593–94).

In the narrative logic of the story, Rachel is not only telling her story orally, but also physically, which here involves her physically interacting with Misto C-----: pushing his foot, looking into his face from a close distance, grabbing his arm, and pushing his hair back. All of these actions, as throughout the story, are evoked with the phrase "jist so."

The story ends not with a return to the frame narrator, Misto C-----, but with a return to the question that began the narrative. It is Rachel who, after praising God for being reunited with her child (only one of seven, it must be remembered), answers the question about her joyful persona with: "'Oh, no Misto C-----, *I* hain't had no trouble. An' no *joy!*" (594, italics in original). If Misto C----- expected a humorous story from Aunt Rachel because of her tendency toward laughter, Rachel's narrative provides a different kind of emotional response, and the end of the story provides a different kind of punch line than Misto C----- might have expected. It is possible to read her final line as a form of comic release in which the tension of the narrator's original question—"[H]ow is that you've lived sixty years and never had any trouble?" (591)—is answered with a statement where meanings are tied up in their vernacular status. In other words, the question is how the reader interprets the tone of Rachel's statement, with its multiple negations and its distinct emphasis on "*I*" and "*joy!*" Whereas Rachel's manner at the beginning of the story was jolly, at the end, the "smile in her voice" may very well be a wry, dismissive, or otherwise superior manifestation of a humorous attitude towards the narrator.

While "A True Story" maintains a formal link with southern frontier humor, and with southern content more generally, its reversal of the narrative power of gentleman narrator and vernacular speaker, and its powerful dramatization of the sorrow of slavery, create a considerable distance between the cultural work of Twain's humor and that of the Old

Southwest. The fact that the narrator does not react to the story within the narrative is telling in terms of the cultural impact of the story. Edward Piacentino reads the ending as a possible equivocation on Twain's part, because Misto C-----'s "silence blocks and obscures any direct affirmation of how Rachel's story has affected him" ("Two Perspectives" 85). Placing the story in the context of southern frontier tales might show the lack of closing frame as a challenge to the formal conventions of that genre. The frame story allowed southern frontier authors to comment upon the vernacular story through the voice of the "self-controlled gentleman," defusing the main thrust of subversion from vernacular speakers (Lynn, 64–65). By choosing not to comment upon the story or its meanings, Misto C----- reinscribes and reinforces Rachel's narrative force without containing any of the power of the story. Misto C----- as narrator and implied author of the story provides a subtle, yet powerful, commentary on the story by re-telling it "word for word as I heard it," allowing himself to be portrayed as naïve about Rachel's history and his own assumptions about race.

III

> I cannot remember that in Mr. Clemens's books I have ever been asked to join him in laughing at any good or really fine thing. But I do not mean to leave him with this negative praise; I mean to say of him that as Shakespeare, according to Mr. Lowell's saying, was the first to make poetry all poetical, Mark Twain was the first to make humor all humorous.
>
> –William Dean Howells, "Mark Twain" (781)

At some point in the mid-nineteenth century, the imaginary frontier line moved out of the Old Southwest and into the new Southwest, extending rapidly after the Mexican-American War through Texas and to the Pacific Ocean. The view of Mark Twain as the "culmination" of southern frontier humor has privileged the frontier aspect of the label while evading the southern portion, especially in the focus on the "Jumping Frog" sketch as the primary example of Twain's Old Southwest writing. Just as Mark Twain largely evaded the Civil War by heading west, classifying his western writings as the culmination of a southern tradition evades the cultural questions raised by the end of slavery and the politics of Reconstruction.

In his early career—roughly from 1863 through 1873—Mark Twain himself largely avoided questions of southern racial and gender politics.[6] During this time, Mark Twain was characterized—by critics and by Samuel Clemens—as a western humorist. As he personally transitioned from his Whig upbringing, through stages as a Confederate sympathizer to Union man, eventually becoming a staunch Republican, Samuel Clemens largely steered clear of linking "Mark Twain," his public persona, with any specific political positions or parties. Only after his marriage into a strongly abolitionist family and move to the staunchly Republican Nook Farm suburb of Hartford did "Mark Twain" begin taking stronger political stances.[7]

The fact that it was published in the *Atlantic Monthly*—the bastion of both the northern literary establishment and the anti-slavery establishment—distanced "A True Story" from the basic traditions of southwestern humor, marking the clearest break with the newspaper-based traditions that influenced Twain. His first published piece in the *Atlantic Monthly*, "A True Story" represented an increase in literary prestige and a culmination in Twain's shifting professional status, as he largely abandoned the trappings of the professional humorist for the life of a professional man of letters. In the early 1870s, Twain quit the rigors of newspaper work (editing and contributing to both the *Buffalo Express* and the New York periodical, the *Galaxy*) for a more settled life as an author. His status as regular contributor to the *Atlantic* for the remainder of the decade put him in the professional company of James Russell Lowell and Oliver Wendell Holmes, of Henry James Jr. and Bret Harte. Most importantly, it put him in the company of William Dean Howells, who most consistently promoted Mark Twain as something more than a mere humorist, in both his role as editor of the *Atlantic* and as a personal friend and editor.

Professionally, the humorists of the southwestern tradition were largely writers by avocation rather than vocation. They worked as lawyers, doctors, judges, editors, and the like and published largely pseudonymously, first in newspapers and then in collected book form. This model was not unique to southern authors and was followed by a number of regional humor traditions. What was unique about Mark Twain was his pursuit of humor as a career, a decision not traceable to southern frontier influences. As Twain rose to national prominence as a humorist in the second half of the 1860s, critics characterized him largely as a western humorist, and as part of a new class of professional humorists, originally newspapermen, who created comic personae that enabled them to earn their living as "humorists." This profession was modeled on the success of "Artemus Ward" (Charles Farrar Browne), a newspaper humorist who developed into an author published in magazines and books, and who parlayed that success into a lucrative career as a platform lecturer.[8] Mark Twain's immediate professional company consisted of literary comedians—Artemus Ward, Petroleum Vesuvius Nasby, and Josh Billings—and western humorists who sought literary and pecuniary success in the East, especially Bret Harte. From 1865 to 1882, book reviews and literary discussions portray Mark Twain almost exclusively as first a western and then a national, "American" humorist.

Founded in 1857, the *Atlantic Monthly* aimed to promote both anti-slavery politics and a national literary culture. The intellectual coterie involved in the founding of the magazine was not a narrow, conservative group intent on maintaining a rigid class status, but a relatively tolerant array of intellectuals dedicated to the publication and dissemination of aesthetic and ethical work that would uplift the larger American culture (Sedgwick 24). The *Atlantic* promoted a culture of letters based on intellectual openness and broadminded discussion of politics, religion, science, and literature. When applied to the South, these goals conflicted throughout the Civil War and its aftermath, and the magazine's anti-slavery politics precluded most southern viewpoints until the 1870s.

Greatly influenced by both the intellectual and editorial views of Lowell, the magazine aimed to balance discussion of contemporary subjects—from slavery to international relations to sewer systems—with analysis and criticism of literary works of permanent artistic status. In his role as founding editor, Lowell promoted a close attention to local conditions in fiction and promoted important work of local color writers, especially regional fiction written by women and focused on New England (Sedgwick 56). This tradition shaped the literary and editorial practices of William Dean Howells, who encouraged local color fiction writers from all regions of the nation. Howells brought a number of western and southern writers—including Bret Harte, Charles Warren Stoddard, George Washington Cable, Mary Noailles Murfree, and Mark Twain—to the attention of the *Atlantic*'s audience. The *Atlantic* promoted humor as an expression of American literature, but its editors and readers preferred "quality" humor that aspired to artistic or moral purpose.

In submitting "A True Story" to Howells, Twain acknowledged the change the piece represented, writing, "I enclose also a 'True Story' which has no humor in it. You can pay as lightly as you choose for that, if you want it, for it is rather out of my line."[9] Howells found the piece to be of such interest that he set it in proof, sent it to Twain, and rushed it into print within two weeks: "I've kept the True Story which I think is extremely good and touching with the best and reallest kind of black talk in it. . . . This little story delights me more and more: I wish I had about forty of 'em!"[10] Howells later wrote that the magazine paid Twain twenty dollars per page for the story, "a rate unexampled in our modest history." He went on to explain:

> I myself felt that we were throwing in the highest recognition of his writing as literature, along with a sum we could ill afford; but the late Mr. Houghton, who had then become owner and paymaster, had no such reflection to please him in the headlong outlay. He had always believed that Mark Twain was literature, and it was his zeal and courage which justified me in asking for more and more contributions from him, though at a lower rate. (Howells, "Recollections," 601)[11]

Mark Twain's focus on the South as a subject provides evidence that there was a national market for stories about southern life in the postbellum era, a market domestic in both the domestic sense and in the location of a majority of local color stories.

Publishing "A True Story" in the *Atlantic Monthly* symbolized both Mark Twain's move into a New England culture of letters and his turn to the South as a subject. "A True Story" was followed in 1875 in the *Atlantic* by the "Old Times on the Mississippi" series. Republished in *Sketches, New and Old* (1875), "A True Story" is the centerpiece of Howells's review in the *Atlantic*, in which he notes that the story "resulted, we remember, in some confusion of the average critical mind, when it was first published . . ." (Howells, [unsigned review] 750). It is unclear here whether Howells is referring to a general critical confusion, for which there is little textual evidence, or to his own confusion as an "average" critical figure. He holds that critics, viewing Mark Twain as a humorist, were confused by the story and classified it as a humorous piece, fearing "a lurking joke." For Howells, the piece was something more:

> Not above two or three notices out of hundreds recognized A True Story for what it was, namely, a study of character as true to life itself, strong, tender, and most movingly pathetic in its perfect fidelity to the tragic fact. We beg the reader to turn to it again in this book. We can assure him that he has a great surprise and a strong emotion in store for him. The rugged truth of the sketch leaves all other stories of slave life infinitely far behind and reveals a gift in the author for the simple dramatic report of reality which we have seen equaled in no other American writer. (750–51)

Here we have the critical inception, in the *Atlantic Monthly*, of Twain not only as a quality humorist but also as an author capable of realist works of great power. Twain's humor, Howells writes, "seems such plain and simple fun at first, doubling and turning upon itself till you wonder why Mr. Clemens has ever been left out of the list of our *subtle* humorists" (749). As in his appraisal of Lowell, Howells praises Twain's "growing seriousness of meaning in the apparently unmoralized drolling, which must result from the humorist's second thought of political and social absurdities" (749.) The moral quality of Twain's humor would become increasingly important in Howells's critical promotion of the humorist's works as a permanent part of the American canon, which the *Atlantic* and Howells wished to promote.

"A True Story" sheds light—artistically, professionally, and culturally—both on Mark Twain's relationship to the genre of southern frontier humor, and on his evolving relationship with the South and the representation of race and gender in the postbellum years. Twain's story adopts the frame narrative and vernacular narrator of the southwestern tale, but the vernacular speaker literally and figuratively breaks the mold with her narrative, reversing the cultural work of southwestern humor. In so doing, Aunt Rachel refuses the containment of political and cultural threats central to frame tales. By giving voice to a powerful black woman in a magazine dedicated both to creating a national literary culture and to promoting racial progress, Mark Twain's "A True Story" posits a different kind of culmination of southern frontier humor. Instead of an artistic high point, the reversal of cultural values dramatized in the story of Aunt Rachel might be seen as the ethical culmination of a southern literature that had struggled and would continue to struggle with seeing the humanity of African Americans.

IV

What, then, might it mean for the study of literary history that Mark Twain has been seen as a "culmination" of southern frontier humor? By coming to a point—either an end point or a high one—with Mark Twain, the humor of the Old Southwest takes a small, but important role in shaping the literary canon. If the humor of Mark Twain—"the Lincoln of our literature," in Howells's formation—was directly shaped by southern frontier humor, then that genre may be clearly linked to the canonical. The link between southern frontier humor and Mark Twain invests the former with a dignity to which the genre on its own has staked little claim. As James Cox has argued, "All these humorists might have been forgotten had not Mark Twain, whose whole genius was rooted in the tradition, made his way into the dominant culture and, by placating the moral sense in an absolutely disarming way, released more humor for more people than the old 'gentlemen' would have believed possible" (Cox, 112). The backward glow of canonicity might be seen in Cohen and Dillingham's summary of the first introduction to their anthology: "From Mark Twain on into the twentieth century, Old Southwestern humor has remained alive in writers like Erskine Caldwell and Robert Penn Warren. In the work of William Faulkner, who read humor of the Old Southwest with great pleasure, it shows signs of living forever" (xl).

In his summative essay on the genre, James Cox argues that the major difference between northern and southern humor in the antebellum era was the southwestern "threat to divorce pleasure from morality" (103). The presence of gentlemen narrators helped ease the moral threat of the uncontrolled vernacular characters, but one hallmark of the genre is a grotesque violence that threatens to overwhelm moral sense. As Cox notes, when the "implicit meanness" of southwestern humor came to the surface, as in a story by Henry Clay Lewis, "many and many a civilized person could never publically acknowledge he had privately laughed . . ." (110). If canonicity is based on either artistic or ethical excellence, judgments that may rely on historical contingency, then southwestern humor may remain a subordinate genre, even if certain stories are worth considering as works of art. If, on the other hand, literary scholars examine southern frontier humor as a central genre in the history of both American humor and southern literature, then the problem of canonicity might disappear—no matter the relationship between Mark Twain and the humor of the Old Southwest.

Focusing on Mark Twain as the culmination of the tradition might also mean that authors who followed after—the declension, as it were—are forgotten, either actively or passively. While the frontier line of southern frontier humor may have moved west into the new Southwest stretching from Texas to California, the literature of the South did not cease to exist, nor did it cease to be influenced by the forms and subjects that came before. What might be elided in taking Mark Twain as a culmination is the continued use of humor—artistically and culturally—by white authors to support social systems in which the presumed superiority of elite, white males was reinforced, sometimes through the use of formal traits of southern frontier humor. The success of Mark Twain's story in the *Atlantic Monthly* was an early example of local color writing, which, with its southern versions of the plantation story written by white authors like Thomas Nelson Page and Sherwood Bonner, increasingly used humorous narrators to help encourage the sectional reconciliation and justify the racial inequalities of Jim Crow America.

By reintroducing a "southern" perspective to a national audience in the *Atlantic Monthly* and other national magazines, local color fiction revised southern literary traditions—including key aspects of southern frontier humor—to address central issues about race, gender, and representation. Divided by the clear demarcation of the Civil War, the transition from southern frontier humor to southern local color fiction involves several key transitions: from frontier wilderness to the harmonious plantation, from public action to private life, from violent humor to romantic sentiment, and from slave to servant. Such shifts are content based, transitioning from mostly white, lower-class vernacular speakers with tales of dehumanized violence, to mostly black, lower-class vernacular speakers with tales of humanized sentiment. While not all southern local color fiction of the postbellum period was clearly related to southern frontier humor, the use of frame tales and vernacular narrators continued in many stories of the period.

Viewing "A True Story" as a point of transition between southern frontier humor and local color fiction shows both the linkages and disjunctures in pre- and post-Civil War southern writing. Twain's story, as an early example of southern local color writing, challenged prevailing stereotypes of black characters through Rachel's powerful narrative, which literally and figuratively shifted the narrative dynamic between oral storyteller and narrator. Aunt Rachel's transgressive voice, briefly heard in Mark Twain's story, was largely silenced by the minstrel stereotypes of "Mammies" and "Uncles" until Mark Twain's later novels, the plantation stories of Charles Chesnutt, and the writings of other African American writers challenged the prevailing stereotypes that helped underwrite the logic of Jim Crow America.

NOTES

1. That DeVoto follows this assertion with the observation, "Simplifications are dangerous," should remind the scholar that questions of influence and connection between literary figures, schools, and periods might not be clearly traced lines so much as sketches used to make sense of a complicated field of relations.
2. Ed Piacentino has recently argued for the importance of "A True Story" to the local color dialect sketch that was becoming popular after the Civil War ("Recontextualizing," 31–32). My argument suggests that Twain's story might function as a key point of transition—aesthetically, historically, and geographically—between southern frontier humor and post-war local color fiction.
3. Paul Rodgers has shown that scholars had long debated the link between southwestern humor and the "Jumping Frog" story, and he argues that Twain's melding of the southwestern frame tale with a deadpan style influenced by Artemus Ward created important differences between Twain's tale and its formal antecedents (273–77).
4. The critical genesis of this question seems to be Kenneth Lynn's thesis that the Whig politics of the majority of southern frontier authors implied that the stories aimed "[t]o convert the entire community to the temperate values of Whiggery [which] was the ultimate purpose of Southwestern humor, and the frame was the place where those values were most overtly insisted on" (65).
5. The fact of the story being true—or at least based on a story told by an African American servant of the Langdon family called "Auntie Cord"—complicates the story, but this would not have been known by readers of the *Atlantic*. The factual basis of the story should not prevent it from being read as a literary piece, especially since Twain claimed the main revision he made to the story was to "begin it at the beginning, instead of the middle, as she did—& ~~worked~~ traveled both ways." SLC to William Dean Howells, 2 Sept 1874, Elmira, N.Y. (*UCCL 02473*). http://www.marktwainproject.org/xtf/view?docId=letters/UCCL02473.xml;style=letter;brand=mtp. For the origins of the story see Wisbery, and Conroy and Sloane.
6. This is not to say that the subjects of race and gender were absent from his work, but that these subjects showed up in different ways—in writings about the Chinese, Native Americans, and Hawaiians, for example.

7. While Colonel Beriah Sellers and his slice of Missouri in *The Gilded Age* (1873) might resonate with aspects of southwestern humor, that novel's mélange of satire, character, and cultural purpose make it less directly linked to the question of Mark Twain's relationship to the South.
8. David E. E. Sloane had the best argument for the influence of "literary comedians" on Mark Twain's career, especially as a corrective for an earlier focus on southwestern humor. Sloane notes that Twain's humor is not fully explained by either southwestern humor or the literary comedians, but that literary comedy "does provide a sense of the origin of his ethics and the centrality of his jokes in developing his ethical viewpoints" (3–4). I would argue that his ethical stance was also shaped by a northeastern view of humor closely linked to the *Atlantic Monthly*.
9. SLC to William Dean Howells, 2 Sept 1874, Elmira, NY (*UCCL 02473*).
10. From Mark Twain and William D. Howells, *Mark Twain-Howells Letters: The Correspondence of Samuel L. Clemens & William D. Howells, 1869–1910*; the first quote is I:17 (Sept 8, 1874), 22-3 (UCLC 32046) and the second from I:18 (Sept 17, 1874), 24-5 (UCLC 32047).
11. William Dean Howells, "Recollections of an Atlantic Editorship" 601.

WORKS CITED

Cohen, Hennig, and William B. Dillingham, eds. *Humor of the Old Southwest*. Boston: Houghton Mifflin, 1964. Print.

———, ed. *Humor of the Old Southwest*. Third Edition. Athens: University of Georgia Press, 1994. Print.

Conroy, Terry, and David E. E. Sloane. "'A True Story' Confirmed: 'How a Slave Mother Found Her Son.'" *Studies in American Humor*, 3:22 (2010): 147–53. Print.

Covici, Pascal. "Mark Twain and the Humor of the Old Southwest." In M. Thomas Inge, *The Frontier Humorists: Critical Views*. Hamden, CT: Archon, 1975. 233–58. Print.

Cox, James. "Humor of the Old Southwest." In *The Comic Imagination in American Literature*, Ed. Louis D. Rubin Jr. New Brunswick, NJ: Rutgers University Press, 1973. 101–12. Print.

DeVoto, Bernard. *Mark Twain's America*. Boston: Houghton Mifflin, 1932. Print.

Harris, George W. *Sut Lovingood: Yarns Spun by a "Nat'ral Born Durn'd Fool*. New York: Dick & Fitzgerald, 1867. Print.

Howells, William Dean. "Mark Twain." *The Century*, 24:5 (Sept. 1882): 780–84. Print.

———. [unsigned review of *Sketches. New and Old*]. *Atlantic Monthly*, 6:218 (Dec. 1875). 749–51. Print.

———. "Recollections of an Atlantic Editorship." *Atlantic Monthly* 100:5 (Nov. 1907). 594–606. Print.

Inge, M. Thomas. *The Frontier Humorists: Critical Views*. Hamden, CT: Archon, 1975. Print.

Inge, M. Thomas, and Ed Piacentino, eds. *Southern Frontier Humor: An Anthology*. Columbia: University of Missouri Press, 2010. Print.

———, eds. *The Humor of the Old South*. Lexington: University Press of Kentucky, 2001. Print.

Justus, James H. *Fetching the Old Southwest: Humorous Writing from Longstreet to Twain.* Columbia: University of Missouri Press, 2004. Print.

Lynn, Kenneth Schuyler. *Mark Twain and Southwestern Humor.* Boston: Little, Brown, 1959. Print.

Piacentino, Ed. "Contesting the Boundaries of Race and Gender in Old Southwestern Humor." *Southern Literary Journal* 32.2 (2000): 116–40. Print.

———, ed. *The Enduring Legacy of Old Southwest Humor.* Baton Rouge: Louisiana State University Press, 2006. Print.

———. "Recontextualizing Mark Twain's 'A True Story.'" *Mark Twain Annual,* 9 (2011): 31–43. Print.

———. "Two Perspectives on Racial Oppression: Doesticks and Mark Twain." *Studies in American Humor* 3:22 (2010): 69–90. Print.

Rodgers, Paul C., Jr. "Artemus Ward and Mark Twain's 'Jumping Frog.'" *Nineteenth-Century Fiction* 28 (1973): 273–86. Print.

Romine, Scott. "Darkness Visible: Race and Pollution in Southwestern Humor." In M. Thomas Inge and Edward J. Piacentino, *The Humor of the Old South.* Lexington: University Press of Kentucky, 2001. 72–83. Print.

Sedgwick, Ellery. *The Atlantic Monthly, 1857–1909: Yankee Humanism at High Tide and Ebb.* Amherst: University of Massachusetts Press, 1994. Print.

Shackford, James Atkins. "David Crockett, the Legend and Symbol." In M. Thomas Inge, *The Frontier Humorists: Critical Views.* Hamden, CT: Archon, 1975. Print. 208–18.

Sloane, David E. E. *Mark Twain as a Literary Comedian.* Baton Rouge: Louisiana State University Press, 1979. Print.

Twain, Mark. "A True Story, Repeated Word for Word As I Heard It." *Atlantic Monthly,* 34:205 (Nov. 1874): 591–94. Print.

Twain, Mark, and William D. Howells. *Mark Twain-Howells Letters: The Correspondence of Samuel L. Clemens & William D. Howells, 1869–1910.* Ed. Henry Nash Smith and William Gibson. Cambridge, MA: Harvard University Press, 1960. Print.

Wallace-Sanders, Kimberly. *Mammy: A Century of Race, Gender, and Southern Memory.* Ann Arbor: University of Michigan Press, 2008. Print.

Wisbey, Herbert A., Jr. "The True Story of Auntie Cord." *Mark Twain Society Bulletin,* 4:2 (June 1981): 1–5. Print.

MORPHING ONCE AGAIN

From Jack to Simon Suggs to Aunt Lucille

WINIFRED MORGAN

TRICKSTERS RESEMBLE SHIT IN THAT THEY ELICIT HILARITY OR gravity, sometimes both. They are both ubiquitous.[1] Neither is welcome in polite company. One indication that the characters Jack, found in oral tales developed in the hills and hollows of Appalachia, Johnson Jones Hooper's Simon Suggs, and Mark Childress's Aunt Lucille belong to a trickster tradition is that the same generalizations can be made about them. The Jack tales that developed in America over the last several centuries and the wily and usually reprehensible "heroes" of the early nineteenth century are often presumed to be time-bound. In fact, all three characters are American—specifically southern—avatars of the constantly changing trickster. Each is a type of Euro-American trickster that has reemerged during late twentieth and early twenty-first century in the fiction of contemporary southern writers such as John Kennedy Toole, Mark Childress, and Clyde Edgerton.

Despite the sometimes vile and horrible things they do, tricksters are generally valued by the cultures that repeat their stories. Tricksters are always two-sided: neither moral nor immoral, they are oblivious to both. Nothing constrains tricksters, neither gender nor death—much less morality or inhibitions. They cannot be pinned down. They tend to be quite sexually active. Sometimes they help; sometimes they hinder. They are slippery, known for their ability to slip out of traps, to fit through small spaces. They are weak characters that use their weakness and wile to outwit the strong. Demi-gods, they can never be totally defeated. They destroy the old and create the new.[2]

Before tricksters appeared in contemporary southern literature, the tricksters of the Old Southwest entertained nineteenth-century reading audiences of sporting papers. Before tricksters from the Old Southwest appeared, oral Jack tales spread throughout and beyond the Appalachians.

Before the Jack tales, still other trickster tales were told around ancient fire pits. Tricksters are both indestructible and universal. For the most part, Euro-American tricksters in contemporary southern literature are con artists with roots in Anglo-American folklore.

Jack-Tales

Though additionally related to still earlier con men, the con artist or flim-flam man of American popular and literary culture can be traced back to oral traditions about Yankee peddlers[3] and the backwoods schemers found in the humor of the Old Southwest. These traditions themselves have ties to Appalachian Jack tales[4]—best known in the relatively "safe for children" story of "Jack and the Beanstalk," which remains current in American popular culture. Since children are the primary contemporary audience of most Jack tales, and since these trickster tales have been best preserved among people with close ties to their small Primitive Baptist mountain churches, not surprisingly most of the tales lack the salacious content of other trickster traditions. Nonetheless, according to contributors to William McCarthy's *Jack Tales in Two Worlds* (xiv, xxxii, 8, 60), Jack tales have been and sometimes remain ribald, even though the tales are bowdlerized for audiences with women—and especially with children—in attendance. The core of some of the more suggestive Jack tales can be traced back to stories that also appear in Chaucer's *Canterbury Tales.* Thus "How Jack Solved the Hardest Riddle," told by Donald Davis, parallels "The Wife of Bath's Tale." In addition, Davis's "The Time Jack Fooled the Miller" relies on the same trick as appears in Chaucer's "The Reeve's Tale." Apparently, outside the hearing of women and children, many Jack tales take on racy overtones.

"Jack and the Beanstalk" and other Jack tales belong to a cycle in English and Irish oral literature that migrated to North America during the seventeenth and eighteenth centuries. The tales have parallels in much of European oral literature.[5] Quite often Jack is a blatant trickster[6] who pretends to be foolish—and sometimes he is indeed foolish. In America, particularly among the Appalachian hills and hollows where they developed most prominently and where they were influenced by other traditions, the setting of the Jack Tales became Americanized; Jack himself became a local boy with qualities the community valued. Though often devious, he is usually a hard worker, generous, and imaginative. Since Jack is always on the lookout for ways to get ahead, he has to leave home and go on the road.

In Jack tales, the line between Jack's feigned and real foolishness blurs because sometimes, as one writer says, his "foolishness borders on stupidity" (Glassie 82). But one can never know for sure: Often his "foolishness" is a form of wisdom. One tale has Jack trading down a sizable inheritance for objects of decreasing material value until he has gotten rid of all of his encumbrances and is "happy."[7] Whether Jack is a wise fool or just stupid is left to the listener/reader to decide. Sometimes the youngest of several sons, Jack has to fend for himself because his older brothers have already received all of their father's bequests. His family doubts his ability and fears that Jack is "a little foolish and uncertain . . . and quare" (Dorson, *Burying* 173).

More than in African American or American Indian trickster traditions, Euro-American Jack tales call upon magical objects to help the hero. Hence the tales highlight the storyteller's rather than the trickster hero's ability to imagine "something else." Many of the Jack tales bring the reader back to childhood and listening to fairy tales such as "East of the Sun and West of the Moon," as echoed in Donald Davis's "The Time Jack Helped the King Catch His Girls" (133–48). Nonetheless, though the Jack tales are full of marvels, the tricksters of oral folk literature are not gods, just fortunate in their wit—and, occasionally, their fortuitous access to magical artifacts.

While Euro-American tricksters—and particularly Jack—have to depend on one sort of chance or another, Jack's chance is of a particular type. Jack has personal qualities that prepare for good luck: Either he performs good deeds for others and they reciprocate with magical gifts, or he uses his native wit to out-maneuver opponents and achieve his good fortune. The American Jack differs from his European predecessors in that his success depends less on using magic than using his own "mental resources"—and perhaps encouragement from other mortals when he confronts a magical creature. Regardless of how they succeed, Jack and latter-day Euro-American tricksters are unstoppable. Like their counterparts in other traditions, they just keep going. As a former American Folklore Society president says of Jack, these tricksters are "unafraid, iconoclastic, and inventive" (Radner 275). The same can be said of the "heroes" of the Old Southwest frontier and of contemporary tricksters portrayed by Toole, Childress, and Edgerton.

Not always, but often, Jack uses his innate wit to right a wrong. He balances justice's scales, as in "Big Jack and Little Jack" (Chase *Jack Tales,* 67–75), when Little Jack turns the tables on a cruel "king" who hires workers but does not feed them and then cuts "strops" out of their backs if they complain. Perhaps more typically, Jack balances social and economic scales by improving his own lot. In one Jack tale, "The Time Jack Stole the Cows" (Perdue 119–31), Jack is caught in the dark one night in the woods, where he has been hunting. He finds a house with no one home, so he has something to eat and falls asleep. Unfortunately, this is the home of fourteen-foot giants who have not "brushed their teeth in 27 years," or bathed in thirty-one or forty-two years. The giants are robbers and do not believe Jack when he pretends he is, too. However, they let him try to back up his lie, and on three successive days, he manages to trick a local farmer out of a cow. The giants like eating the cows Jack brings them, so they let him live a while longer. Then Jack brags that he can steal as much in an hour as they have in year. Of course, they do not believe him. So he goes to the sheriff, turns in the giants, and receives half of their ill-gotten gains as his reward. A good son, he brings his mother to live in the giants' now-empty house. Unlike African American and American Indian tricksters, Jack is dissatisfied with his lot, rather than oppressed. Jack's pursuit of happiness usually centers on seeking his fortune.

Southern Flimflam Men

As Jack tales accommodated themselves to North America, their characters took on American attitudes, and their settings became localized. However, elements of their magical *märchen* origins remain. Jack's descendants (including both early nineteenth-century Yankee peddlers and southern flimflam men), though clearly related to Old World rogues, are still more American than Jack in their speech and attitudes. The Duke and Dauphin, whom Huck encounters on the Mississippi River, are just as cruel and soulless as the tormenters of Lazarillo de Tormes; on the other hand, their exaggerations are more comical. Huck himself is far more innocent than Lazarillo. There is something timeless about rogues like Huck's Duke and Dauphin. The assumption is that every society grows its own malefactors, yet in the American heartland, the good-hearted Huck manages to sidestep their machinations and finally slip out of the traps they set for him. William Faulkner's reivers are also thieves and liars; the adult reivers demonstrate active libidos and are certainly con men. Yet they, too, evince a certain innocence—from the conniving Ned McCaslin and over-muscled child-man Boon Hoggenbeck (who "rents" his Miss Corrie for a weekend as often as he can afford her price), to the eleven-year-old man-child Lucius Priest, who cannot escape his sense of guilt at being involved in non-virtue. In the end, Faulkner's whole "reminiscence" retains a sense of the wonder tale, with the good and traditional people foreordained to triumph.

Con Men from the Old Southwest

During the boom and bust "flush times" of the 1840s, popular sporting papers publishing news, verse, and fictional sketches chronicled the adventures of confidence men who were distinctly American tricksters. Scattered through these publications memorializing the humor of the Old Southwest, wily backwoods con men reflected the social order writers had observed rather than heard from oral sources.

There is something so ingenuously bold-faced about the confidence games rapscallions from Old Southwest sketches play that readers laugh both at and with them—as in a favorite anecdote relating how Simon Suggs Jr. escapes from jail dressed in his "widow's" clothes, while she takes his place in his coffin. He gets safely away, too, even though she "obstinately refuse[s] to be buried in [his] place when she [gets] to the grave" (Baldwin 139). The protagonists of Old Southwest tales assume that dupes deserve their ignominious fates and generally glory in language that rubs in their opponents' defeat and their own triumph. The contemporary notion that no one can cheat an honest man has close ties to the contention that the society as well as the person confiding in con men often reveal inherent moral flaws. To the trickster, such a confiding personality smacks of at least naiveté, inviting manipulation. So much is apparent in Augustus Baldwin Longstreet's "The Horse Swap," when the man who is "a *little* the best man at a horse-swap that ever [anyone] got hold of" gets a bit "snappish" on realizing he has traded a pathetic looking little horse with an open sore on its back for one that looks fine but is deaf and blind (21).

In contrast with the good-heartedness and youthful mischievousness of Huckleberry Finn, for example, humor about con men in the Old Southwest often feels vindictive and assumes the worst about human behavior. The tricksters of Old Southwest humor demonstrate the worst aspects of individualism, while Huck demonstrates the best. Readers of or listeners to the tales of Augustus Longstreet and others have to achieve a level of intellectual detachment to find the humor in what are for the most part cruel jokes. Old Southwest tricksters are opportunists, adapting to circumstances. Yet although the phrase "confidence man" came in to currency only during the 1840s in the United States, tricksters from many eras would agree with Simon Suggs's aphoristic encapsulation of his "ethical system": "IT IS GOOD TO BE SHIFTY IN A NEW COUNTRY" (Hooper 12). Huck may shave a few ethical corners; however, he does not purposely set out to cheat good people. In fact, he finds good in some whom most of his fellow citizens would probably be leery of.

The frontiersmen of the Old Southwest were struggling to assert their independence and establish themselves in a hostile and often violent milieu. They generally proved more than adequate at dealing with the claims to social and political hegemony that eastern and northern elites tried to assert. Their struggles and those of Jack as they elbow their way ahead, insisting on their worth, find an echo in the late twentieth- and early twenty-first century literary tricksters of John Kennedy Toole, Mark Childress, and Clyde Edgerton.

Modern Southern Literary Tricksters

Whether a trickster, that most protean of characters, represents a savior or destructive force is a matter of perspective. Folk sayings have always emphasized this point: "It's all in where you sit, how far the man in the balcony can spit," or less crassly, "It depends on whose ox is gored." Toole, Childress, and Edgerton shade their narratives, however, to demonstrate how—regardless of their intent or what they do—the tricksters in their fiction actually benefit the world they live in.

John Kennedy Toole's Ignatius Reilly

Even funny tricksters are destructive. At the center of John Kennedy Toole's *A Confederacy of Dunces* waddles a trickster happy to contribute his bit of chaos to a universe he despises. Ignatius Reilly is totally anarchic and certainly hard to pigeonhole. One writer settles for calling the novel itself an example of "comic grotesque" fiction (Nelson). Toole's central character is so self-absorbed and so delusional that his tricks flow from only a few motives endemic to all tricksters: ensuring his own physical comfort, self-glorification, and self-protection. Yet regardless of his motives, Reilly effectively changes everyone he encounters. He even helps a fair number of others.

Although many readers have found the mix of characters in Toole's *A Confederacy of Dunces* satisfying in themselves, Random House editor Robert Gottlieb finally passed on recommending the novel for publication because he could not find any "reason" for its anarchy. Rather than a plot, the novel offers readers a concoction of characters and contrivances. Lucinda MacKethan's characterization of the novel as a depiction of comic "immersion in a city representing the perverse heart of modernity[,]" however, points to Toole's trickster opposing not injustice but modern attempts to quell creativity and imagination. No trickster will stand for that. Toole's Ignatius Reilly does not.

Years after Toole's suicide, his determined mother finally badgered Walker Percy into reading the manuscript, and Percy in turn persuaded Louisiana State University Press to venture a limited press run of 2,500 copies.[8] Despite the novel's farce and over-the-top satire, another difficulty Toole and later his mother encountered in getting the book published may lie in the central character: Reilly is physically disgusting and morally limited—a trickster. Walker Percy's foreword refers to Reilly as a "slob extraordinary" (vi), too gentle a description. Reilly is unwashed and grossly overweight. He belches and masturbates into his already filthy sheets while he pencils overwritten though half-baked ideas in Big Chief tablets. When he does leave his mother's house, he is comically attired and socially inept. He spouts spurious academic jargon,[9] demands his own prerogatives, but is quick to call attention to the quirks and limitations of other characters. In applying for a job, he berates would-be employers. Particularly at the opening, readers find little to like or admire in Reilly, yet his trickster spirit holds the novel together, and the other characters' successes are directly related to his whims.

In the course of the event-filled and character-stuffed novel, Reilly encounters a swirl of lively characters from a few select New Orleans settings: outside a department store, inside a dreary bar that is at once sleazy and pathetic, and at Reilly's two places of work. Reilly precipitates anarchy and chaos. For no better reason than he feels like it, he composes an insulting letter to a customer, forges the signature of his boss, Gus Levy, and mails the letter. The recipient's reaction threatens to bankrupt Levy. Later on, realizing his actions might have some unwanted consequences for *himself* as well as for Levy, Reilly rather ineffectively lies to protect himself. For the most part, however, his lies have little purpose other than annoying his listeners. As an article of personal faith, he believes in his own innate intellectual superiority, though his language—a mix of cliché and bombast—hardly supports this conviction. Rather than deal with the mess he has achieved, he flees town.

But despite his apparent ineptitude—and without actually intending to—Ignatius Reilly creates a new world. By the novel's end, his actions have caused his mother to realize she can find a new mate. Because of Reilly, Gus Levy realizes he can revive his company and control his termagant wife. Because of Reilly, a bungling policeman is credited with breaking up sales of pornography to children. Even the inept bargirl is offered her dream job as an exotic dancer, and a malingering janitor is slated to receive an award while the police arrest a pornographer and her minion. Reilly has actually—though probably only temporarily—bettered the world he inhabits.

Mark Childress's female tricksters

LUCILLE VINSON—Part of what characterizes Euro-American—particularly southern—tricksters is the sense that no matter what they do, no matter how unlikely the outcome, they will somehow not only survive but even thrive. Certainly Lucille Vinson, the narrator's aunt in Mark Childress's *Crazy in Alabama*, demonstrates this quality. Early reviews of the novel use phrases like "craziness rules" (See) and "gruesomely entertaining" (Larue). The narrator's Aunt Lucille beheads her husband, leaves her six children with their long-suffering grandmother, flees across the country, gets her chance to make a splash as a femme fatale on *The Beverly Hillbillies*, and is finally caught and convicted of murder. But she gets off with a suspended sentence and then lives happily afterward with a smitten beau. While she is "going along," Lucille manages to escape one trap after another, win a small fortune at roulette, and thoroughly enjoy a series of illicit sexual encounters. At the novel's end, she is almost thirty years older but still intent on inveigling her nephew to get her a part in a new movie. Mark Childress says that he thinks of himself as a storyteller rather than an "artist" (Caton 39). As a storyteller, Childress falls heir to a southern oral tradition characterized by a strong admixture of trickster exaggeration. Except for her gender, Aunt Lucille is a typical Euro-American trickster. Her original circumstances are not harsh, but once she decides they warrant extreme action, she quickly deals with her husband's petty tyranny and demanding children before performing the twentieth-century version of Huck's "lighting out for the territory."

GEORGIA BOTTOMS—In Georgia Bottoms, the title character of his 2011 novel, Mark Childress creates another resilient female trickster, constantly knocked down but never defeated. Georgia is dealt a less than stellar hand by fate and her own choices: Her mother is slipping into dementia; her charming but reckless younger brother drinks, even directly after his AA meetings and before meetings with his parole officer; she schedules a huge annual women's luncheon for September 11, 2001; out of the blue, her unacknowledged twenty-year-old black son shows up in her racist town. And yet, Georgia keeps bouncing back from disasters. Even as she and her family escape *into* New Orleans during early August of 2005—as virtually all other traffic flows out of town and away from Hurricane Katrina—readers recognize that Georgia will somehow find a way to thrive there.

Unfettered by moral qualms, Georgia organizes her life to suit herself. Over the better part of twenty years, Georgia has built up her bank account by selling handmade folk-art quilts made by old African American descendants of slaves. *Somehow* the town has the impression that Georgia makes the quilts during the evenings she spends in her room above the old stable behind her family home. Actually, she uses that small apartment as a place to meet the local men who gratefully thank her—following a sliding scale geared to how much each can afford—for playing out their sexual fantasies. Each of the six men believes he is her only lover. She, on the other hand, thinks of them all as clients or patients, "not lovers" (Childress 39).

Unlike Ignatius Reilly, Georgia is smarter that those around her. She knows that in a world where most people are only simulating rectitude, by telling the truth she can defeat her strongest enemy. Georgia routs her minister by telling the truth about her relationship with him and those with her other "patients" to the entire congregation at Sunday services. Plainly, the only way to defeat Georgia is actually to live what one professes. In an odd sort of way, she is the town's conscience. If Georgia's two minister "clients" were as devoted to their wives and their callings as the elderly man who holds the post during an interregnum between their tenures, they would be invulnerable. Most people in Six Points, however, are flawed men and women, prime targets for someone with Georgia's talents.

Though amoral, Georgia is not a villain. She tries to protect the feelings and reputation of her closeted lesbian friend, the mayor. She never really loses patience with her racist mother and irresponsible brother. She comes to care for her son, in whom she recognizes bits of her youthful self. She allows herself to care for both of the ministers who ultimately betray her. Everyone in Six Points, Alabama, readers are told, loves Georgia. She is a culture hero to townspeople because she understands them. Even when they do not realize it, she works to make them comfortable. Her efforts smooth the way for the annexation of the African American section to Six Points, so that it can access city services. She thinks of her relationships with her clients as saving their marriages.

Georgia Bottoms has a surreal quality to it. Despite its coincidences and bizarre characters, it is no more ludicrous or unbelievable, of course, than an oral trickster tale or the tales of the Old Southwest. Georgia Bottoms deals with twenty-first century chaos. Sometimes she tames it; sometimes she creates it. Aunt Lucille and Georgia offer glimpses of how twentieth- and twenty-first-century female tricksters might function. Presumably the weaker sex, they use their powers—unbridled sexuality and amorality—to escape the traps in which their culture attempts to confine them. Lucille and Georgia are relaxed and able to survive any catastrophe. Typical Euro-American tricksters, they assume that ultimately they are smarter than others, and they can always find a way to manipulate the people around them. Since the men around them are hypocrites, they succeed.

Clyde Edgerton's conflicted moralists

WESLEY BENFIELD—Another southerner, Wesley Benfield in Clyde Edgerton's *Walking Across Egypt,* is something of a trickster wannabe. A sixteen-year-old thief and braggart with murky antecedents, he seldom considers anything beyond how to satisfy his appetites for food and sex. He escapes from a youth correctional center, but having borrowed first a choir robe to blend in at church and later a car from one of the churchgoers, he is still cornered by the sheriff and his deputies at the home of Mattie Rigsbee, the woman he rather wishes were his grandmother. (Like traditional tricksters from oral literature, Wesley's most significant feminine relationship is with an old woman. Mattie is Wesley's protector, and Wesley resembles the feisty stray dog Mattie feeds against her better judgment.) Wesley is an unprepossessing hero—young, awkward, a relatively ineffective schemer. Yet he is also a transformer, and as he says (though with considerable exaggeration) to the deputy who has missed capturing him in a church choir loft, "I can just about be anywhere I want to at anytime I want to" (*Walking* 167). In any case, wherever Wesley lands, somehow he never settles down.

In *Walking Across Egypt,* as well as in the next Edgerton novel featuring Wesley Benfield, *Killer Diller,* Wesley demonstrates traits commonly encountered in Euro-American tricksters: He is individualistic and inclined to focus entirely on his own needs and desires, and he has an outsider's penchant for spotting the failings of those around him. Yet he is also drawn to Mattie Rigsbee, who represents the good in his society. Perhaps because of her rectitude, one critic even sees Mattie as the novels' "primary character" (Huggins 91). Though almost never found in traditional tricksters—especially in popular fiction—the tension between self-serving individualism and the communal good lies at the core of Edgerton's two novels. American individualism has always strained against the pull of what is good for the community. While in their extreme forms these values are always at odds, the United States glorifies both the lone individual and collective effort. That tension is reflected in Euro-American tricksters. In Wesley's case, although he can be a hustler, he is more mischievous than acquisitive. Like Huck, he is a young innocent functioning in a world of hypocrisy.

In *Killer Diller,* Wesley is older—twenty-four—and if not exactly mature, somewhat toned down owing to Mattie Rigsbee's authentically

Christian influence. He is still a trickster (for example, he switches a donor's nameplate from a classroom to a broom closet just for the fun of it) and still fixated on sex. Yet he also ponders moral questions in a fashion that would never occur to a full-blown trickster. Innocent, rather than totally amoral like a traditional trickster, Wesley turns his intelligence and honesty against the pseudo-Christianity that surrounds him at his cleaning job. In spite of Wesley's trickster instincts and in contrast with that his bosses, Wesley's Christianity is sincere.[10]

Powerful men and women instinctively recognize that tricksters can upset their carefully constructed plans. So, of course, they try to marginalize the tricksters. In *Killer Diller* the comfortable men who administer a small Baptist university, more focused on fund-raising and encouraging small, careful virtues than on either education or the gospel, know that tricksters are bound to stir up trouble. Tricksters always upset the expectations of anyone who emphasizes conformity at the expense of creativity. In *Killer Diller*, contrast to Wesley and oblivious to his language's contradiction, a new dean explains the university administration's values by explaining to Wesley's band of musicians that "[h]ierarchy is . . . the cornerstone of American democracy" (188).

Almost all of Ballard University's administrators come from a military background and prefer coercion to debate; they confuse coercing with convincing others.[11] At the pinnacle of the school's hierarchy, Ballard's all-male administration believes that its role is to limit the damage nonconformists might inflict on their closed system. Having thrown a fright into Ballard's leaders, at the end of the novel Wesley and his band, the Wandering Stars (an exemplary trickster name), head out on Interstate 95. Edgerton paints Wesley's opponents as larcenous and therefore fair game, but in any case they and the milieu they foster seem deadly because they are boring. The limited virtues and simplistic "correctness" of Ballard's administrators beg for a trickster's correction.

HENRY DAMPIER—In 2008, Edgerton introduced still another innocent trickster, Henry Dampier, who readers are told from the first, is "hungry for adventure and good food" (*Bible* 3). At twenty, Henry is still, as the narrator says, a "boy" (4). Henry has been raised by his Aunt Dorie and Uncle Jack. While the former encourages conventional virtues, the latter teaches him to love fishing. Uncle Jack smells like alcohol, cigars, and the inside of a truck. Because of unspecified trouble, Jack skips town just as Henry is about to enter adolescence. Earlier indications that Jack is apt to "acquire" things he may not necessarily pay for suggest that he is smart to choose this moment to leave. Even after Henry has been officially saved in his Pentecostal church, he retains a bit of Uncle Jack's influence. It is true that he spends a great deal of his time reading and puzzling over biblical passages; in fact, the youthful Henry makes his living as a Bible salesman. Yet he is selling free Bibles he got from the Chicago Bible Society.

At fourteen, Henry told his cousin Carson that he did not intend to have sex until he married. At twenty, he is clearly ready to change his mind. From the first Henry is something of a Huck Finn; most of his "vices" are relatively small human failings. Despite his infractions against his family's strict Pentecostal code, he is an innocent. That characteristic is part of his appeal for Preston Clearwater, the conniving car thief who picks Henry up and hires him as a driver. In contrast with the naïve Henry, who is conflicted over biblical inerrancy, Clearwater's reflection after killing someone who objected to his stealing a car jack is that "[h]e didn't like to shoot people, but sometimes it just happened because it was the only way to get through some problem to a place where he had to be" (135). For most of the novel, Henry actually believes he is working with an FBI operation engaged in infiltrating a car theft ring. Finally, however, Henry figures out that Clearwater is a thief and a murderer, so he tells the police what has happened. The local police chief does not believe him. Later, the Atlanta police investigate, although they decide not to prosecute Henry for his part in the operation, given "a lack of evidence of criminal intent" (229). By the end of the novel, Henry has earned a sizable salary working for Clearwater, abetting Clearwater in stealing one safe and a number of cars. Albeit in self-defense, he has also shot Clearwater to death and kidnapped the retarded son of one of Clearwater's murder victims. Replete with hilarious comic touches, Henry's tale echoes that of his predecessor Jack in "The Time Jack Stole the Cows," in that Edgerton's protagonist has acquired loot as well as experience. On his honeymoon with the girl he met along the way, Henry discusses with her what they will call their first son. Henry leans toward "Jack" as a good choice.

Henry's eponymous Uncle Jack appears to play a minor role in *The Bible Salesman;* nonetheless, as Henry's earthy mentor, his role is significant. He offers the child Henry an alternative to the boy's otherwise circumscribed upbringing. The novel's reviewers generally focus on Henry's difficulties with the Christian fundamentalism in which he has been raised, and the novel's division into chapters with biblical names, as well as Henry's puzzling over biblical contradictions, encourages this focus. Yet Henry's early training by Uncle Jack, his tie to a culture even older than that of the local church, fuels the tension between what Aunt Dorrie and her preacher have taught and what Henry works out for himself. Uncle Jack would fit right in among the characters who inhabit the tales of the Old Southwest: He is an earthy "good old boy" who cannot envision anything better than a day fishing with the youthful Henry. While at nine Henry already wonders how God can be tired enough to need rest on the seventh day, Uncle Jack thinks such quibbling is pointless. According to him, boys need Sunday school "like a dog needs a spoon" (51). Although the Sunday school indoctrination Henry received as a child has influenced him, he is not a villain like Clearwater. Nonetheless, his experience on the road and his uncle's early influence cause much of his fundamentalist training to wash away, much as the rain washes "Jesus Saves" from Carson's bumper stickers, leaving behind only his pedestrian printing business's name and address. Instead of giving his child a biblical name, Henry acknowledges his uncle's influence by choosing Jack as a suitable name for his son.

In a fictional world where tricksters function, anything can happen—though perhaps not in the way the tricksters intended. In their single-minded focus on what they want, Wesley Benfield, Henry Dampier, and Ignatius Reilly, and Lucille Vinson and Georgia Bottoms are all seeking their fortune. Their success may also spell success for others, but for these tricksters those effects are peripheral. Contemporary literary tricksters have a little Jack in them—and more than a little of the con man. Moralists decry their shenanigans, but they are funny. Since tricksters hold a mirror up to society, they also cause others to reflect on their own failings and collusions. Readers recognize the ways the tricksters have broken up staid patterns that needed shattering. Euro-American tricksters are not usually as competent or as in charge as Hermes or Loki, but their single-minded pursuit of their own self-interest alters and often improves the world they live in. Even those who disapprove of latter-day fictional tricksters enjoy the tales they inhabit, and regardless of contemporary attitudes toward them, tricksters are everywhere.

NOTES

1. Far more decorously, Lewis Hyde refers to tricksters being found wherever a society has "dirt" it wants to hide.
2. The anthropologist Barbara Babcock (162–63) lists sixteen characteristics that set a true trickster apart from other entities.
3. Despite the challenge in tracing the oral roots of popular culture tricksters an unpublished 1965 master's thesis by Joseph John Arpad does demonstrate ties that several popularizers of Brother Jonathan (the most frequently used name for the trickster Yankee peddler) had with John Wesley Jarvis, a witty antebellum American painter and raconteur known for his stories about Yankee peddlers and tricksters. In addition, H. E. Dickson shows that at least one stage Yankee, a comedian named Charles Mathews, was indebted to Jarvis for part of his repertoire of American sketches.
4. Traditional oral tales about a character called Jack surface in Virginia, West Virginia, Tennessee, Kentucky, Pennsylvania, New York, Missouri, and Arkansas, but these disparate tales lack the coherence of the North Carolina Beech Mountain tales first published in Richard Chase's 1943 collection, *The Jack Tales.* Whether or not Chase's collection reflects a larger collection of coherent tales remains arguable.
5. A number of sources, including Henry Glassie, (82, 83), Richard Chase ("Origins" 190–92), and Carl Lindal (in McCarthy xvii), agree the Jack tales represent a merging of multiple traditions, especially Scotch-Irish and German traditions, but also French and, of course, British traditions.
6. Nonetheless, as C. Paige Gutierrez points out, in the Beech Mountain tales she examined, Jack's success in half of the Jack tales depends on magic rather than "trickery and quick-thinking" (98).
7. "Jack and His Lump of Silver," 25–26, in Charles L. Perdue.
8. According to *Publishers Weekly,* each of those copies now sells for $2,000 in the rare book market (Summer). A more recent blog in the *Chronicle of Higher Education* carries a story that quotes Mary Katherine Callaway, the director of Louisiana State University Press, who spells out just how well the novel has done for the press: "The novel is, quite simply, a phenomenon. It has sold steadily since its first year, spurred on by winning the Pulitzer Prize for Fiction in 1981, and by word of mouth from countless readers. . . . Today, the press continues to sell the book in hardcover and large-print hardcover editions, and we have licensed translations in over 26 languages, as well as English paperback, audio, and e-book editions" ("'A Confederacy of Dunces,' Still Strong").
9. Toole wrote his M.A. thesis on John Lyly's sixteenth-century *Eupheus,* a text known for its ornate convoluted prose; Toole presumably enjoyed parodying the style in Reilly's pretentious "pensées."
10. W. Todd Martin makes the case that Edgerton's protagonists have a lover's quarrel with southern Baptists, as the tricksters force "other characters . . . to confront the limitations of their views" (260) because these characters' views focus on respectability rather than—to paraphrase Isaiah—turning their hearts to be healed (Isa. 6:10).
11. Dean Daren's 2006 interview with him throws light on many of the attitudes (including Edgerton's distaste for militarism) suggested by his fiction.

WORKS CITED

Arpad, Joseph John. "David Crockett: An Original." Masters thesis. University of Iowa. 1965. Print.

Babcock, Barbara. "'A Tolerated Margin of Mess': The Trickster and his Tales Reconsidered." *Journal of the Folklore Institute* 9 (1975): 147–86; rpt. *Critical Essays on Native American Literature*, ed. Andrew Wiget. Boston: Hall, 1985. 153–85. Print.

Baldwin, Joseph G. *The Flush Times of Alabama and Mississippi: A Series of Sketches.* New York: Appleton, 1854. Print.

Caton, Bill. *Fighting Words: Words on Writing from 21 of the Heart of Dixie's Best Contemporary Authors.* Montgomery, AL: Black Belt, 1995. Print

Chase, Richard. *The Jack Tales: Folktales Told by R. M. Ward and His Kindred in the Beech Mountain Section of Western North Carolina and by Other Descendants of Council Harmon (1803–1896) Elsewhere in the Southern Mountains; With Three Tales from Wise County Virginia.* Boston: Houghton, 1943. Print.

———. "The Origin of 'The Jack Tales.'" *Southern Folklore Quarterly* 3 (1939): 189–91. Print.

Childress, Mark. *Crazy in Alabama.* New York: Ballantine, 1993. Print.

———. *Georgia Bottoms.* New York: Little, 2011. Print.

"'A Confederacy of Dunces,' Still Strong at 30," *Chronicle of Higher Education.* http://chronicle.com/blogPost/A-Confeeracy-of-Dunces/24140/?sid+at&utm_source=at&utm_medium=en. Web. 21 May 2010.

Davis, Donald. *Jack Always Seeks His Fortune: Authentic Appalachian Jack Tales.* Little Rock, AR: August House, 1992. Print.

Dean, Daren. "A Conversation with Clyde Edgerton." *Image: A Journal of the Arts & Religion* 59 (Summer 2006): 67–78. Print.

Dickson, H. E. "A Note on Charles Mathews' Use of American Humor." *American Literature* 12 (1940): 78–83. Print.

Dorson, Richard. *Burying the Wind: Regional Folklore in the United States.* Chicago: University of Chicago Press, 1964. Print.

Edgerton, Clyde. *The Bible Salesman.* New York: Little, 2008. Print.

———. *Killer Diller.* Chapel Hill, NC: Algonquin; rpt. New York: Ballantine, 1992. Print.

———. *Walking Across Egypt.* Chapel Hill, NC: Algonquin; rpt. New York: Ballantine, 1987. Print.

Glassie, Henrie. "Three Southern Mountain Jack Tales." *Tennessee Folklore Society Bulletin* 30 (1964): 82–102. Print.

Gutierrez, C. Paige. "The Jack Tale: A Definition of a Folk Tale Sub-Genre." *North Carolina Folklore Journal* 26 (1978): 85–110. Print.

Hooper, Johnson Jones. *Some Adventures of Capt. Simon Suggs.* (1843–1851). Upper Saddle River, NJ: Literature House, 1970. Print.

Huggins Cynthia E. "Witnessing by Example: Southern Baptists in Clyde Edgerton's *Walking Across Egypt* and *Killer Diller.*" *Southern Quarterly,* 35:3 (1997): 91–96. Print.

Hyde, Lewis. *Trickster Makes This World: Mischief, Myth, and Art.* New York: Farrar, Straus and Giroux, 1998. Print.

Larue, Dorie. Review of "*Crazy in Alabama.*" *Southern Quarterly* 32:2 (1994): 161. Print.

Longstreet, A. B. *Georgia Scenes: Characters, Incidents, etc. in the First Half Century of the Republic.* 1835; rpt. New York: Sagamore, 1954. Print.

MacKethan, Lucinda. "Redeeming Blackness: Urban Allegories of O'Connor, Percy and Toole." *Studies in the Literary Imagination* 27:2 (1994): 29–40. *EBSCOhost.* Web. 8 Oct. 2003.

Martin, W. Todd. "Where Trouble Sleeps: Clyde Edgerton's Criticism of Moralistic Christianity." *Renascence* 53 (2001): 257–66. Print.

McCarthy, William Bernard, ed. *Jack in Two Worlds: Contemporary North American Tales and Their Tellers.* Chapel Hill: University of North Carolina Press, 1994. Print.

Nelson, William. "The Comic Grotesque in Recent Fiction." *Thalia* 5:2 (1982): 36–40. Print.

Perdue, Charles L., Jr., ed. *Outwitting the Devil: Jack Tales from Wise County, Virginia.* Santa Fe, NM: Ancient City, 1987. Print.

Radner, Joan N. "AFS Now and Tomorrow: The View from the Stepladder". *(AFS Presidential Address, 28 October 2000). Journal of American Folklore* 114.453 (2001): 263–76. Print.

See, Carolyn. "Book World: Characters of Every Stripe." Review of *Crazy in Alabama* by Mark Childress. *Washington Post* 27 August 1994: C2. Print.

Summer, Bob. "Honoring 'Dunces.'" *Publishers Weekly* 20 Mar. 2000: 23. Print.

Toole, John Kennedy. *A Confederacy of Dunces.* Baton Rouge: Louisiana State University Press, 1980. Print.

ANANCY'S WEB/SUT'S STRATAGEMS

Humor, Race, and Trickery in Jamaica and the Old Southwest

JOHN LOWE

OVER THE CENTURIES, TRICKSTER TALES AND STORIES HAVE been generated in most parts of the world, and many of them found their way to North America via the slave ships that supported the plantation economy of the New World but also disseminated the people of the African diaspora. One of the chief exports from Western Africa was the Ashanti people, whose folklore centered on the spider trickster Anansi/Anancy. As the opposite of Nyame, the creator and namer, Anancy represents humor, chaos, and ambiguity, all of which of course have an interrelationship with creativity. His disorienting yet invigorating activities are a useful counterbalance to the stability (which can be overly rigid) of Nyame[1] (Christen 6, 7). While he maintains his arachnid identity in some of the stories, he often takes on human form and deceives all sorts of people.[2] Yet many of his activities are creative and beneficial; destruction often becomes a way of clearing the ground for new forms.[3]

In the New World, Anancy appeared wherever the Ashanti people (from present-day Ghana and Ivory Coast) were enslaved—but particularly in Jamaica, where Anancy tales, often referred to as "Anansesem," remain popular to this day. Anancy, like many Native American tricksters, is mischievous, profane, and unable to control his voracious appetites. At one point, he is said to be "the biggest rascal in the world" (62). In the Bahamas he was said to be "B'Nansi—or Nansi, Boy Nasty, or Gulumbanansi, a trickster and hero, either boy, man, or monkey" (Crowley 29). Also, similar to what appears in the Native American tales, the concept of Anancy occupying a position between man and god, with his mythical web sometimes pictured as a ladder to heaven is common among inheritors of the Ashanti.[4] As many critics have noted, Anancy resembles African Americans' Brer Rabbit, a weak creature who uses what blacks call "mother wit" to get the better of larger animals. As such, Anancy also has an African analogue in the signifying monkey, who often tricks and outmaneuvers larger creatures such as the lion and the elephant through subterfuge and wily "signifying." These small-dimensioned tricksters were chosen by enslaved people to stand for the "ways out of no way" they had to construct. Anancy originally worked his web in West Africa, in what we now know as Ghana. As Robert Pelton has stated, "He is both fooler and fool, maker and unmade, wily and stupid, subtle and gross, the High God's accomplice and his rival" (28–29).

This description also applies to the fools, knaves, and confidence men of the Old Southwest humor genre of the nineteenth-century US South. Characters such as Simon Suggs and Sut Lovingood especially come to mind, with their wiliness, greed, outsized appetites, and generally gross appearance and behavior. Also, in the printed versions of both Old Southwest humor and the Anancy stories, a redactor took down the tales (which of course began in oral culture), and attempted in retelling them to reproduce the story in the language of the original teller, whose salty vernacular added a great deal of appeal for the general reader. In the case of the Old Southwest humorists, most redactors, as has often been noted, were members of the professional class, and they usually spun the tales out to make them virtual short stories. In some cases the tales were invented, but the large majority of them came from folk sources. Similarly, the Anancy stories have almost always come to us from white redactors/collectors (Martha Warren Beckwith and Walter Jekyll are early examples), who use proper English to foreground and explain the significance of their collections. By contrast, the Old Southwest tales, as has often been noted, usually have a frame story narrated by a white professional of some sort in proper English, while the tales themselves feature dialect-dripping characters who employ voluptuous vernacular. In the Anancy stories the animals/tricksters/human protagonists all speak in dialect and vernacular.

Anancy, like Simon Suggs and Sut Lovingood, is a transgressor who delights in breaking boundaries. Circulating stories about these figures create a communal discourse, one that sifts and ponders cosmic issues through humor. Anancy stories, like other trickster tales, often center on inordinate appetite, greed, and outsized transgressions of social norms. As such, all these tales feature the body and its appetites, functions, and grotesque manifestations as grist for comedy and symbolic nodes of narrative connections. At the same time, they function as a warning to children to behave and follow a more orderly path—thus the concluding "John Mandora me choose none," or as Daryl Dance records it, "Jack Mandora, me no choose none" (12) (a third example from Beckwith's 1924 collection is the final "Jackman dora, choose none" [10]). In all three variations, taletellers are admitting that Anancy does wicked things, as the incantation is directed to Jack Mandora, the gatekeeper of heaven; "choose none" indicates the teller himself rejects Anancy as a model. This formulaic element indicates how ritualistic Anancy stories tend to be.

Rituals, of course, are often part of sequences of instruction. Karl Kroeber has remarked that "Stories teach skill in living. . . . A story teaches skill in a specific way of life, a culture . . . [which] cannot be divorced from long-term engagement in its performances" (82). Obviously, the orally delivered Anancy tales involve performance in a way that the Old Southwest tales don't, being confined to the written page. Nevertheless, one could argue that both traditions "teach skill in living" by emphasizing creative approaches to problems, providing moral instruction through hilarious negative examples, and offering examples of how humor can offer an indirect approach to very serious problems, such as racial oppression or the rigors of frontier life.[5]

As these remarks suggest, the Anancy tales are much closer to the people themselves than the Old Southwest humor stories were. Why is this? Perhaps because the former served a more intimate and necessary service: release from oppressive circumstances. In Jamaica, as in most of the Caribbean, the folk were mostly black. Although slavery officially ended in Jamaica in 1838, colonial social structures kept whites in control well into the twentieth century. The two chief early redactors in Jamaica, Walter Jekyll and Martha Warren Beckwith, understood the important historical and cultural aspects of the material, and wanted to present the tales just as they heard them—in the vernacular, yes, but without their own interpolations. In both the Old Southwest humor genre and the Anancy tradition, however, the core material is always oral. Slaves in Jamaica were from West Africa—many from what we now call Ghana—and had no written language. Their store of legends, tales, jokes, riddles, and songs came over with them on the Middle Passage and found new registers after contact with the landscape of the Caribbean and British colonial rule. In

Jamaica, where there were far fewer whites than in the American South, Africans managed to maintain many more cultural remnants from the Old World—including linguistic elements, which punctuate black island vernacular. In the Old Southwest humor era, many backwoods denizens were also illiterate and just as reliant on oral tradition. Clearly, however, the wisdom of the folk narrators and of the animal figures in Jamaica stand out somewhat more in contrast to the proper but oppressive standard English of the island's white arbiters. Still, in both modes, vernacular "wisdom" challenges the standard English of ruling elites, dismantling its authority, unmasking its pretensions and restrictions, and offering a liberated, more democratic alternative.[6] In both traditions, too, some of the stories have British antecedents, but they have been transformed and intermingled with African (Jamaica) and southern frontier elements.[7]

Operating from this perspective, James Justus has observed that the Old Southwest writers were intent on rendering written versions of oral tale telling, and that the "defining feature" of their work is the human voice. Indeed, he feels, straightforward narrative is never the primary object of the stories (Justus 323). Such is certainly true of the Anancy tales, which over time often lost a clear narrative progression, but which were retained because of interest in the other elements. In both Old Southwest humor and Jamaica, the confidence man/trickster employs language to achieve his ends. In virtually every case, the deception he creates is directly subsequent to his creation of a community of interests between himself and his dupe(s). He creates the opportunity he desires at the crossroads of accident, when he runs across something he wants, usually in the possession of someone else. The "spur" to "prick the sides of his intent" is usually hunger or lust, but it can be sheer perversity as well.

Orality inevitably involves performance, and a key factor in the reputation of the trickster man of words is his ability to lie. In both traditions, the rewards of skillful lying can usually be measured materially in the form of filched monies, food, or females, although the accompanying fall of the dupe can be featured just as prominently. We find outrageous liars in both the Old Southwest and Jamaica, liars who shamelessly hoodwink anybody, anytime, anywhere for personal gain—or sometimes, for sheer knavery's sake. Joseph Glover Baldwin's notorious Ovid Bolus, Esq, Attorney at Law, from *The Flush Times of Alabama and Mississippi,* offers a fine example of a figure that glories in his fabrications. Another figure that delights in self-promoting hyperbole is David Crockett. Here we find a commonality with African American culture: Zora Neale Hurston tells us that story-telling sessions in black rural communities are called "telling lies." In world cultures everywhere, skillful liars and flamboyant boasters are rightly considered artists, unless their lies work mischief rather than cause amusement.

Thus while Old Southwest humor stories comprise a written archive, there is no doubt that the stories themselves have their origin in oral culture, just as the Anancy stories do. As such, both traditions stem from folk culture. Jan Harold Brunvand's definition of folklore is "those materials in culture that circulate traditionally among members of any group in different versions" (5). But Bakhtin goes further; he declares that "folk culture . . . at all states of its development has opposed the official culture of the ruling classes and evolved its own conception of the world, its own forms and imagery" (473). We see this evolution clearly in examples of Old Southwest humor and the Anancy tales where elite postures and figures are relentlessly laid low—uncrowned—through the wily machinations of folk tricksters.

Often, however, the primary motive for lying is not democratic, but Darwinian; more often than not, the lies are born of need, especially hunger. Anancy is a thief, a liar, and is quite willing to sacrifice others to save himself; indeed, in one story, he feeds all six of his children and his wife to Tiger to avoid being eaten himself (Beckwith 9–10), an extreme that has no parallel in Old Southwest humor.

Still, hunger drives many narratives in that genre, too. As I have stated, one of the southwest tricksters who has analogues in Jamaican tales is Simon Suggs, particularly in his charade as a repentant sinner in the sketch "The Captain Attends a Camp Meeting." When his wife informs him the larder is nigh empty, he declares, "Damn it! *Somebody* must suffer!"(qtd. in Inge and Piacentino 104) and he means somebody he will victimize, not his family. The instigation for the story, hunger, is a constant thematic and narrative engine in the Anancy tales. Taking food by cunning from another animal—often this takes the form of the victim's own fat—is the most recurrent theme in the cycle of tales. Suggs, of course, uses his "confessions" before the congregation to take the pulpit from the minister, thereby enabling him to raise a collection that the good parson could have had himself. In the course of the tale, we discover the lechery and avarice of the good parson, but the entire company, including the women, use religious hysteria as a front for exhibitionism, groping, and general sexual abandon.[8] "Amid all this confusion and excitement Suggs stood unmoved. He viewed the whole affair as a grand deception—a sort of 'opposition line' running against his own, and looked on with a sort of professional jealousy" (qtd. in Inge and Piacentino 106). In the Anancy stories, as in many trickster tales from around the world, the narrative is generated by hunger: "One great hungry time, Anansi couldn't get anyt'into to eat . . ." (Beckwith 1). Hunger sets things in motion. Appetite is ever the instigator of action, and often, of mischief. Certainly the leading figures of Old Southwest humor favor their appetites as well. Also, Anancy, like the other smaller trickster figures, invents stratagem to foil larger foes. For Anancy, that is often the Tiger, who in one story is tied through trickery to a tree by Anancy and then killed by a hunter. In other tales, Anancy tricks Lion and ties him up. And like the Uncle Remus stories, where Brer Rabbit tricks Brer Fox into wearing a bridle and letting Brer Rabbit ride him, Anancy uses Tiger as a riding horse. (Beckwith 5, 6).

In the U.S. South and in Jamaica, too, the trickster figure craftily plays on his dupe's often hypocritical performance of piety to secure food, money, or a woman. In an Anancy tale, "Parson Puss and Parson Dog," the title figures duel over who will officiate at the wedding of Toad and a "pretty Indian girl" (a nod to the South Asian immigrants to Jamaica, and another analogue to the Uncle Remus stories, where Brer Rabbit courts Miss Meadow's daughter). Parson Puss's wife is the organist at the event, where Parson Dog is tricked into leaving. Returning, he is enraged at Parson Puss, who is celebrating his victory by dancing with all the pretty girls and bad-mouthing Parson Dog. At story's end, the two revert to their animal identities, when Dog—significantly, not "Parson Dog" at this point—chases Puss (again, not "Parson Puss") up a tree: "An' from that day that why Dog an' Puss can't 'gree till now," followed by the traditional "Jack Mandora me no choose any" (Jekyll 92–93). Despite the looser structure of the Anancy tales, they are quite regular in this ritual conclusion, which is required when Anancy has done something reprehensible that the auditors of the tale should not copy. Jack Mandora is the mythical keeper of the door of heaven, so the narrator is precluding being shut out of heaven by declaring "me no choose none," that is, I have never acted the way Anancy did.

While the story just considered is technically an Anancy tale (the spider/man is a guest at the event), it is also a satire of rival ministers, a subject that plays a leading role in many African American narratives, such as Zora Neale Hurston's novel *Jonah's Gourd Vine* and the play she co-wrote with Langston Hughes, *Mule Bone*. Under the surface of these references to ministers lurks the figure of the Obeah man, who offered up a form of African religion comparable to that of Cuba's Santeria, Haiti's vodun, and the coastal US South's hoodoo. One of the recurring figures in the Anancy tales is a character who is said to be a "witchboy" or "witchwoman," which should be read as a practitioner of the African-derived religion, obeah.

In another story centering on religion, "How Monkey Manage Annancy," Monkey is too smart for Anancy's pious hypocrisy, which the latter shares with many tricksters of the Old Southwest. His family cupboard bare, Anancy summons his friends Cow, Sheep, Goat, Hog, and Monkey to pay respects to his dead father (who turns out to be a banana barrel covered by a sheet in a bed). Reverend Cow leads the others in, but Monkey wisely refuses to go, as Anancy locks the door. After crying over the "body" and urging Reverend Cow to pray, Anancy kills his friends and eats them. Bearing no ill will to the rightly suspicious Monkey, he gives him some of the meat (Jekyll 21). The Anancy stories endlessly repeat horrific events like this. Anancy regularly tricks and eats one or more of these "friends," and he himself is often killed at tale's end. Similarly, many of the courtship tales involve Anancy hankering after a young girl, and then tricking her and/or her parents into letting him marry her. The tales echo the coyote and raven stories of Native Americans, in that the mythic figures never really die. Moreover, the deaths themselves are not the point, but rather the manner of the trickery. While the Old Southwest stories don't involve characters resurrected from the dead, they too often seem more interested in the strategy of the trickster than in the particulars of the characters or their ultimate fates.

Anancy in one tale pretends to be a preacher in Monkey country, where he sets up an oven and tells the monkeys they have to go in to be christened. He goes in first before it gets hot to make them think it is safe. Coming out, he ushers them in. Shutting the door, he roasts and then eats them. But a little monkey watches and goes to the next monkey country to warn them; when Anancy arrives and tries the same strategy there, they shut him in the oven when he performs the example, and he gets eaten ("Christen Christen," Beckwith, 47).

In "Annancy in Crab Country," the trickster, posing as a preacher in order to entrap tasty crabs, fails to attract a crowd, so he brings several friends with him to start a congregation. When that doesn't work, he gets his friends to play music at the services. That failing, too, he invites the crabs to witness him baptizing his friends, which makes the crabs agree to be "baptized" in a barrel. Anancy performs these crab baptisms with boiling water, thereby finally making a tasty meal. In several stories that feature Anancy's death, he is burned "till him belly burst" (Beckwith 50), a fitting punishment for a creature with such a voracious appetite.

Another religious dimension of the Anancy tales, however, has no analogue in Old Southwest humor. As in Native American narratives, many of the Anancy stories explain how things came to be. "Anancy and Brother Tiger" ends with the former fleeing the latter and taking refuge, in spider form, in the rafters. The tale ends, "From that, Tiger live in the wood till now, an' Annancy in the housetop" (Jekyll 9). More generally, however, Anancy, like trickster figures everywhere, is a comedian, whose antics help us deal with feared subjects more easily. By drawing dreaded things into the open, tricksters enable us to face them. Accordingly, although Anancy's usual opponents are other animals, he also duels with personifications of Fire, the Devil, and Death, lending a cosmic element to his repertoire, but also illustrating how his tales enable auditors to confront terrible things in life through humor and narrative.

Further, although Simon Suggs's injunction that it is best to be shifty in a new country implies shape shifting, Old Southwest humor characters can at best feign an identity, wear a disguise, or misrepresent themselves through actions, reference, and gesture. Both Simon Suggs and Sut Lovingood, for instance, pretend to be reformed sinners in order to fleece camp meeting congregations; so do Twain's King and Duke, who also, like Huck himself in that novel, wear various disguises.[9] Anancy can do all this, but he can also change from human to animal at will. Transformation and trickery are his hallmarks, but he seems to be partly divine, since he miraculously appears in yet another story after being killed in a prior one, and this is true for his rivals such as Tiger, Monkey, Hog, too. In the "creation stories" his antics often result in positive benefits for mankind, as when he employs deception to secure fire, the sun, the moon, or the stars for mankind.

Another key difference between the two sets of stories lies in the various aspects of society that are presented in the stories. The frontier was rough, crude, and often lawless; it did, however, have institutions and social conventions that could be used as frame stories. Quilting bees, court sessions, religious revivals, church meetings, and boarding houses offered appealing settings for rambunctious rapscallions. Tricks, in order to be amusing, have to upset something orderly, and such units were ripe for unsettling. The Anancy tales, by contrast, were created by an enslaved people who had to be much more circumspect in their narration. One, two, or three levels of masking might be employed in order to veil the underlying messages of tales that were, at bottom, critiques of slavery and, later, racial repression. Accordingly, the first level of disguise came in the traditional African guise of animal fables, wherein the characters—even though they might wear clothes and carry on very human activities—are ostensibly animals. The difference in species, of course, often was meant to signify racial or tribal difference. Still, the African American creators of the story also drew from social units such as the black church and the country store, in addition to the jungle that covered the interior mountains of Jamaica. We might remember, also, that many of the Old Southwest tales are set and/or told in the wilderness, often around a campfire.

Trickster tales are about many things, but most of them concern both chance in this world and the related realm of narrative chance. Anancy, like Sut Lovingood and Simon Suggs, is always alert to chance. In Anancy's case, it is often a chance to grab some unexpectedly available food. But all three figures also look for opportunities to create sheer mischief, particularly when it upsets the structures and mechanisms of controlling figures, be it those in the animal realm or backwoods society. That Anancy is also a force for liberation—specifically the liberation of enslaved people of color—is obvious in the ways in which his subversion and stratagem offer a means of survival, getting nourishment from those who would otherwise deny him sustenance. In a metaphysical sense, the tales (obviously coded so as not to attract the animus of those in power) offer both hope and amusement. At the same time, however, they constitute warnings, in that Anancy, when he isn't careful and is greedy or actively evil, is struck down, even killed. Like the Native American tricksters, he is a negative example to children, who are instructed by both his positive and his negative aspects.

Yet another similarity in the traditions is the subversive, indirect quality of the tales. As many have noted, most of the Old Southwest humorists presented themselves through masks, or as "anonymous." Others chose to write under the cover of pseudonyms. They did so to protect themselves in several ways. First, the literary man was not regarded as a man of substance in antebellum southern culture. Second, moral white culture would naturally suspect authors of such pieces of sharing the sometimes hedonistic, sometimes mischievous, and more often, diabolic aspects of the featured tricksters. African American tricksters, by contrast, employing African modes of myth, comedy, and signification (an ancient tradition of the continent) adjusted their heritage to fit the new culture, flora, and fauna of the tropical US, inserting Brer Rabbit for the signifying monkey, and Brer Fox, Brer Bear, and Brer Wolf for the Elephant, Lion, and Tiger. A major difference in the new approach, however, was that many of the tales were now quite clearly radical significations not just on the powerful, but on the enslavers. As such, these tales were heavily coded and rebellious, and kept the spirit of resistance flickering, a prospect of revolution. Masters, beguiled as the enslaved intended, found the tales charming inventions of a childlike people. Joel Chandler Harris's popularization of tales that actually have chilling inner cores featuring torture, cruel deaths, and brutal denouements demonstrated white readers' myopia to material that had a comic surface.[10]

A story that has most in common with Brer Rabbit tales is the one in which Anancy tricks Tiger into getting into a pot ("Shut up in the Pot," Beckwith 19), whereupon he is boiled, and the hungry children of Anancy get fed (repeating the ever-present hunger theme we have seen before). Similarly, in the Brer Rabbit story, the wolf is tricked into the pot and boiled to death. Remember, Uncle Remus enchants both the plantation mistress and her little boy with his animal fables; neither sees through to the horror hidden at the heart of the stories. Jamaican tales were no different. Anancy's frequent victims—especially Tiger—are clearly stand-ins: first, for slave masters, and later, for white landowners and politicians who continued to oppress the island's African-descended citizens after emancipation. Yet, white Jamaicans also delighted in the tales and told them to their children. This turn of events is not surprising. Folk narratives, Bakhtin demonstrates, are always ambivalent (12), and sometimes, as these tales reveal, they can be paradoxical. Humorous surfaces masking horrific inner meanings are quite common in the subversive stratagem of the oppressed.

As noted above, like African American and Native American folktales, the Anancy stories sometimes feature an account of how things came to be, as in "Long-shirt," where we learn why Mr. Ram-goat has such an unpleasant smell, a tale akin to the Uncle Remus story about how Brer Rabbit's luxurious long tail got cut off to a nub. We don't find this kind of stories in the Old Southwest humor tradition, perhaps because the latter level of myth is more earth-bound and realistic, despite its tendency toward exaggeration. Further, some of the African-derived stories that found New World versions told by blacks in the American South also have analogs in Jamaica. But because ethnicity is their central subject, similar tales are not found in Old Southwest humor. We are all familiar with the Uncle Remus story of the race between the tortoise and the hare. The Ashanti original found an avatar in Jamaica in the tale of the race between the toad and the donkey. As in the Uncle Remus tale, Toad, like Tortoise, has many children, and he stations them at various checkpoints in the race. In this version, "all Toads look alike" (corresponding to the white southern dictum that all blacks look alike), so Toad can park himself early on at the finish line and appear to have won the race, proving Donkey was right to be suspicious of the entire procedure. Like Anancy, "Toad is a very trickified thing" (Jekyll 39).

Another thing the traditions have in common is the curious appeal of tricksters, despite their wicked schemes and machinations, their gluttony, greed, and sloth, and their frequent betrayal of friends, spouses, parents, and children. Anancy has always been the most beloved figure in Caribbean folklore. In Native American oral culture, Coyote, equally problematical morally, is also a universal favorite, as is their African counterpart, the signifying monkey. Shiftiness, in whatever country, is not only valuable, it seems it is admired—even though the reader/witness would never get too close to such a figure, and would be horrified if anyone accused him or her of approving trickster antics. It is easy to understand why the circum-Caribbean audience for all these figures grew fond of them. The victory of the seemingly powerless and sometimes smaller figure over the dominant and often larger characters (and in the Old Southwest tales, richer and more socially prominent ones) always strikes a chord—and not just in the US, which supposedly has a soft spot for all underdogs. In Longstreet's "The Horse Swap," Peter Ketch is a good example of this kind of character (Inge and Piacentino 28–33), and we find a female version in the crafty Dolly of James Edward Henry's "My Man Dick" (Inge and Piacentino 213–23).

It isn't the fall of the mighty that causes laughter. The real payoff for readers and listeners is the clever stratagem—what African Americans call "mother wit"—that bring victory to the trickster, or sometimes, to the trickster's opponent. Further, shiftiness is crucially important for slackers, who are everywhere in Old Southwest humor.[11] One of the motifs we find in both traditions is the laziness of the trickster. Anancy has an industrious wife, who plants a field, but he won't help, being "so lazy he would never do any work" (Beckwith 25). He pretends to die and sneaks out of his grave every night to eat the peas. As in many other stories, he is caught by a tar baby the family sets in the field. At the end of the tale, it is said that "Anansi was so ashamed that he climb up beneath the rafters an' there he is to this day," thereby transforming the parable about laziness, greed, and deception into a creation tale (how things came to be) about why spiders stay in the rafters. One of my favorite jokes, which my grandmother from rural Georgia told me, certainly must come from that tradition. Old Clem, a wastrel with a large and starving family, was sprawled on his shack's porch with a jug of hooch. A generous neighbor came by in his wagon and told Clem he had a load of corn to give him. Clem drew up on one elbow and asked, "Is it shucked?"

Lazy figures, however, can rise to the occasion when survival is at stake. Anancy stories, even more than Old Southwest humor tales, are often brutal, pitting close relatives against each other in fights to the death. One of Anancy's children names himself "Cunnie-mo'n-father" and repeatedly outwits not just Anancy, but also his then compatriot, Tiger. Subsequently, Anancy and Tiger try to kill Cunnie-mo'n-father, but fail, and at the end of the tale, Anancy is tricked into a coffin that is thrown into the sea, where his son has told him he will find sheep. The end of the tale reads, "An' that was the las' of poor Anansi in *that* story" (31), an ending rather like that of cartoon segments featuring the roadrunner and Wily Coyote. And in fact, Anancy is often tricked at the end of a tale, several times by a signifying monkey who watches Anancy's tricks and then reverses them on him. ("The Yam-Hills" 39; "Fling-a-mile" 42). On another occasion, Tiger tells Anancy he can feed by reaching inside a cow and pulling tripe out, but when he does so, the cow runs away and scrapes Anancy against stones, thereby accounting for his white belly. We have thus both a creation story and an example of the trickster tricked (11).

Similarly, Old Southwest humor heroes get tricked on occasion as well.[12] The duping of the hero is in keeping with the mythic history of tricksters, who occupy a position between gods and men. If they succeeded always, they would be too close to the gods, which would damage their valuable functions as emissaries between gods and men, and as tricksters who steal gifts from above for those below (as in the case of the trickster Prometheus, who brings man fire). When the trickster is tricked, the tales double back on themselves, providing corrective humor. But such tales are also, perhaps, a form of self-reflexive humor especially noticeable in African American and Jewish American humor. Freud called this sort of joking protective humor. Rather than suffer the insults of others, the joker inflicts comic barbs on himself.

In African American humor, self-reflective humor is largely confined to jokes and tales told within the race. Langston Hughes called this type of humor "Jokes Negroes Tell on Themselves." Many of these tales take the form of the origin tales, as in a classic joke about how African Americans came to be black. One day God summons all people to wash in the river of life. Some people dally along the way, taking their own good time. When they finally arrive, all the water is has been used to wash the others white. Only mud, which the latecomers scoop up with their hands, is left. Thus blacks only have white hands and soles. That's what happens when you're late! (Hughes 23). The joke is an affectionate take on what blacks call "C.P.T." Someone who arrives late to a party might say, "We're keeping C. P. Time" (colored people time). Interestingly, immigrants from India kid about how they are guilty of keeping I.S.T. ("Indian standard time").

When Old Southwest humor tricksters use self-reflective humor, it is usually part of a scheme to disarm their dupes, who tend to let down their guard after hearing the con man denigrate his own intelligence or ability. Simon Suggs employs this technique at a camp meeting, posing as a poor but repentant sinner. On a more romantic note, the title figure of "Major Jones Pops the Question" forces Miss Mary to accept his Christmas present by climbing in a bag and almost freezing to death on the porch before she opens this "gift" in the morning. "The gals laughed themselves almost to deth" as the meal-covered major is revealed, but he gets his girl by making himself a comic butt (Cohen and Dillingham 122–26).

One of the most important collections of Anancy tales was compiled by Martha Warren Beckwith, whose two-volume *Jamaica Anansi Stories* was published in 1924 by the American Folklore Society. The volumes include music recorded in the field by Helen Roberts. Beckwith, who served as president of the society from 1932 to 1933, was a major contributor to ethnography and folklore, which she gathered mainly from the Caribbean and the Pacific. Like her great contemporary Zora Neale Hurston, she studied anthropology under Franz Boas at Columbia, which provided her with a firm scientific platform for her ethnographic work. In addition to her Anansi volumes, she published *Black Roadways: A Study of Jamaican Folk-Life* (1929), which garnered the praise of the eminent anthropologist Melville Herskovits, a noted Africanist, who called Beckwith's book the "first ethnographic study of the life of any New World Negro" (332–38). Her research was based on interviews with over sixty "negro story-tellers in the remote country districts of Jamaica" in 1919 (xi). Later, Hurston, too, would travel to Jamaica to collect stories, which she included in her landmark study, *Tell My Horse* (1938). Throughout her visits to the outback, Hurston noted parallels between cultural phenomena: "First we talked about things that are generally talked about in Jamaica. Brother Anansi, the Spider, that great cultural hero of West Africa who is personated in Haiti by Ti Malice and in the United States by Brer Rabbit" (25). As Hurston was keenly aware, one of the key differences between these groups of taletellers was race. Old Southwest humor characters are often poor, but all the genre's leading figures are white and therefore enjoy privileges denied southern blacks. Most of the Anancy stories have their origins in slave cultures, where the tellers of the tales had to employ masking devices to avoid the ire of whites. After emancipation, some changes occurred in the structures and subjects of the tales, but their basis in slavery dictated that some forms of narration and characterization remained constant, particularly since political control remained in the hands of whites until contemporary times.

On the other hand, both genres originated during periods of slavery and reflect the conditions taletellers were experiencing. One group was white, living in a frontier, which to them is a "new country," as Simon Suggs puts it. Against their will many Africans were living in a new country, too, and they would no doubt agree with Johnson Jones Hooper's Simon Suggs that it is always "good to be shifty in a new country." As in a famous episode involving Anancy's son, Cunnie-mo'n-father, Simon pulls a card trick scam on his own father (but doesn't kill him, as Cunnie-mo'n-father does in the Jamaican story). Seizing the possibilities of chance and accident, Anancy points to stratagem oppressed people can create if they will only look sharp and exercise their "mother-wit."

The wild countryside of the Old Southwest provides an appropriately rough background for grifter tales. Still, the boastful "roarers" of these narrations often trumpet their community as a unique Eden (a prominent example is Jim Doggett in Thomas Bangs Thorpe's "The Big Bear of Arkansas" [Inge and Piacentino 129–38]). The Anancy narrators, in contrast, rarely apostrophize their surroundings, which are full of dangers for oppressed people of color. Yet in both traditions, place has much to do with virtually every aspect of the story. Certainly the most pertinent commonality is the driving dynamo in both—humor—which in both cases proceeds from the folk, what Bakhtin called the voice of the "village square," a place that generates a communal voice and folklore. African compounds had such a space, where griots held forth on public occasions, and respected elders told tales, too. The same was true of slave quarters. As Lewis Hyde has indicated, all trickster figures like to hang out in doorways, because that's where many accidents that change things take place. Eshu, the Yoruba trickster, the god of the crossroads, is just such a vagrant at the door between heaven and earth, signifying his liminal space between gods and man, a space he occupies just like coyote and raven.

Similarly, the tricksters of Old Southwestern humor congregate at social "doorways" and "crossroads" where people meet or congregate—country stores, church events, camp meetings, races, cockfights, and so on. Hanging out at such places also suggests, of course, that like Coyote, Raven, or Wolverine in Native American stories, trickster is often presented in tales as a negative example, particularly for children in the audience.

We need to remember a difference, too: Frontiers are often characterized by violence, as was particularly the case in the Old Southwest. Escape from chaos into the enveloping and often protective wilderness was always possible, however, and white figures could move through these areas with impunity. Jamaican slaves, by contrast, experienced violence in a more confined, domestic arena called the plantation. Slavery, as far as black Jamaicans were concerned, was akin to the frontier state of lawlessness. Yes, there were laws, but they were written by white people, and slaves had no legal rights to speak of. Thus the violence of masters and overseers became another version of lawlessness.

Very often, the tales include three figures, which usually include Anancy and another, stronger animal, such as Tiger. The third figure is most often Monkey, the one being who can sometimes get the better of Anancy. Monkey in this respect is an avatar of the "signifying monkey" of African mythology, who has been presented and dissected so memorably by Henry Louis Gates Jr. In a variation of this pattern, Anancy's sidekick in many of his adventures is Tacoomah (Tacoma or Tacuma in some versions) who, as Daryl Dance points out, is sometimes Anancy's buddy, sometimes his spouse, or son, or neighbor. Harold Courlander has suggested Tacoomah/Tacuma may refer to the Ashanti name for Anancy's son, Intikuma (129). Often these two figures vie for a prize to be wrested from the same victim. They also frequently engage in verbal dueling, always a key component of folk humor. These trios characterize many Old Southwest humor tales too, as in the aforementioned "The Captain Attends a Camp Meeting," where the title figure vies with Bela Bugg for the parishioners' contributions, with the dupe(s) filling out the triangle. In that tale Bugg is clearly figured as just a more refined kind of confidence man. Perhaps the most hilarious use of this comic triangle in a "religious" tale, George Washington Harris's "Parson John Bullen's Lizards," features a similar configuration made up of Parson John, Sut Lovingood, and the parishioners they wish to dupe (Inge and Piacentino 75–80). "Good nature make nanny-goat lost him tail." Goat formerly had a long bushy tail, but one day when Goat and the spider, Anansi, were out together, rain fell and Goat good-naturedly held her tail over Anansi to keep him dry. When the rain was over, Anansi cut Goat's tail off, and ever since, goats have had stumps for tails" (Beckwith II 54).

Another way to look at the similarities between Anancy and Sut/Suggs figures is to consider Lewis Hyde's observations about the relation of classic trickster figures to the American confidence man: "[S]ome have even argued that the confidence man is a covert American hero. We enjoy it when he comes to town, even if a few people get their bank accounts drained, because he embodies things that are actually true about America but cannot be openly declared (as, for example, the degree to which capitalism lets us steal from our neighbors, or the degree to which institutions like the stock market require the same kind of confidence that criminal con men need)" (11).

Old Southwest humor and Anancy tales still have meaning for the US and Jamaican cultures of today. According to Daryl Dance, Anancy tales have long comprised the largest group of folk materials in Jamaica, and they continue to be told there to this day. Further, Anancy appears as a character or symbol in poetry, tales, and novels of leading Jamaican and West Indian writers (Dance 11).[13] Thus we have a parallel to the literary tradition that in some ways culminated in the work of Mark Twain. It is also easy to see Twain's effect on subsequent writers, as is evident in the work of contemporary southern writers such as Harry Crews, Rick Bragg, Michael Malone, Carl Hiassen, Lisa Alther, Rita Mae Brown, Jeff Foxworthy, Percival Everett, Ishmael Reed, and many others, who are keeping the frontier humor of earlier times alive in new places and formats, including the Internet.

Why are we still intrigued by these tales in the twenty-first century? Gerald Vizenor, the distinguished Native American writer and critic, has suggested that the trickster is by his nature postmodern: "The trickster is a communal sign in a comic narrative; the comic *holotrope* (the whole figuration) is a consonance in tribal discourse . . . comic world views are communal; chance is more significant than 'moral ruin' . . . " (9). Further, Joseph Meeker has stated that "[t]he comic mode of human behavior represented in literature is the closest art has come to describing man as an adaptive animal" (192). Further, Old Southwest humor scoundrels and Anancy, as spirits of disorder, nevertheless give man hope, for their boisterous, irreverent, often chaotic interventions demonstrate the possibility of creating ruptures in rigid cultures, which can lead to new forms and modes of being. As Karl Kerenyi has noted, the trickster is the enemy of boundaries; his mission is "to add disorder to order and so make a whole, to render possible, within the fixed bounds of what is permitted, an experience of what is not permitted" (185).

As this brief comparison has indicated, Old Southwestern humor and Anancy tales come from very different origins, yet they also share many qualities. Both genres can be creative, exuberant, or even heroic—especially in the brave subversive humor slaves created in masked form directly in front of their masters. But both traditions also demonstrate that humor can be cruel, malicious, sexist, stereotypical, and exploitive. The great Caribbean poet and critic Edward Kamau Brathwaite has written about "nation language," which though based in English, the imposed language, was created by "the people who were brought to the Caribbean, not the official English now, but the language of slaves and labourers," which includes remnants of the African languages brought to the islands, especially that of the Congo, Yoruba, and Ashanti peoples. As we have seen, the Ashanti influence was pronounced in Jamaica, especially in the Anansi stories. Brathwaite is careful, however, to distinguish "nation language" from demeaning "dialect," which he rightly states is often seen as "bad English," adding, "caricature speaks in dialect" (13). This "nation language" originated in oral expression, and its values are the reverberations of the human voice. Therefore the oral language is closely aligned with song—and many of the Anansy stories were meant to be sung. As Brathwaite notes, when the stories are written they lose part of their meaning (17). This so-called "nation language" is found in many places, such as Shango cults, Baptist services, yard theatres, ring games, and at tea meetings. Most venerably, perhaps, we find it in the *anansesem*. The "nation language" Brathwaite endorses found eloquent, epic expression in Andrew Salkey's Jackson's 1983 long poem, *Jamaica: An Epic Poem Exploring the Historical Foundations of Jamaica Society*, which uses the island's vernacular to deflect the imposed British history that preceded independence. Claiming a kinship with Anancy ("I ol' as Anancy") the speaker reminds us of Anancy's foundational importance:

> "Spider Man,
> Wes' African
> an' Wes' Indian,
> nearish total Caribbean Man!
> You spring out o' you' own 'ead,
> 'Cross Atlantic, over Sargasso,
> an' you lan' up 'monst the pickney them.
> You too sweet, Anancy!" (101)

Ernest Hemingway famously opined that all of American literature that really counted stemmed from Mark Twain's *Huckleberry Finn*, which for the first time demonstrated all the possibilities of American vernacular. Maybe what he meant wasn't too far removed from Brathwaite's notion of "nation language." We know, of course, how powerfully influenced Twain was by the rich vernaculars of the United States, which he had absorbed on riverboats, in stagecoaches, in western mines, and around campfires. As Shelley Fisher Fishkin has demonstrated, he was also powerfully influenced by African American vernacular, and he was well aware of the vast influence it had on other speech communities of the nation. Always mining for new literary gold, he found it first of all, however, in the cultural mirror of Old Southwest humor, which like the Anancy tales offered up "nation language," animated by trickster discourses and antics, yes, but also by rambunctious verbal performances that proceeded directly out of what Zora Neale Hurston called "mouth almighty," the voices of the common people. The redactors of Old Southwest humor and the Anancy tradition understood the power of these utterances. The parallel legacies of these traditions continue to sustain us and amuse us, and they need to be understood as sustaining streams of wisdom that have many underlying similarities.

NOTES

1. For a full description of Anansi's African avatar, see Barker and Sinclair, Herskovits and Herskovits, Meyerowitz, and Pelton.
2. An example of Anancy in human form: In one tale he is hired to herd sheep, gradually stealing them from his employer. He tricks Tiger into attending a ball in sheep's clothing, and then tells all present this is the thief, thereby securing the reward of two hundred pounds and the boss's daughter, while Tiger gets ten years in prison.
3. In this essay I am privileging the name "Anancy," but the trickster also appears as Nancy, Annancy, Ananse, or Anansi; all these names come from the Akan word for spider.
4. For an analysis of Native American trickster traditions and verbal performance, see Lowe, "Coyote Jokebook" (1994).
5. The Anancy tales have been collected and published for children. A notable example is Philip M. Sherlock's *Anansi the Spider Man: Jamaican Folk Tales* (1954), illustrated by Marcia Brown.
6. Since the early twentieth century, when Jekyll and Beckwith made their collections, Anancy tales have continued to be told, collected, and analyzed. These tales have also found new forms through the performances of new generations. While I have profited from the many fine insights Daryl Dance includes in the introduction to her collection of tales from Jamaica, I have not used the stories she found in the 1980s, as they are not as close to the time of the Old Southwest humorists as those collected by Jekyll and Beckwith.

7. For examples of this, see Jekyll, xxvi–xxvii, and Piacentino, 7.
8. We see this again in George Washington Harris's similar "Parson John Bullen's Lizards" (Inge and Piacentino, 75–80). The tradition of women using religion as a vehicle for sexual activity perhaps reached an apogee in Sister Bessie of Erskine Caldwell's *Tobacco Road* (1932), a twentieth-century classic clearly inspired by Old Southwest humor.
9. In *Huckleberry* Finn, the King and the Duke notoriously represent themselves as British relatives of the Wilks girls. Twain likely had in mind Simon Suggs passing himself off as General Thomas Witherspoon, a rich hog drover from Kentucky who appears in "Simon Fights the Tiger" (Cohen and Dillingham 217–26).
10. In Walter Jekyll's 1907 collection, *Jamaican Song and Story: Annancy Stories, Digging Songs, Ring Tune and Dancing Tunes*, the introduction by Alice Werner makes a link between Jamaica and US South by stating, "[O]ne is very glad to find Mr. Jekyll doing for Jamaica what Mr. Chandler Harris, *e.g.* has done for Georgia" (xii).
11. As always, Sut Lovingood and Simon Suggs are classic examples, but so is Billy Fishback in Kittrell Warren's *Life and Public Services of an Army Straggler* (excerpted in Cohen and Dillingham, 360–75).
12. Some examples may be found in Augustus Baldwin Longstreet's "The Horse Swap," Johnson Jones Hooper's "The Captain Attends a Camp-Meeting," and Charles F. M. Noland's "Pete Whetstone and the Mail Boy" (Inge and Piacentino 28–33; 103–111; 56, respectively).
13. See also Joyce Jonas's *Anancy in the Great House* (1990), which usefully examines mythic and folk dimensions of contemporary West Indian fiction.

WORKS CITED

Bakhtin, Mikhail. *Rabelais and His World*. Trans. Hélène Iswolsky. Bloomington: Indiana University Press, 1984. Print.

Barker, W. H., and Cecilia Sinclair. *West African Folk-Tales*. 1917; London: Sheldon Press, 1928. Print.

Barrett, Leonard. *The Sun and the Drum: African Roots in Jamaican Folk Tradition*. Kingston, Jamaica: Sangster's Book Stores, 1976. Print.

Beckwith, Martha Warren. *Black Roadways: A Study of Jamaican Folk Life*. Chapel Hill: University of North Carolina Press, 1929. Print.

———. *Jamaica Anansi Stories*. New York: American Folklore Society, 1924. Print.

Brathwaite, Edward Kamau. *History of the Voice: The Development of Nation Language in Anglophone Caribbean Poetry*. London, England: New Beacon Books, 1984. Print.

Brunvand, Jan Harold. *The Study of American Folklore: An Introduction*. New York: Norton, 1968. Print.

Cohen, Hennig, and William B. Dillingham. *Humor of the Old Southwest*. 2nd ed. Athens: University of Georgia Press, 1975. Print.

Courlander, Harold. *A Treasury of Afro-American Folklore*. New York: Crown, 1976. Print.

Crowley, Daniel J. *I Could Talk Old-Story Good: Creativity in Bahamian Folklore*. Berkeley: University of California Press, 1966. Print.

Dance, Daryl. *Folklore from Contemporary Jamaicans*. Knoxville: University of Tennessee Press, 1985. Print.

Evers, David H. *William Faulkner, William James, and the American Pragmatic Tradition*. Baton Rouge: Louisiana State University Press, 2008. Print.

Goveia, Elsa V. *A Study on the Historiography of the British West Indies to the End of the Nineteenth Century*. Washington, DC: Howard University Press, 1980. Print.

Herskovits, Frances, and Melville Herskovits. "Tales in Pidgin English from Ashanti." *Journal of American Folklore* 50 (1937): 60–62. Print.

Herskovits, Melville. Review of *Black Roadways*. *Journal of American Folklore* 43.169 (1930): 332–38. Print.

Hooper, Johnson Jones. "The Captain Attends a Camp Meeting." *Southern Frontier Humor: An Anthology*. Ed. M. Thomas Inge and Ed Piacentino. Columbia: University of Missouri Press, 2010. 103–111. Print.

Hughes, Langston. "Jokes Negroes Tell on Themselves." *Negro Digest* 9.8 (1951): 21–25.

Hurston, Zora Neale. *Tell My Horse: Voodoo and Life in Haiti and Jamaica*. 1938. New York: Harper & Row, 1990. Print.

Inge, M. Thomas, ed. *The Frontier Humorists: Critical Views*. Hamden, CT: Archon Books, 1975. Print.

Inge, M. Thomas, and Ed Piacentino, eds. *Southern Frontier Humor: An Anthology*. Columbia: University of Missouri Press, 2010. Print.

Jekyll, Walter. *Jamaican Song and Story*. 1907; rpt. New York: Dover, 1966. Print.

Jonas, Joyce. *Anancy in the Great House: Ways of Reading West Indian Fiction*. New York: Greenwood, 1990. Print.

Justus, James. *Fetching the Old Southwest: Humorous Writing from Longstreet to Twain*. Columbia: University of Missouri Press, 2004. Print.

Kerényi, Karl. "The Trickster in Relation to Greek Mythology." Trans. R. F. C. Hull. Commentary to Paul Radin, *The Trickster: A Study in American Indian Mythology*. New York: Schocken, 1972. 195–211. Print.

Kroeber, Karl. "Deconstructionist Criticism and American Indian Literatures." *Boundary 2: A Journal of Post Modern Literature and Culture*, 7.3 (1979): 73–89. Print.

Lowe, John. "Coyote's Jokebook: Humor in Native American Literature and Culture." *Dictionary of Native American Literature*. Ed. Andrew Wiget. New York: Garland, 1994. Print.

Meeker, Joseph. *The Comedy of Survival: Studies in Literary Ecology*. New York: Scribners, 1972. Print.

Meyerowitz, Eva Lewin-Richter. *The Akan of Ghana*. London, England: Faber and Faber, 1958. Print.

Pelton, Robert. *The Trickster in West Africa: A Study of Mythic Irony and Sacred Delight*. Berkeley: University of California Press, 1980. Print.

Piacentino, Ed. "Intersecting Paths: The Humor of the Old Southwest as Intertext." *The Enduring Legacy of Old Southwest Humor*. Ed. Ed Piacentino. Baton Rouge: Louisiana State University Press, 2006. 1–35. Print.

Salkey, Andrew. *Jamaica*. London, England: Hutchinson, 1973. Print.

Sherlock, Philip M. *Anansi the Spider Man: Jamaican Folk Tales.* New York: Thomas Y. Crowell, 1954. Print.

Vizenor, Gerald, ed. *Narrative Chance: Postmodern Discourse on Native American Indian Literatures.* 1989; Norman: University of Oklahoma Press, 1993. Print.

POSTMODERN HUMOR *ANTE LITTERAM*

Self-Reflexivity, Incongruity, and Dialect in George Washington Harris's Yarns Spun

MARK S. GRAYBILL

When Milton Rickels wrote, in his 1959 essay on George Washington Harris's imagery, that among the humorists of the Old Southwest, "Harris was among the least interesting in the variety of his plots, but at the same time the most intense in his vision, and the most self-conscious in his use of language" (173), he did not mean "self-conscious" in the postmodern sense. Rickels likely could not have imagined the self-reflexive extremes to which American writers of fiction such as John Barth, Thomas Pynchon, and Kurt Vonnegut—or a southern heir to Harris such as Barry Hannah—would push language in the coming years. Yet, though a product of a different time and culture, Harris's linguistic gymnastics do fit rather comfortably beside those of postmodern writers. Harris's self-reflexive discourse is most evident in the heavy inflection that characterizes the speech of his protagonist, Sut Lovingood. Ostensibly deployed for purposes of realism, the dialect in Harris's Lovingood tales becomes a sophisticated aesthetic experiment. The proliferation of punctuation and strange-looking combinations of letters on the page make it difficult to forget we are reading fiction, pointing up the elasticity of language, the incongruity between signifier and signified—and, of course, Harris's own intellect and ingenuity.

To what degree, though, does Harris's use of self-conscious, or self-reflexive language account for the humor in his stories? That is the question that this essay seeks to answer. It is one that has not much interested commentators on Harris's work. Indeed, even as well known an inheritor of the Old Southwestern style and disposition as Harry Crews may have avoided the Sut Lovingood stories because of Harris's adventures with dialect, as Frank W. Shelton surmises. Citing Crews's comment that for the writer trying to represent southern speech, "The first thing you wanna do is to get rid of what I call 'Uncle Remus' dialect, gross misspelling or phonetically spelling everything," Shelton laments that though Crews "would have recognized kindred spirits in Harris and Sut," he may, like countless other readers through the years, have been "put off by" Harris's extravagant representation of oral speech (124). As I will argue, however, a large part of the humor in Harris's tales lies in the exaggerated quality of the words themselves. In order to give this assertion appropriate context and complexity, however, it is advisable to consider Harris's language—both that employed by Sut, and by his more polished and circumspect interlocutor, George—in light not only of postmodern aesthetics, but also of the major theories of humor.

Theorizing (Old Southwestern) Humor: Superiority, Relief, and Incongruity

While those who study Harris's work (and that of his fellow Old Southwestern humorists) have occasionally touched upon the three major theories of humor, no one has fleshed them out in detail. This oversight is surprising, because each model offers considerable insight into Harris's comic modus operandi. At first blush, the superiority theory seems to define the humor of the Sut stories most accurately. Plato and Aristotle were the first to put forth the notion that laughter occurs when we witness something bad happen to someone we regard as inferior, though both regard this phenomenon with a good deal of ambivalence. The fullest early articulation of this idea of humor, though, comes from the seventeenth-century philosopher Thomas Hobbes, who posits that "[t]he passion of laughter is nothing else but *sudden glory* arising from some sudden *conception* of some *eminency* in ourselves, by *comparison* with the *infirmity* of others, or with our own infirmity" (46, italics original). Subsequent theorists have argued convincingly that this principle does not account for all humor. John Morreall, for example, observes that people "can laugh on being tickled, on seeing a magic trick, or on running into an old friend," all without the kind of "self-evaluation" necessary for feelings of superiority

(129). Yet the notion of superiority, and the displacement or subversion of it, arguably serves as the axis on which Old Southwestern humor turns. For example, the frame narrator convention found so frequently in these works sets up a series of hierarchies that conditions the laughter that they elicit. The intellectual, urbane "outsider" regards with superciliousness (sometimes overtly, sometimes tacitly) the hicks and yokels whom he meets and whose exploits he often conveys. The native "insiders" whom he looks down upon view him (again, at times clandestinely, at times more aggressively) as a learned but naïve dolt who is disconnected from reality—as what my mother, who grew up in the foothills of southwestern Virginia, would call an "educated idiot." And the reader takes in the exploits of both groups with amusement, pleasure, and perhaps, as Plato suggests, a mixture of malice and pain.

There is malice and pain aplenty in Sut's world, most of it perpetrated by him, and this is where the superiority theory seems most helpful in understanding Harris's humor. Whether Sut is breaking up a camp meeting and publicly humiliating Parson Bullen by compelling him to strip naked by releasing a batch of lizards up his pant leg, or reducing to physical pain and social chaos Sicily Burns's wedding reception with a crazed bull and hives of angry bees, or convincing the "niggar" Major and several other townsfolk that Major is a reanimated corpse possessed by the devil by dint of some red and white pain and amateur ventriloquism, he consistently glories in the misfortune of others. Indeed, in never failing to embrace his own identity as a "nat'ral born durn'd fool," Sut invites his learned friend, George, as well as the reader each to indulge their own sense of superiority over him. According to the superiority theory, Sut's antics qualify as humor, though, because their outlandishness and because the exaggerated quality of the language used to describe them (about which more later) distance and distort them, keeping us from taking them too seriously. Noel Polk suggests as much when he asks about the goings-on in "Hen Bailey's Reformation," "We are not actually expected to believe—are we?—that the mole . . . actually, literally, crawls up Hen's pantsleg and through his anus, chasing that lizard out of Hen's stomach, into his esophagus, and then out of his mouth?" (154). Aristotle explains that "[t]he ridiculous . . . is some error or ugliness that is painless and has not harmful effects," and offers as an example "the comic mask" of Greek drama, which "is ugly and distorted but causes no pain" (45). Sut and the world that he inhabits are certainly ugly, Polk suggests, but ultimately they cause no real pain.

Perhaps, though, this generalization overlooks the possibility, indeed the probability, that some readers do experience discomfort when faced with Sut's behavior—for example, his unabashed racism toward Major (and the deceased Cesar) in "Frustrating a Funeral." The relief theory of humor might help explain how we resolve this kind of reaction into laughter. The two thinkers most associated with this theory are the philosopher Herbert Spencer and the psychologist/philosopher/literary critic Sigmund Freud. Their perspectives, though different in detail, both hold "the view that humorous laughter is a manifestation of the release of nervous excitement or emotional tension" (Bardon 470). Perhaps more than any of his contemporaries, Harris demonstrates the ability to build up tension within his reader, until he or she must release it in the physical (and mental) action of laughing. As many perceptive readers of Sut's yarns have noted, they frequently pulse with sexual energy; his very surname is our first hint. Milton Rickels observes that Sut's "philosophy insists on the joy of sex" (118), as this famous statement in "Sicily Burns's Wedding" illustrates: "Men wer made a-purpus jis tu eat, drink, an' fur stayin awake in the yearly part ove the nites: an' wimen wer made tu cook the vittils, mix the sperits, an' help the men du the stayin awake" (Harris 88). William Lenz deftly explains how Sut projects his erotic desires onto the widows in "Mrs. Yardley's Quilting," how he describes them using "animal imagery [that] emphasizes . . . [their] earthiness and the type of skin-to-skin contact he anticipates." Lenz argues that "the escalating accumulation of heated details—from their abject submission to their 'naik-veins a-throbbin'"—suggests "frustration rather than consummation" (192). Lenz's Sut seems much more repressed than Rickels's, but what is most critical to understanding the humor in the sexually charged descriptions is that they create a reservoir of tension within the reader—not necessarily sexual tension, but a combination of intellectual and emotional tension which, if Spencer, Freud, and their followers are correct, is best relieved through laughter at key points in the reading process.

The opening of "Mrs. Yardley's Quilting" might provide a better illustration of how Harris steadily builds up tension—again, a feeling that need not have anything to do with sex. Indeed, the topic of Sut and George's conversation is not eros, but thanatos:

"THAR'S one durn'd nasty muddy job, an' I is jis' glad enuf tu take a ho'n ur two, on the straingth ove hit."

"What have you been doing, Sut?"

"Helpin tu salt ole Missis Yardley down."

"What do you mean by that?"

"Fixin her fur rotten comfurtably, kiverin her up wif sile, tu keep the buzzards frum cheatin the wurms."

"Oh, you have been helping to bury a woman." (134)

For the reader who can decipher the dialect without too much difficulty, the punch line here—the point at which the feeling of discomfort likely dissipates into laughter—is Sut's graphic, matter-of-fact, some might say callous, characterization of interment as a necessity "tu keep the buzzards frum cheatin the wurms." For the reader who finds Sut's heavy accent more problematic, George's "translation" in more polite language releases the pent-up energy—though for this type of reader, that energy may be caused as much by cognitive stress as by discomfort over Sut's inappropriate verbal treatment of the deceased.

What of that dialect, though? Given its ubiquity in every Sut Lovingood yarn, it must contribute significantly to the humor. I would argue that the incongruity theory best illuminates this aspect of Harris's comic genius. This theory is associated most with Immanuel Kant and Arthur Schopenhauer, who, like Spencer and Freud, conceive of incongruity in similar but not identical ways. The incongruity paradigm has been articulated more recently and more economically by John Morreall as humor that arises out of "conflict between something we perceive, remember, or imagine, on the one hand, and our conceptual patterns with their attendant expectations, on the other" (189). One can begin to imagine the importance of language, which inevitably shapes our conceptual patterns, to such an explanation of humor. Jerry Palmer, a leading humor theorist, cites an example of humorous incongruity in Aristotle that demonstrates the centrality of words to comic incongruity: "In the *Rhetoric* [Aristotle] indicates that an effective device, which may result in laughter, is to set up a particular expectation in the audience, and then to contradict or subvert it: 'He walked, and under his feet were sores,' where the audience would expect something like 'stones' as the last word'" (94). Though Palmer does not comment on it, the humor in Aristotle's example depends heavily on the substitution of one word for another.

Many Harris scholars have already noted the way in which Sut's imagery and metaphors rely on incongruity, even if they have not explicitly discussed such figures of speech in terms of theory. In one of the earliest twentieth-century discussions of Harris's work, Walter Blair notices that "[r]ecited in Sut's drawl," numerous memorable episodes "contrast amusingly with the rhetorical framework language"—that is, George's commentary. Blair continues:

> Harris seemed to realize the possibilities of ludicrous antithesis in language, for he liked to put Sut's talk alongside of flowery passages or of learned language in which big words predominated. Humorous, too, is the contrast between the circumstances under which Sut tells his tale and the harrowing scenes he describes. (89)

While Blair considerably overstates the number of "flowery passages" in the yarns, his overall point is well taken. Consider the "ludicrous antithesis in language" present in this celebrated passage from "Old Burns's Bull-Ride":

> Jis' look at me! Did yu ever see sich a sampil ove a human afore? I feels like I'd be glad *tu be* dead, only I'se feard ove the dyin. I don't keer fur herearter, fur hits onpossibil fur me tu hev ara soul. Who ever seed a soul in jis' sich a rack heap ove bones an' rags es this? I's nuffin but sum new-fangil'd sort ove beas', a sorter cross atween a crazy ole monkey an' a durn'd wore-out hominy-mill. (106–7)

The passage draws its humor largely from an incongruity of concept, as Sut describes himself as part monkey, part (dilapidated and useless) machine. But in addition to this bizarre metaphor—which Shelley Armitage labels an example of "fabulation" (230)—what catches the reader's eye are the exaggerated, phonetically rendered clusters of symbols that paradoxically are and are not English. Such a situation reminds me of Jerry Palmer's analysis of a joke that exemplifies the incongruity thesis: "'Doctor, come at once! Our baby swallowed a fountain pen! 'I'll be right over. What are you doing in the meantime?' 'Using a pencil.'" Palmer argues that this incongruity requires "a bifurcated logical process, which leads the listener to judge that the state of affairs portrayed is simultaneously highly implausible and just a little bit plausible" (95–96). This "logic of the absurd," as Palmer calls it (96), saturates Sut's narration, both at the conceptual level and at the level of the written word, the sign. That the proudly uneducated and ever-vital Sut, a man of action rather than words, should use this flamboyant and barely sensible verbiage to express existential angst only deepens the humorous incongruity. While there is evidence that Harris was conservative in his politics and his religion, Sut's yarns make it clear that Harris was radical in his art, and his experimentations with language suggest interesting parallels with the postmodern writers who came upon the literary scene approximately a century after his death.

Incongruity, Self-Reflexity, and the Postmodern Aesthetic

Armitage's invocation of "fabulation," a term coined by Robert Scholes, has already suggested Harris's surprising kinship with postmodernist authors. Scholes defines fabulation as "fiction that offers us a world clearly and radically discontinuous from the one we know, yet returns to confront that known world in some cognitive way" (61). Though Harris is often celebrated for his sharp-eyed, hardnosed realism, the language in which he has Sut speak continually defamiliarizes the environment, especially the social milieu through which he rampages. Works of fabulation

> violate, in various ways, standard novelistic [or narrative] expectations by drastic . . . experiments with subject matter, form, style, temporal sequence, and fusions of the everyday, the fantastic, the mythical, and the nightmarish, in renderings that blur traditional distinctions between what is serious or trivial, horrible or ludicrous, tragic or comic. (Abrahams and Harpham 232)

While it would be a stretch to say that every item on in this list of aesthetic strategies is illustrative of Harris's work, his experimentation with style is undeniable, as is the disharmonious yet pleasurable tone described in the last clause. Though critics rarely acknowledge as much with explicit reference to humor theory, to the extent that postmodern fiction is funny, I would argue that it often is, the incongruity paradigm often providing the best explanation for why it is.

Such is the case with metafiction or self-reflexive fiction, arguably the dominant, most representative genre of postmodern narrative. According to Patricia Waugh, "Metafiction is a term given to fictional writing which self-consciously and systematically draws attention to its status as an artifact in order to pose questions about the relationship between fiction and reality" (2). While I and many other critics prefer the term self-reflexive, because it is broader and relaxes the expectations created by Waugh's use of the word "systematically," this definition provides a useful starting point in discussing the humor in postmodern fiction generally and Harris's surprisingly prescient work specifically. Self-reflexivity thrives on incongruity; incongruity is its lifeblood. By drawing attention to the fact that it is fiction, incongruity violates our expectations of reality—or the literary equivalent, realism—and exploits, to quote Morreall again, the inevitable "conflict between something we perceive, remember, or imagine, on the one hand, and our conceptual patterns with their attendant expectations, on the other." As has been demonstrated, we often laugh at Sut not because we can relate readily to the world he describes, but because his metaphors and his dialect flamboyantly distort that world. His language allows us the detachment that humor almost always requires—a detachment famously acknowledged by Henri Bergson in his essay on "Laughter":

> Indifference is [humor's] natural environment, for laughter has no greater foe than emotion. I do not mean that we could not laugh at a person who inspires us with great pity, for instance, or even with affection, but in such a case we must, for the moment, put our affection out of court and impose silence upon our pity. . . . To produce the whole of its effect, then, the comic demands something like a momentary anesthesia of the heart. Its appeal is to intelligence, pure and simple. (215)

When we are made aware that something that pretends to be real is not—as I think we are time and again in Sut's narration—such "momentary anesthesia of the heart" occurs much more easily.

The notion that Harris employs a kind of pre-postmodern self-reflexivity might seem a stretch to some. But considering the five passages with which Waugh opens her book—one each by Laurence Sterne, B. S. Johnson, Ronald Sukenick, Donald Barthelme, and John Fowles—and her subsequent discussion of them, it becomes clear to me how much Harris's mode of humor overlaps with these writers' wit. Waugh's analysis could be applied, nearly whole, to the Lovingood yarns. Although each excerpt Waugh highlights bears the unique style and vision of its author, each demonstrates at least

> two or three of the following: a celebration of the power of the creative imagination together with an uncertainty about the validity of its representations; an extreme self-consciousness about language, literary form and the act of writing fiction; a pervasive insecurity about the relationship of fiction to reality; a parodic, playful, excessive or deceptively naïve style of writing. (2)

Shortly, I will discuss in detail the way that Harris's comic language rides the tense boundary between "creative imagination" and "uncertainty about the validity of its representations," and between belief in "literary form" and "a pervasive insecurity about the relationship" of that form to reality. For the moment, though, the last set of qualities Waugh lays out is the most immediately intriguing vis-à-vis Harris's fiction. The "style" of that fiction is "parodic" in its exaggeration of normal, civilized discourse, playful in its spirited commitment to freedom of act and expression (in a later chapter, Waugh elaborates on the idea that metafictional play stems from the quest for freedom, from an "emphasis on the importance of discovering fresh combinations in probability and risk" [42], a statement that recalls both Harris's and Sut's attitudes), and simultaneously "excessive" and "deceptively naïve" in its style, owing to Sut's maniacally creative yet raw and untutored language.

Again, Harris's use of dialect is crucial here. As mentioned earlier, numerous critics and readers have been put off by it. Acting on the discomfort expressed by Carvel Collins and others, Brom Weber famously tried to "clean up" the dialect in his 1954 edition of the yarns. In his essay defending that and other editorial decisions, Weber writes,

> With all due respect to Harris' art, his dialect is one of its least valuable achievements. Its faults include inconsistent misspellings for humorous effect as well as rendition of dialect terms in a confusing and unsystematic variety of forms. A prime requisite for first-person narration, which Sut employs is that the narrator use only one language—his own—rather than several languages interchangeably. (112–13)

Looking back on these comments through the prism of postmodern aesthetics generally and Mikhail Bakhtin's ideas about heteroglossia and dialogism specifically, Weber's complaint seems stuffy and a little naïve. Clearly grounded in realist assumptions about fiction, Weber's perspective is rather obviously not up to the challenge posed by Harris's art, which is not nearly as committed to realism as is often supposed. But still more contemporary critics have rejected Harris's use of dialect. In an essay that traces Harris's influence on William Faulkner's creation of Jason Compson in *The Sound and the Fury*, for example, Stephen M. Ross praises Harris's "brilliance and consistency of image" and the "constant motion" of his language, but finds his use of "eye-dialect" to be "cumbersome" (280–81). While Ross is correct about the energy and inventiveness of Sut's language and its influence on Faulkner, he misses the virtuoso humor on display in the "eye-dialect." Ross's term even suggests the reflexive character of Harris's writing, as it points to the act of a person reading the words on the page, of becoming aware of the aesthetic, crafted properties of the language, if he or she slows down enough to ponder them. The opening of "Parson John Bullen's Lizards" serves as a good illustration. The first thing the reader sees, of course, is the poster offering a reward for Sut, so that justice may be meted out for his disruptive behavior in church:

> AIT ($8) DULLARS REW-ARD.
> 'TENSHUN BELEVERS AND KONSTABLES! KETCH 'IM!KETCH 'IM!
>
> THIS kash wil be pade in korn, ur uther projuce, tu be kolected at ur about nex camp meetin, *ur thararter*, by eny wun what ketches him, fur the karkus ove a sartin wun SUT LOVINGOOD, dead ur alive, ur ailin, an' safely giv over tu the purtectin care ove Parson

John Bullin, ur lef' well tied, at Squire Mackjunkins, fur the raisin ove the devil pussonely, an' permiskusly discumfurtin the wimen very powerful, an' skeerin ove folks generly a heap, an' bustin up a promisin, big warm meetin, an' a makin the wickid larf, an' wus, an' wus, insultin ove the passun orful.

Test, JEHU WETHERO.

Sined by me,

JOHN BULLEN, the passun (48)

Right next to the most bombastically humorous touches here—for example, the ridiculous size of Bullen's self-righteous indignation, underscored in his repetition of "an' wus" in speaking of his maltreatment by Sut—is the crucial detail, at first easily overlooked, that the document is rendered in exactly the same distorted, exaggerated version of backwoods speech.

As the incongruity theory makes clear, humor works by violating our expectations, and here, Harris plays with the reader's preconception of a difference between the sloppiness of speech and the formality of writing. Bullen's notice provides Harris with an especially potent comic opportunity, because while the reader may be seduced by the illusion that Sut is speaking throughout his tales (though, again, Harris goes to great lengths to disrupt that illusion), Bullen's words are *supposed* to be writing. Thus, were Bullen's words presented as actual speech, they would be funny—but not nearly as funny as they are when seen on the page, in writing, on a document that Harris asks us to envision. Harris emphasizes the outrageousness of Bullen's writing by contrasting it immediately with the smoothness of George, the frame-narrator, who registers his curiosity about the sign's "bloodthirsty spirit, its style, and above all, its chirography" (376). The final word here, which means penmanship, exemplifies George's advanced vocabulary, but also reminds us again that despite all evidence to the contrary, Bullen has actually *written* these exotic clusters of sound.

As Ed Piacentino observes, "antebellum southern humor . . . [is] a mode especially known for its orality" (24). Piacentino explains, though, that such orality has become textualized, indeed intertextualized, and that this process accounts for its continuing power in the culture. In Harris's case, I would argue, speech is only half the story. As Parson Bullen's wanted poster demonstrates, much of the humor arises out of the discrepancy, the tension, the incongruity between the oral and the symbolic. The dialect used primarily by Sut—and by other local figures such as Bullen as well—will not let the reader forget about that incongruity, and Harris continually finds new ways to play it up. The inconsistency noted by Weber should probably be read as intentional, as Harris wants to keep his experiments with language fresh. If the reader becomes too comfortable, and the fictionalized written speech of his characters becomes too familiar, the author risks losing his comic edge. Like all great, edgy humor, Harris's addresses some serious matters. Specifically, as Waugh would put it, it raises questions about the "relationship between fiction and reality," and especially about the potential discord between language, (especially literature) and the world to which it is supposed to refer.

"The Hole Ove Hit": Sut's Self-Reflexive Musings on Language and Literature

Earlier, I briefly discussed the exchange between Sut and George that opens "Mrs. Yardley's Quilting" as an example of the way Harris builds tension that must be relieved through laughter, suggesting that release arrives with the reader's realization that Sut is colorfully describing Mrs. Yardley's burial. Between this opening and the rest of his tale proper, though, Sut reflects on how well, compared to him, George is served by words. In response to George's statement, "Oh, you have been helping to bury a woman," Sut exclaims, "That's hit, by golly! Now why the devil can't I 'splain mysef like yu? I ladles out my words at randum, like a calf kickin at yaller-jackids; yu jis' rolls em out tu the pint, like a feller a-layin bricks every one fits. How is it that bricks fits so clost enyhow? Rocks won't ni du hit" (134). The first metaphor that Sut employs to describe his unimpressive word-smithing abilities is typical in its wonderful dissonance, as it moves at breakneck speed from the calm image of the cook in the kitchen to the animal anarchy of the barnyard. The wall building metaphor that follows, though more logical, similarly underscores the jagged, always-about-to-collapse nature of Sut's narration, as opposed to George's regular, structurally sound language. Of course, as countless critics have pointed out, one of the most unique aspects of Harris's brand of Old Southwestern storytelling is the way the bumpkin insider's narration subsumes that of the learned outsider. As a speaker, George disappears for long stretches, leaving Sut's voice in control. Harris seems to be telling his reader, "What I'm constructing here will be ugly—and hilariously so." The passage serves as one of the cleverest moments of self-reflexivity in the entire collection of Lovingood tales.

It also bespeaks, though, a certain apprehension about the referential capacity of language. Later in the story, Sut expresses that anxiety more directly. Describing the kick in the rear he receives from Mr. Yardley when he tries to kiss Yardley's daughter, Sut interrupts the tale to ask, "George, wer yu ever ontu yer hans an' knees, an' let a hell-tarin big, mad ram, wif a ten-yard run, but yu yearnis'ly, jis' onst, right squar ontu the pint ove yer back-bone?" Bewildered by the question, George replies that he has not, and Sut responds, "I wanted tu know ef yu cud hev a realizin' noshun ove my shock. Hits scarcely worth while tu try tu make yu onderstan the case by words only, onless yu hev been tetched in that way" (146–47). Sut, again, is a man of action, one who trusts experience over words. Yet he is also a storyteller, the supposedly secondary narrator who has somehow usurped George's role as the primary voice, and thus relies on language to relate his experiences and establish his very identity. His self-consciousness, which I suspect reflects that of his creator, strikes one as particularly modern—or, as I have been suggesting here, as presciently postmodern. As David Reynolds notes in *Beneath the American Renaissance*, many critics have contended "that beneath the sparkling surface of Harris's humor lurks a profound skepticism" regarding the "mainstream values" of American culture (455). One senses a similar attitude toward language itself—especially literary language—on the part of Harris and his alter ego.

Nowhere is Harris's view of language clearer than in the preface to *Sut Lovingood: Yarns*, which parodies several literary and publishing conventions in a manner that would make any postmodern novelist proud. Harris clearly has fun with the conceit that he, "George," serves as scribe for the illiterate Sut—much the same way that William Faulkner would do, some seventy years later, in his obscure story, "Afternoon of a Cow." That specimen of Old Southwest-inspired absurdity reveals that a man named "Earnest V. Trueblood" has had the responsibility of committing to paper Faulkner's groundbreaking fiction. In his preface, Sut laments, "I jis' tell yu now, I don't like the idear ove yu writin a perduckshun, an' me a-findin the brains." Though a subsequent comment that "[u]sin ether men's brains is es lawful es usin thar plunder, an' jis' es common" suggests that Harris is alluding to the widespread problem of book piracy (ix), he also comically insinuates that despite his lack of facility with standard English, Sut is the "brains" behind this "perdukshun." Though he proclaims himself "a orthur" now (x), Sut several times underscores his anxiety about not being able to write, and about the written word's power as social currency, as in the following excerpt:

> Sumtimes, George, I wishes I cud read an' write, jis' a littil; but then hits bes' es hit am, fur ove all the fools the worild hes tu contend wif, the edicated wuns am the worst; they breeds ni ontu all the devilment a-gwine on. But I wer a-thinkin, ef I cud write mysef, hit wud then *raley* been my book. (ix)

Sut's disdain for "edicated" people, a theme that runs through his tales, is perhaps intensified by his supposed reliance on George to help write those tales. Interesting, too, is the notion of writing as the devil's work. Sut probably suspects that sophisticated use of language makes it easier to perpetrate duplicity. The written word would be particularly dangerous, as it is in a sense even further removed from the real than oral speech.

Sut's suspicion of writing comes through most colorfully, and hilariously, in his initial response to George's decree that his book "must have a preface."

> "[W]hat's the use of . . . [it], in pint ove good sense?" he asks. "Smells tu me sorter like adurned humbug, the hole ove hit—a littil like cuttin ove the Ten Cummandmints intu the rine ove a warter-million; hits jist slashed open an' the inside et outen hit, the rine an' the cummandmints broke all tu pieces an' flung tu the hogs, an' never tho't ove onst—them, nur the 'tarnil fool what cut em thar" (ix).

Sut's first metaphor of the book establishes the special brand of incongruity that he will bring to his humorous metaphors. Who would ever conceive of carving the Ten Commandments into a watermelon? On the most superficial level, Sut makes the well-founded observation that people often do not read prefaces, preferring instead to get quickly to the meat of the book. Sut's doubts about the entire endeavor of writing stories runs deeper, however, as his phrase "the hole ove hit" suggests. Although it is unlikely that Harris intended for "hole" to be a pun, in this case the phonetic spelling creates a deliciously overdetermined moment of self-reflexivity: The "whole" book is a "humbug"—that is, a hoax, a deception. Where the reader expects to find the truth, he finds lies, and where he seeks substance—the kind of capital-T truth associated with religious discourse (say, the Ten Commandments)—he finds absence, the "the inside et outen it," leaving a hole. From Harris's point of view as the author, this description makes sense because Sut and his (mis)adventures, though they may have been inspired by a contemporary of Harris's named Sut Miller (McClary 72–73), are the products of a fecund imagination, as every strange word, phrase, and metaphor reminds us. In an age when fiction was still regarded in some quarters as deleterious to society because of its essential factitiousness, perhaps Harris is slyly acknowledging, in a way that is at once celebratory and derisive, its status as an artful prevarication.

Discussing the comic American metafiction that came to prominence in the decades after World War II, Daniel Green suggests that the humor of this genre emerges from a "radical skepticism [that] informs not merely the epistemology but also the aesthetic assumptions of the novel in its most provocative forms" (242). Writers such as Robert Coover, John Barth, and Gilbert Sorrentino recognized the self-reflexive approach as "a natural extension of the literary and cultural energies of the late 1960s and early 1970s, implicitly asking why the corrosive laughter being directed at other institutions and conventions should not additionally be directed at the governing conventions of fiction as well" (238). Although this skepticism and its concomitant self-reflexive impulse proliferate in postmodern writing more than in that of previous eras, they have been around for ages, as Green acknowledges. He mentions *Don Quixote* and *Tristram Shandy*, two works often regarded as being precociously postmodern, pointing to Sterne's novel especially as "a model of literary comedy that takes the 'literary' itself as a practice in need of comic interrogation" (243).

Harris's Sut Lovingood tales, I would argue, could also serve as such a model. As David Reynolds thesis in *Beneath the American Renaissance* suggests, the tales come out of an era and a region with subversive energies that rival those of the 1960s and 1970s. Sylvia J. Cook judiciously observes that Harris and his fellow humorists "raised, in their exaggerated characterizations and shocking situations, the possibility that the frontier world was not wholly amenable to the operations of right reason and the controls of Christianity" (53). In response to this world, Harris's tales exhibit a "radical skepticism" that exploits the incongruity between speech and writing, popular and elitist culture—and especially truth and fiction—to raise vexing questions even as they generate laughs. Harris's use of dialect, however, sets his work apart from other examples of both Old Southwestern humor and self-reflexive fiction. Sut Lovingood is Harris's version of a traditional character type, identified by Green (with help from Bakhtin) as "the jokester," who can appear variously as a "rogue," a "fool," and/or a "clown." As Green argues in his analysis of Sorrentino's *Mulligan Stew*, "'[C]haracter [is] inseparable from the language in which it is conveyed. Character, like speech in Derrida's analysis, does not precede or exceed writing, but emerges from it" (246). Throughout his yarns, Harris takes great advantage of "character," which means both a written or engraved mark and the personality of a human being. Sut Lovingood's outrageous rhetorical figures, filtered through a dialect so idiosyncratic it sometimes seems hieroglyphic, somehow make him simultaneously a unique, engaging person and a series of letters and symbols that draw attention to his textuality. To paraphrase Jerry Palmer's insight about incongruous humor, we find this joke(ster) to be highly implausible and just a little bit plausible—and we laugh.

WORKS CITED

Abrams, M. H., and Geoffrey Galt Harpham. *A Glossary of Literary Terms*. Ninth edition. N.P.: Wadsworth Cengage Learning, 2009. Print.

Aristotle. "Poetics." Trans. Leon Golden. *The Critical Tradition: Classic Texts and Contemporary Trends*. Ed. David H. Richter. New York: St. Martin's, 1989. 42–65. Print.

Armitage, Shelley. "Seeing Sutly: Visual and Verbal Play in the Work of George Washington Harris." *Sut Lovingood's Nat'ral Born Yarnspinner: Essays on George Washington* Harris. Ed. James E. Caron and M. Thomas Inge. Tuscaloosa: University of Alabama Press, 1996. 228–45. Print.

Bardon, Adrian. "The Philosophy of Humor." *Comedy: A Geographic and Historical Guide*. Vol. 2. Ed. Maurice Charney. Westport, CT: Praeger, 2005. 462–76. Print.

Bergson, Henri. "Laughter." *Comedy: Plays, Theory, and Criticism*. Ed. Marvin Felheim. New York: Harcourt, Brace & World, 1962. 214–29. Print.

Blair, Walter. "George Washington Harris." Caron and Inge 87–93. Print.

Caron, James E., and M. Thomas Inge. *Sut Lovingood's Nat'ral Born Yarnspinner: Essays on George Washington Harris*. Tuscaloosa: University of Alabama Press, 1996. Print.

Cook, Sylvia J. "Camp Meetings, Comedy, and Erskine Caldwell: From the Preposterous to the Absurd." *The Enduring Legacy of Old Southwest* Humor. Ed. Ed Piacentino. Baton Rouge: Louisiana State University Press, 2006. 52–72. Print.

Green, Daniel. "'Terribly Bookish': Mulligan Stew and the Comedy of Self-Reflexivity." *Critique* 41.3 (2000): 327–49. Print.

Harris, George Washington. *Sut Lovingood: Yarns Spun by a "Nat'ral Born Durn'd Fool," Warped and Wove for Public Wear*. Electronic edition. New York: Dick & Fitzgerald, 1867. http://docsouth.unc.edu/southlit/harrisg/menu.html. Web.

Hobbes, Thomas. *The English Works of Thomas Hobbes of Malmesbury*. Vol. 4. Ed. Sir William Molesworth. London, England: John Bohn, 1840. Print.

Lenz, William E. "Sensuality, Revenge, and Freedom: Women in *Sut Lovingood. Yarns Spun by a Nat'ral Born Durn'd Fool*'." Caron and Inge 190–99. Print.

McClary, Ben Harris. "The Real Sut." Caron and Inge 72–73. Print.

Morreall, John, ed. *The Philosophy of Laughter and Humor*. Albany: State University of New York Press, 1987. Print.

Palmer, Jerry. *Taking Humour Seriously*. London, England: Routledge, 1994. Print.

Piacentino, Ed, ed. *The Enduring Legacy of Old Southwest Humor*. Baton Rouge: Louisiana State University Press, 2006. Print.

Piacentino, Ed. "Intersecting Paths: The Humor of the Old Southwest as Intertext." Piacentino, *The Enduring Legacy of Old Southwest Humor*. 1–38.

Polk, Noel. "The Blind Bull, Human Nature: Sut Lovingood and the Damned Human Race." Caron and Inge 148–75. Print.

Reynolds, David S. *Beneath the American Renaissance: The Subversive Imagination in the Age of Emerson and Melville*. New York: Alfred A. Knopf, 1988. Print.

Rickels, Milton. "The Imagery of George Washington Harris." *American Literature* 31.2 (1959): 173–87. Print.

———. "The Fool as Point of View." Caron and Inge 115–25. Print.

Ross, Stephen M. "Jason Compson and Sut Lovingood: Southwestern Humor as Stream of Consciousness." *Studies in the Novel* 8 (1976): 278–90. Print.

Scholes, Robert. *Structural Fabulation: An Essay on Fiction of the Future*. Notre Dame, IN: Notre Dame University Press, 1975. Print.

Shelton, Frank W. "George Washington Harris and Harry Crews." Piacentino 119–30. Print.

Waugh, Patricia. *Metafiction*. New York: Routledge, 1984. Print.

Weber, Brom. "A Note on Edmund Wilson and George Washington Harris." Caron and Inge 108–14. Print.

THE REAL BIG KILL

Authenticity, Ecology, and Narrative in Southern Frontier Humor

JAMES E. BISHOP

ONCE OF THE RICHEST TRADITIONS WITHIN THE GENRE OF OLD Southwest humor is the embellished story of the hunt, emphasizing the resourcefulness, tenacity, and self-reliance of the nineteenth-century American frontiersman. In recounting these stories, southern humorists, taken as a group, depict a veritable massacre of deer, bears, bison, raccoons, wolves, mountain lions, and a plethora of game bird and fish species, many of which faced extinction by the turn of the twentieth century. That the widespread slaughter of animals—what I term the "big kill" in this essay—was an object of humor for nineteenth-century American readers and writers points to several important questions about writers of southern frontier humor and their audiences. To what extent are these stories Americanized versions of European storytelling traditions, and in what ways are they products of the American frontier and the values of the people who lived there? What assumptions about nature were writers of Old Southwest humor making when they wrote these wildly exaggerated hunting stories, and why would these stories have been appealing to their audiences? What can these assumptions tell us about nineteenth-century Americans' attitudes toward the frontier and the natural world?

Writers of southern frontier humor were not the first to exaggerate in their telling of hunting stories. Roman and Greek epics are interspersed with hunting tales meant to illustrate the bravery, skill, and manliness of their heroes. *Beowulf* is, in essence, a hunting yarn. A more direct influence on Old Southwestern humor is *Baron Münchhausen's Narrative of His Marvelous Travels and Campaigns* (1785), by German scientist and tall tale writer Rudolph Raspe. A number of nineteenth-century southern frontier tales appear to be Americanizations of Raspe's hyperbolic hunting stories. That Raspe's tall tales likely had an important influence on writers of American Southwest humor is a point thoroughly elucidated in Walter

Blair's 1984 essay, "A German Connection: Raspe's Baron Munchausen." Blair shows that Raspe's volume was popular in the United States, and he documents the numerous references to Münchhausen in popular American publications that seem to take for granted readers' general familiarity with Münchhausen. In 1822–23, for instance, traveling British comedian Charles Mathews impersonated a character named Major Longbow, who was characterized in both newspaper reports and the show's program as "a modern Munchausen" (Blair 126). Numerous other accounts throughout the nineteenth and early twentieth centuries assumed American awareness of the Münchhausen stories.[1]

Surely the Baron Münchhausen stories were humorous to their original audiences because they placed their intrepid protagonist in unlikely, extravagant, and improbable situations that he overcomes with a combination of guile, panache, and spectacularly good luck. How, then, could the trope of the "big kill" induce laughter in an American context where large-scale destruction of wildlife was neither unlikely nor improbable? Three factors offer the most likely explanations. First, nineteenth-century Americans were astoundingly—and often willfully—oblivious to the widespread devastation of wildlife in the American West, partly because most Americans had never seen the West or witnessed its destruction. Second, frontier ideology mandated "taming" the wilderness to make way for westward expansion. Third, to the extent that Americans witnessed and recognized the environmental destruction that was occurring, the use of self-deprecating humor may have eased their guilt. Southern frontier humor is not, of course, responsible for perpetuating the ideology of environmental devastation that dominated nineteenth-century American policy and practice, but it did play a role in enabling and ennobling it.

Wild exaggeration and whimsical imagination are the qualities for which Raspe's Baron Münchhausen stories were best known when they appeared and for which they are still remembered.[2] Raspe's stories, based loosely upon the life of German nobleman Karl Friedrich Hieronymus, Freiherr von Münchhausen (known as Baron Münchausen or Münchhausen in English), a famous recounter of tall tales. A number of Raspe's Baron Münchhausen tales concern his abilities as a hunter. In one story, for instance, Münchhausen sees through his bedroom window a flock of wild ducks on a nearby pond. He grabs his gun from the corner, runs downstairs, and on his way out of the house accidentally knocks his head against the doorframe. "Fire flew out of my eyes," he recounts, "but it did not prevent my intention" (43). Arriving within firing range of the ducks, Münchhausen discovers that the flint has been dislodged from his gun. The baron, however, improvises: "I presently remembered the effect [the shock of the blow against the doorpost] had on my eyes, therefore opened the pan, leveled my piece against the wild fowls, and my fist against one of my eyes" (44). With the single shot Münchhausen kills "fifty brace of ducks, twenty widgeons, and three couple of teals" (44). Upon completing this portion of the tale, Münchhausen proclaims with endearing understatement, "Presence of mind is the soul of manly exercises" (44).

While offering readers a laugh at Münchhausen's hilariously inventive approach to hunting, Raspe effectively satirizes Enlightenment ideals that privileged science and reason as ways for understanding the world and solving problems. Münchhausen's blazing eye defies all reasonable scientific interpretation. Instead, Raspe affirms what Münchhausen calls "presence of mind," which in this context means a combination of spontaneity, ingenuity, guile, humor, and above all, imagination. It's a useful metaphor, in fact, for the Romantic ideals that had begun to supplant the Age of Enlightenment within European art, literature, and philosophy. As Münchhausen himself points out, "Chance and good luck" (not faith, science, or reason) "often correct our mistakes" (44). Beneath Raspe's fanciful yarn spinning, then, lies a biting satire on the intellectual culture that prevailed in Germany and across Europe during his lifetime. Münchhausen's hunting success happens precisely because of his insistence upon irrational notions rejected by Enlightenment-era scientific rationalism.

When the Baron Münchhausen hunting stories made their way across the Atlantic and were assimilated by American writers and audiences, however, they adopted a different set of meanings, as Americans were developing relationships with their natural environment very different from those of their European kin. Southern frontier writers adapted the Münchhausen pattern to a narrative mode in which the values underpinning the humor in these tales assume conceptions of egalitarianism that resonated with white Americans. By the end of the eighteenth century, in most parts of Europe the upper class owned exclusive rights to hunt in feudal or national territory, so hunting became the domain of elites such as Baron Münchhausen.[3] As hunting became more a luxury than a necessity, the stylized pursuit of it came to be seen by Americans as an effete, upper-class enterprise. Americans, by contrast, saw subsistence hunting as a means of establishing one's worth as a man. Michael Oriard explains, "[E]verything was up for grabs along the frontier—not only were wealth and status there to be won by the most enterprising, rather than the best-born individuals, but the entire social order was to be determined by those who could most effectively impose their will" (6). Any man, regardless of his social status or material wealth, could enjoy success hunting on the American frontier if he possessed the requisite patience, skill, strength, and stamina. According to Annette Kolodny, "In an age that looked with suspicion on the phenomenal fortunes apparently made overnight by factory and mill owners, the west suggested an escape from superfluity, an escape from wealth gained only by investment, and an escape from the exploited labor of the poor" (168). Out of this ideology of self-made frontier manhood grew a rich storytelling tradition designed, in part, to reinforce these egalitarian ideals.

The template for hunting yarns, as expressed through southern frontier humor, is articulated well in William Gilmore Simms's short story "How Sharp Snaffles Got His Capital and Wife." As Simms's narrator explains,

> The hunter who actually inclines to exaggeration is . . . privileged to deal in all the extravagances of invention; nay, he is *required* to do so! To be literal, or confine himself to the bald and naked truth, is not only discreditable, but a *finable* offense! He is, in such a case, made to swallow a long, strong, and difficult potation! He can not be too extravagant in his incidents; but he is also required to exhibit a certain degree of *art*, in their use; and he thus frequently rises into a certain realm of fiction, the ingenuities of which are made to compensate for the exaggerations. (240)

These guidelines articulated by Simms's narrator serve as a metaphor for the way that hunting tales are told through southern frontier writing generally. The stories might be based in truth, but they generally must have some element of exaggeration or fanciful imagery in order to fit effectively within the genre.

The "big kill," as adapted by American travel writers and southern humorists, has a couple of variants. The first, which I call the mythic beast version, centers on an individual animal that has become something of a local legend. For the story to have full effect, the animal must be formidable: a bear, maybe, or a wolf, or a panther. In some stories, the animal has been slaughtering livestock, destroying crops, or attacking people—in some way causing mayhem for a community, thereby providing the hunter with moral justification for dispatching it. More commonly, however, the animal instigates dread not because it has destroyed anything of value, but because it has somehow eluded the community's best hunters. The difficulty in hunting the animal, in such cases, becomes its most threatening quality, perhaps because it reveals the limits of human skill and understanding. There are numerous iterations, but the story generally recounts various efforts made to track and kill the animal, leading hunters into frustrating, embarrassing, humorous, and often dangerous situations. The animal narrowly evades several close encounters before finally, in a dramatic turn of events, the animal meets its doom. The stories often conclude with a sense that justice, or at least equilibrium, has been restored. "It is essential to all of these tales," Oriard argues, "that the struggle between man and beast be expressed as a game—a *fair* contest in which the antagonists meet on equal terms" (9). Not only does the success of the story depend on a sense of equality between the frontiersmen jockeying for supremacy along the frontier, the struggle between humans and wilderness is viewed in similar terms.

Thomas Bangs Thorpe's "The Big Bear of Arkansas," published initially in the New York *Spirit of the Times* in March 1841 and subsequently included in his 1854 volume, *The Hive of "The Bee-Hunter,"* demonstrates the egalitarian essence of the mythic beast trope.[4] The story, recounted on a Mississippi riverboat by Jim Doggett, "a man enjoying perfect health and contentment," with eyes "as sparkling as diamonds" and a disposition "good-natured to simplicity" (28), concerns Doggett's hunt several years earlier for a bear with which he had become obsessed because it had left scratches on trees "eight inches above any in the forests that I knew of" (32). After seeing the scratches, he makes a resolution to himself: "[T]hat bear is mine, or I give up the hunting business" (32). Doggett and his dogs track the bear multiple times over a distance of many miles, but each time the bear manages to outrun them. After a time, he says, "that bear got so sassy, that he used to help himself to a hog off my premises whenever he wanted one; the buzzards followed after what he left, and so, between bear and buzzard, I rather think I got out of pork" (33).[5] A friend of Doggett shoots the bear in the forehead, yet the bear "shook his head as the ball struck it, and then walked down from that tree, as gently as a lady would from a carriage" (33). Finally, after vowing that he "would start that bear, and bring him home with me, or [my neighbors] might divide my settlement among them, the owner having disappeared," he finally finds the bear in the woods and shoots it. Rather than taking credit for his success, however, he insists, "My private opinion is, that the bear was an unhuntable bear, and died when his time come," thus preserving the bear's mythical, even magical essence (35). To further de-emphasize the role of Doggett's own skill, the story finishes with a scatological joke, in which Doggett starts after the bear but is "tripped up by [his] own inexpressibles, which, either from habit or the excitement of the moment, were about [his] heels," creating a decided anticlimax (35).

Doggett's entanglement in his own "inexpressibles" while apparently having a bowel movement, and his inclusion of this information in his telling of the tale, suggest a measure of humility on the hunter's part, reminding readers that even a clumsy, incompetent hunter can get lucky.[6] Additionally, and perhaps more important for the purposes of this discussion, the story suggests respect on the part of the hunter for his intended prey. Partly this may be a gesture of humility; no truly self-respecting hunter aggrandizes his own exploits. But the story also suggests a sense of genuine awe for the bear's canniness, audacity, and sheer size. In many instances of the "big kill," the hunter does not pursue game strictly for food, for sport, or for self-promotion. He does so, paradoxically, out of a sense of admiration. Only because the struggle between man and bear is treated as a fair fight does the hunter earn his right to survive the encounter and establish his place among his peers on the frontier.

Expressing admiration for animals and killing them may strike some modern readers as inherently contradictory, but such likely would not have been the case for nineteenth-century readers. Indeed, some of the most renowned conservationists of the nineteenth century would not have seen affection for and slaughter of animals as a logical inconsistency. John James Audubon, probably the nineteenth century's most meticulous naturalist and most passionate advocate on behalf of birds, nevertheless shot thousands of them. The killing was deemed necessary for production of Audubon's *Ornithological Biography*—including the many richly developed paintings of North American bird life he painted before the advent of photography and high-resolution binoculars—since killing and mounting the birds was the only known way to render accurate images of them. Audubon found and painted so many birds that were novel to science that he was accused of inventing some of them. It was not until he produced the stuffed specimens that he was believed, a fact that highlights a telling paradox: The birds did not "exist" until it was proven through death and preservation that they did. In addition to these practical justifications, however, it is also likely that Audubon simply did not view his passionate advocacy for birds in general as in any way anathema to his destruction of individual specimens. Thorpe and other writers of Old Southwest humor shared Audubon's sense that loving animals and killing them was not necessarily incompatible practices. Indeed, the mythic beast storytelling mode, presented in a way that emphasized respect for animals, might well have formed the basis of a moral code for game hunters. At the same time, however, the mythic beast narrative reinforced the notion, omnipresent in nineteenth-century American culture, that Americans were separate from and perpetually at war with the natural world.

The second variant, which I term the extravagant harvest, offers no such moral or ethical dimension, because it concerns itself almost exclusively with the raw numbers of animals killed, rather than with admiration for individual animals. The more extraordinary the number, the more impressive the hunt. Unlike the mythic beast stories, these are not fair fights between competitors on roughly equal terms. In these stories, prolific hunts rarely have any discernible practical purpose; the numbers are too great to justify as having been achieved for purposes of personal use or consumption. For instance, C. M. Haile's "Pardon Jones" letter, entitled "Letter from Curnel Pardon Jones, To 'Curnel Tom Owen' of the Agricultural Society, with a Tail," published May 29, 1843, in Thomas Bangs Thorpe's New Orleans newspaper, the *Southern Sportsman*, concerns Josiah Flintlock, an "old soger of the revolutionary war," who detests woodpeckers because they "pestered him almost the death" (150, 151). In his desperate hatred of these birds, Josiah orders his son Jack to "draw up some articles agin them infernal woodpeckers" (151). Every man within a three-mile radius signs the paper—an apparently humorous nod to the universally bothersome nature of woodpeckers—and when the men gather on Saturday, they count 6,339 woodpeckers' "scalps" among them (151). That the humor derives from killing vast numbers of birds that are merely annoying is a strong indictment of the author's environmental sensibility, particularly since one famous Louisiana species, the ivory-billed woodpecker, was already rare by the mid-nineteenth century owing to habitat loss.

One of the most memorable tales of the extravagant harvest type is William Gilmore Simms's posthumously published short story, "How Sharp Snaffles Got His Wife and Capital." In this story, a group of hunters gathers at Lying Camp to tell tall tales of their hunting escapades. Among them is Sam "Sharp" Snaffles, a notorious ne'er-do-well and incompetent hunter. The others wheedle Snaffles to tell "the history of how [he] got [his] capital" (241). After some cajoling, Snaffles recounts his efforts to court Mary Ann Hopson ("my Merry Ann, as I calls her," says Snaffles), the daughter of Squire Hopson, who is of the opinion that Snaffles lacks the capital, the wealth, to be a suitable husband for his daughter (242, 247). Feeling despondent after his meeting with Squire Hopson, Snaffles settles down under a tree beside a lake, where he is soon awakened by a "rushing and a roaring and a screaming and a plashing, in the air and in the water, as made you think the univarsal world was coming to an eend" (252). The commotion turns out to be a flock of Canada geese landing on the lake. Snaffles meditates for some time upon a plan to "captivate" the entire flock of forty thousand geese and eventually settles on a scheme to trap them with a giant net.

His plan succeeds—sort of. He manages to ensnare the geese in his net, but "instid of wrapping the eends of [his] lines around the sapling that was standing jest behind [him], what does [he] do but wraps 'em around [his] own thigh—the right thigh, you see—and some of the loops waur hitched round [his] left arm at the same time" (255). The geese, suddenly aware of their entrapment, take off all at once, carrying Snaffles high into the air. After a time, though, they become tired, and they crash-land high in a huge mountain oak. While contemplating his situation, Snaffles falls from his perch and lands in the hollow of the tree, neck deep in peach honey. To make matters even more interesting, a bear climbs down into the hollow to retrieve some honey, enabling Snaffles to grab on to its fur and scramble out of the tree. Upon reaching the outside of the tree hollow, the bear falls out of the tree, breaking its neck. So as a result of spectacular accidents and dumb luck, Snaffles finds himself in possession of several thousand geese, several thousand gallons of honey, and a bear carcass, all of which he liquidates for cash. Next, he purchases the mortgage to Squire Hopson's farm, which he then uses to negotiate Mary Ann's hand in marriage.

In Simms's story, individual animals are never assigned the sort of significance they have in the mythic beast stories; indeed, the animals themselves are barely understood as wild animals, but instead serve as symbols of "capital," the money Snaffles intends to garner from selling them. Indeed, much of the story's humor derives from the incessant "calkilations" Snaffles performs, even as he is hanging upside down fifty feet off the ground, ensnared in his own homemade goose net. Snaffles is hardly the sort of man for whom dispassionate "calkilations" seem like an effective strategy, and thus his machinations strike the reader as incongruously funny. In order for the humor to work, though, one must forget what was happening on an enormous scale to the fauna of the North American continent during the nineteenth century. Canada geese were in serious decline by the second half of the century, and the giant Canada goose subspecies was believed to be extinct by the 1950s.[7]

"The Pigeon Roost," included in Hardin E. Taliaferro's volume, *Fisher's River (North Carolina) Scenes and Characters*, is narrated by Uncle Davy Lane, who asserts that "a man will git tired out on one kind o' meat"—in this case, turkey—thus explaining his determination to hunt "a mighty pigeon-roost down in the Little Mountings" (79). Lane locates the roost in a grove of trees. There are so many birds there, the tree limbs sag under the pigeons' enormous weight. Lane loads his gun and "commence[s] blazin' away at the pigeons like thunder and lightnin'," forgetting that he has hitched his horse to one of the limbs (80). The pigeons alight from the branches, which swing upward, carrying Lane's horse high off the ground. "Soon as I got him down," Davy boasts, "I piked fur home with my pigeons, and we made uvry pan and pot stink with 'um fur one whet, and they made us all as sassy as a Tar River feller when he gits his belly full uv fresh herrin'" (84). Taliaferro's story, published in 1859, portends the demise of the passenger pigeon, and in so doing reminds us of the failure of imagination that contributed to their extinction. One nineteenth-century observer in Ontario claimed to have seen a flock of passenger pigeons one mile wide and three hundred miles long taking fourteen hours to pass a single point, an estimated 3.5 billion birds in that one flock alone (Sullivan 210). Yet by 1896, after several decades of profligate destruction—often abetted by government policy—the last major flock of passenger pigeons, numbering 250,000 birds, was systematically wiped out by professional hunters in Michigan. Why did this happen? Not for reasons any more sophisticated than men getting "tired out on one kind o' meat."

Did Simms, Taliaferro, and other writers of their generation understand the ecological implications of the large-scale hunting that provides much of the humor in their stories? The simple answer is no; ecology, as we understand it today, is a twentieth-century concept. The first American book of ecological science, written by Frederic Clements, wasn't published until 1905. One did not need to be an ecologist, however, to see the damaging effects of unrestrained, unrestricted hunting on the wildlife of North America. Indeed, some efforts were made in the nineteenth century to slow overharvesting of certain species. In 1857, for instance, a bill was brought before the Ohio state legislature seeking protection for the passenger pigeon. In response, a select committee of the state senate filed a report stating, "The passenger pigeon needs no protection. Wonderfully prolific, having the vast forests of the North as its breeding grounds, traveling hundreds of miles in search of food, it is here today and elsewhere tomorrow, and no ordinary destruction can lessen them, or be missed from the myriads that are yearly produced" (Hornaday i). Even as early as the late eighteenth century, some Americans noticed—and were attentive to—the environmental consequences of "taming" the frontier. In his travel narrative *Journey into Northern Pennsylvania and the State of New York*, published in 1801, J. Hector St. John de Crévecoeur quotes a settler who offered a stinging rebuke to his contemporaries on the frontier: "The second generation will regret bitterly that their fathers destroyed so much!" (257). There were some, then, raising the alarm over the practices of the day, but these voices were drowned out by those of commerce and the ideology of the limitless frontier. They were also ignored, by and large, by writers of southern frontier humor.

The problem, however, is not that writers depicted fantastic hunting stories and that readers found these stories funny. Trouble arises when southern frontier humor leaves the impression that readers are getting the "real," or "authentic," American frontier experience. Scholars such as Nathaniel Lewis and Patricia Limerick have examined the trope of authenticity as it applies to what Limerick—in a mildly derisive way—refers to as "the Real West." Even as writers of southern frontier humor use the strategy of wild embellishment, they frequently do so not for evident satirical purposes, but to bolster their claims about the "real" hardiness of frontier Americans. Real frontiersmen, the narratives suggest, are the sorts of folks who spin yarns around the campfire about their hunting escapades. In doing so, they inadvertently expose the irony and tragedy of American frontier ideology: Americans were busy destroying the very animals and landscapes that they identified with the "real" America. One wonders if the catastrophic ecological events on the nineteenth-century American frontier are examples of life imitating art, or vice-versa.

Whereas the Baron Münchhausen stories were read in Europe as political satire and viewed as humorously absurd (the Baron's astounding feats included riding cannonballs, traveling to the moon, and escaping from a swamp by pulling himself up by his own hair—or bootstraps, depending on who tells the story), American adaptations of this storytelling mode reflect uniquely American attitudes about animals and the landscape. Many Americans, particularly white males, identified with conceptions of masculinity embedded in the stories. Indeed, what had been a preposterous notion in the Baron Münchhausen stories—the idea that a single man (or, in the case of the Crockett almanacs, a single "shemale") could, or would, kill hundreds of animals—became a reality in nineteenth-century America. Indeed, it was the reality of the stories—or at least the possibility of truth, rather than the exaggerations therein—that would have been most compelling to nineteenth-century Americans. I disagree, then, with those critics who have suggested that southern frontier writing, particularly when it depicts hunting, is defined centrally by a propensity toward exaggeration. I suggest, in fact, that quite the opposite was true. Even cases of exaggeration in southern frontier writing are intended in some way as gestures of authenticity illuminating certain truths, as they were perceived by the authors and their readers, about life on the American frontier.

One text in which the distinction between fiction and nonfiction becomes especially muddy, and which demonstrates the destructive potential of the "big kill" narrative, is the so-called autobiography of David Crockett. *A Narrative of the Life of David Crockett*—ghost written by Thomas Chilton, who interviewed Crockett extensively and compiled his written materials—catalogs Crockett's move westward from eastern

Tennessee, his participation in the Creek War, his hunting adventures, and his political career in the Tennessee House of Representatives and the United States Congress.[8] Published in 1834, during Crockett's failed attempt at re-election to the US House of Representatives, the book is, at its heart, a campaign biography. Several chapters are devoted to tales of Crockett's hunting escapades. Bears in particular play an important role in these stories. Crockett boasts not only about the fierceness of individual bears that he has killed, but also the raw numbers of killed animals, making his book somewhat different from other authors' accounts emphasizing the difficulty and heroism of hunts for wily individual creatures. In late 1812, for instance, Crockett "had killed in all, up to that time, fifty-eight bears, during the fall and winter," and by spring he "took a notion to hunt a little more, and in about one month . . . killed forty-seven more, which made one hundred and five bears [he] had killed in less than one year" (193–94). Crockett's skills as a hunter reaffirmed his status as a folk hero, a strategy that played well with nineteenth-century Americans, who had become obsessed with the ideal of frontier manhood as expressed through James Fenimore Cooper's Leatherstocking tales and other books that romanticized life on the American frontier. Historian Richard Slotkin argues that Crockett "embodied the western ambition for self-improvement and the attainment of equality (equated with economic prosperity) and whose career reflected the concept of economics and politics as a hunt, in which he who bags the most and biggest prey is the best man" (464). Crockett's success as a politician, particularly as a representative of the state of Tennessee—then a frontier state—was based on his appeal as a frontiersman.[9] It is unclear whether or not the stories themselves actually happened as they appear in the almanacs, but this is an insignificant matter. Crockett's hunting feats *could* have happened, and indeed *were* happening, on a scale that should have been alarming to nineteenth-century Americans. Crockett's stories borrow from the Münchhausen template, adapt them to an American context and storytelling style, and present them to an American audience as nonfiction[10]—all with intent to glorify Crockett, probably for political purposes. They were highly successful in doing so, as evidenced by Crockett's re-election to Congress and his subsequent immortalization in American folk mythology. Few nineteenth-century Americans were troubled by the environmental consequences of the frontier ideology that Crockett epitomized.

Wild West hero "Buffalo Bill" Cody killed nearly five thousand buffalo by his own count over seventeen months in 1867 and 1868. Less than two decades later, the American bison had been virtually extirpated from the North American continent. Yet Cody is remembered not as a bloodthirsty wastrel, but as an extraordinary showman and a symbol of authentic Americana. To understand the environmental history of nineteenth-century America and to make sense of Americans' destruction of so many of the things they believed made their continent special, it is instructive to examine the popular literature of the time. The "big kill" narrative in Old Southwest humor, placed in its historical context, enables us to see that humorous renderings of embellished hunting stories may have obscured Americans' ability to see the real environmental destruction that was happening around them, much in the way that frontier humor may have blunted their attentiveness to racism, gender inequality, and rural poverty. I do not mean to promote the prudish view that it is unacceptable to laugh at stories that are, by twenty-first century standards, politically incorrect. I do, however, think it is appropriate to ask, "Wait, why was that funny?" Only by doing so can we reflect upon the attitudes that enabled nineteenth-century Americans to look the other way while large-scale species extermination and habitat loss were occurring, and only through a similarly heightened awareness in our own historical era can we develop a deeper and more respectful relationship with the natural environment that sustains us.

NOTES

1. Blair's article lists a number of these references because, as he suggests, "they go to prove that [Raspe's] telling, rather than others, were likely sources of American retellings" (128).
2. Terry Gilliam's 1988 film adaptation, *The Adventures of Baron Munchausen*, for instance, plays up the protagonist's childlike imagination, ingenuity, and sly sense of humor.
3. The significance of this proprietary view of game can be seen, for instance, in the Robin Hood legends, in which one of the primary charges against the outlaws is that they hunt the king's deer.
4. Other bear stories following a similar template include Henry Clay Lewis's "The Indefatigable Bear Hunter," Alexander G. McNutt's "A Swim for a Deer," and Charles F. M. Noland's "Pete Whetstone's Bear Hunt." All of these stories can be found in Cohen and Dillingham's *Humor of the Old Southwest* (1964).
5. Americans on the frontier did, of course, face real threats from wild animals. I choose not to emphasize this dimension of the story, in this case, because Thorpe's narrator is

not initially concerned with protecting his farm. Only after he initiates the chase does the bear become emboldened to start stealing his livestock.

6. We should be careful taking gestures of humility such as this entirely at face value. Nicholas W. Proctor points out that "[w]hen hunters composed hunting narratives, they usually featured their own triumphs. In essence, storytelling acted as another form of trophy taking—one that could potentially appeal to a national audience" (39).
7. In recent years, Canada geese populations in some areas have grown substantially—so dramatically, in fact, that many consider them pests (for their droppings, the bacteria in their droppings, the noise they make, and their often confrontational behavior). Expansion of their numbers can be explained by the removal of natural predators and an abundance of protected water sources (such as on golf courses, in public parks and beaches, and in planned communities). Large flocks of Canada geese have established permanent residence in Chesapeake Bay, on Virginia's James River, and in the Research Triangle area of North Carolina (Raleigh, Durham, Chapel Hill). For an excellent history of Canada geese, see Harold C. Hanson, *The Giant Canada Goose*, 2nd edition, Carbondale: Southern Illinois University Press, 1997.
8. In the early 1950s, Crockett biographer James Atkins Shackford unearthed two letters in Crockett's hand that reveal the true authorship of Crockett's autobiography. For more details, see Shackford, "The Author of David Crockett's Autobiography."
9. For a fuller discussion of the association between manliness and hunting in nineteenth-century America, see Rotundo, *American Manhood: Transformations in Masculinity from the Revolution to the Modern Era* 227.
10. Psychologist Rolf A. Zwaan has demonstrated a relationship between the genre of the source (his study examines readers' responses to literary texts and news sources) and the way readers process information. One might suppose, then, that nineteenth-century readers were more likely to perceive David Crockett's "autobiography" as a relatively honest account of "real" happenings than as a typical Old Southwest tall tale. See Zwaan "The Effect of Genre Expectations on Text Comprehension" 920–33.

WORKS CITED

Blair, Walter. "A German Connection: Raspe's Baron Munchausen." In *Critical Essays on American Humor*. Ed. William Bedford Clark and W. Craig Turner. Boston: G. K. Hall, 1984. 123–39. Print.

Cohen, Hennig, and William B. Dillingham, eds. *Humor of the Old Southwest*. Boston: Houghton Mifflin, 1964.

Crévecoeur, J. Hector St. John de. *Journey into Northern Pennsylvania and the State of New York*. Trans. Clarissa S. Bostelmann. Ann Arbor: University of Michigan Press, 1964. Print.

Crockett, David. *A Narrative of the Life of David Crockett*. Ed. Thomas Chilton. Lincoln: University of Nebraska Press, 1987. Print.

Fielder, Leslie. *Love and Death in the American Novel*. New York: Stein and Day, 1966. Print.

Haile, C. M. "Letter from Curnel Pardon Jones, To 'Curnel Tom Owen' of the Agricultural Society, with a Tail." *C. M. Haile's "Pardon Jones" Letters: Old Southwest Humor from Antebellum Louisiana.* Ed. Ed Piacentino. Baton Rouge: Louisiana State University Press, 2009. 149–52. Print.

Hanson, Harold C. *The Giant Canada Goose.* 2nd ed. Carbondale: Southern Illinois University Press, 1997. Print.

Hornaday, William Temple. *Our Vanishing Wild Life.* New York: New York Zoological Society, 1913. Print.

Kimmel, Michael. *Manhood in America: A Cultural History.* New York: Oxford University Press, 2006. Print.

Kolodny, Annette. *The Land Before Her: Fantasy and Experience of the American Frontiers, 1630–1860.* Chapel Hill: University of North Carolina Press, 1984. Print.

Lewis, Nathaniel. *Unsettling the Literary West: Authenticity and Authorship.* Lincoln: University of Nebraska Press, 1981. Print.

McHugh, Tom. *The Time of the Buffalo.* Lincoln: University of Nebraska Press, 1994. Print.

Oriard, Michael. "Shifty in a New Country: Games in Southwestern Humor." *Southern Literary Journal* 12.2 (1980): 3–28.

Proctor, Nicholas W. *Bathed in Blood: Hunting and Mastery in the Old South.* Charlottesville: University of Virginia Press, 2002.

Raspe, Rudolph Erich. *The Surprising Adventures of Baron Munchausen.* Doylestown, PA: Wildside Press, 2001. Print.

Rotundo, E. Anthony. *American Manhood: Transformations in Masculinity from the Revolution to the Modern Era.* New York: Basic Books, 1993. Print.

Seton, Ernest Thompson. *Life Histories of Northern Animals.* New York: Scribner's, 1989. Print.

Shackford, James Atkins. "The Author of David Crockett's Autobiography." *Boston Public Library Quarterly* 3 (1951): 294–304. Print.

Simms, William Gilmore. "How Sharp Snaffles Got His Capital and Wife." 1870. *Tales of the South.* Ed. Mary Ann Wimsatt. Columbia: University of South Carolina Press, 1996: 237–79. Print.

Slotkin, Richard. *Regeneration through Violence: The Mythology of the American Frontier, 1600–1860.* Norman: University of Oklahoma Press, 1973. Print.

Sullivan, Jerry. *Hunting Frogs on Elston.* Chicago: University of Chicago Press, 2004. Print.

Taliaferro, Hardin E. *Fisher's River (North Carolina) Scenes and Characters.* New York: Harper & Brothers, 1859. Print.

Thorpe, Thomas Bangs. *The Hive of "The Bee Hunter": A Repository of Sketches, Including Peculiar American Character, Scenery, and Rural Sports.* New York: Appleton, 1854. Print.

Zwaan, Rolf A. "The Effect of Genre Expectations on Text Comprehension." *Journal of Experiential Psychology, Learning, Memory & Cognition* 20.4 (1994): 920–33. Print.

CONTRIBUTORS

JAMES E. BISHOP is assistant professor of English at Young Harris College in Georgia. He has published articles on American writers J. Hector St. John de Créveceour, John Muir, and John Graves. Currently he is at work on an anthology, *Currents of the Universal Being: Explorations in the Literature of Energy*, which he is co-editing with Kyhl Lyndgaard and Scott Slovic.

BRUCE BLANSETT is a graduate student studying English literature at Virginia Tech. He received a bachelor of arts degree in English from the University of Virginia's College at Wise, while also cultivating his love for math and science. Bruce's chief research interests include African American literature, literature of the nineteenth century, gender studies, and the influence of science on social phenomena and the written word.

MARK S. GRAYBILL is an associate professor of English at Widener University in suburban Philadelphia. He has published scholarly articles on Barry Hannah, James Dickey, John Gardner, Bobbie Ann Mason, and Bruce Springsteen, among others. Currently, he is co-editing a collection of essays on representations of evil in popular music of the twentieth and twentieth-first centuries.

JENNIFER A. HUGHES is an assistant professor of English at Young Harris College in Georgia, where she teaches courses in early American literature, humor, romanticism, women's literature, and southern/Appalachian literature. Her publications include "Turning the Century" in *A Concise Companion to American Fiction 1900–1950* (co-authored with Michael A. Elliot; Blackwell, 2008) and "The Politics of Incongruity in Paul Laurence Dunbar's The Fanatics" (*African American Review*, Summer 2007). She is currently revising her dissertation, *Telling Laughter: Hilarity and Democracy in the Nineteenth-Century United States*, into a book.

JOHN LOWE is the Barbara Lester Methvin Distinguished Professor of Southern Literature at the University of Georgia. He is the author or editor of seven books, including *Jump at the Sun: Zora Neale Hurston's Cosmic Comedy* (1994) and the recently completed *Calypso Magnolia: The Caribbean Side of the South* (forthcoming).

GRETCHEN MARTIN is an associate professor of American Literature, with special interest in southern literature, at the University of Virginia's College at Wise. She also teaches African American literature and literary theory. She is the author of *The Frontier Roots of American Realism* (2007) and has published her work in *Southern Literary Journal, Mississippi Quarterly, South Atlantic Review, Southern Studies, North Carolina Literary Review, and Studies in American Humor.*

KATHRYN MCKEE is McMullan Associate Professor of Southern Studies and English at the University of Mississippi. She is co-editor, with Deborah Barker, of *American Cinema and the Southern Imaginary* (2011), and her articles have appeared in various journals, including *American Literature, Legacy, Southern Literary Journal,* and *Mississippi Quarterly.*

WINIFRED MORGAN, Professor of English, Edgewood College, has a long-term fascination with tricksters. Her 1988 book, *Brother Jonathan: An American Icon* (University of Delaware Press) explores the role of a Yankee trickster in American popular culture. Her interest in southern literature is demonstrated by chapters and articles in *American Studies* and *CEA Critic.*

ED PIACENTINO is a professor emeritus of English at High Point University in North Carolina and editor of the scholarly journal *Studies in American Humor.* A specialist in the literature and culture of the American South, he has published widely and extensively in the field, having authored or edited seven books, most recently *Southern Frontier Humor: An Anthology* (Missouri 2010), with M. Thomas Inge, and has also contributed chapters to books and numerous articles and reviews to scholarly journals.

TRACY WUSTER received his PhD in American studies from the University of Texas at Austin in 2011. He has published articles on Steve Martin, Mark Twain and Hawaii, and Mark Twain and England. He is the founding chair of the Humor Studies Caucus of the American Studies Association.

INDEX

www.ingramcontent.com/pod-product-compliance
Lightning Source LLC
Chambersburg PA
CBHW060805310726
48980CB00002B/238
* 9 7 8 1 6 1 7 0 3 7 6 8 9 *